Acting in British Tele

Tom Cantrell and Christopher Hogg

Acting in British Television

First published 2017 by
PALGRAVE

Palgrave in the UK is an imprint of Macmillan Publishers Limited, registered in England, company number 785998, of 4 Crinan Street, London, N1 9XW.

Palgrave® and Macmillan® are registered trademarks in the United States, the United Kingdom, Europe and other countries.

ISBN 978–1–137–47021–8 hardback
ISBN 978–1–137–47020–1 paperback

This book is printed on paper suitable for recycling and made from fully managed and sustained forest sources. Logging, pulping and manufacturing processes are expected to conform to the environmental regulations of the country of origin.

A catalogue record for this book is available from the British Library.

A catalog record for this book is available from the Library of Congress.

In memory of Ray – the boss of the remote control
—Christopher

For Anna. And the bump
—Tom

Contents

List of Images   ix
Notes on Authors   xi
Acknowledgements   xiii

1 Acting in British Television: A General Introduction   1
   References   11
   Notes   13

2 Soap Opera   15
   Introduction   15
   The Case Studies   17
   Interviews   19
   Acting in Soap Opera   58
   Conclusion   74
   References   76
   Notes   77

3 Police and Medical Drama   79
   Introduction   79
   The Case Studies   84
   Interviews   87
   Acting in Police and Medical Drama   123
   Conclusion   140
   References   142
   Notes   143

4 Comedy   145
   Introduction   145
   The Case Studies   147

Interviews   154
Acting in Television Comedy   188
Conclusion   203
References   205
Notes   207

5 Period Drama   209
Introduction   209
The Case Studies   214
Interviews   217
Acting in Period Drama   252
Conclusion   264
References   266
Notes   268

6 Acting in British Television: A General Conclusion   269

Index   277

List of Images

Image 1   Julie Hesmondhalgh's first appearance as Hayley in
          Coronation Street   64
Image 2   Gary Beadle as Paul Trueman in *EastEnders*   72
Image 3   Ken Stott as DI John Rebus in *Rebus*   124
Image 4   John Hannah as DI John Rebus in *Rebus*   131
Image 5   Paul Henshall as medical student Dean West in *Holby City* 134
Image 6   Nina Sosanya as Lucy Freeman in *W1A*   190
Image 7   Rebecca Front and Roger Allam as Nicola Murray
          MP and Peter Mannion MP in *The Thick of It*   196
Image 8   Jack Farthing as George Warleggan in *Poldark*   260
Image 9   Lesley Nicol as Mrs Patmore in *Downton Abbey*   263

Notes on Authors

Tom Cantrell

Dr Tom Cantrell is Senior Lecturer and Head of Theatre at the University of York. He has published widely on screen and stage acting, including *Playing for Real: Actors on Playing Real People* (Palgrave 2010, co-edited with Mary Luckhurst) and *Acting in Documentary Theatre* (Palgrave 2013). He has published articles in *Studies in Theatre and Performance*, *Drama Online*, the *Journal of British Cinema and Television* and *Critical Studies in Television*. His edited collection, *Exploring Television Acting*, co-edited with Christopher Hogg, will be published this year by Bloomsbury.

Christopher Hogg

Dr Christopher Hogg is Senior Lecturer in Television Theory at the University of Westminster. His research interests lie primarily in British television drama but also include such areas as media adaptation and translation, and screen representations of the past. He has published television-related work in a number of journals, including the *Journal of British Cinema and Television*, the *New Review of Film and Television Studies* and *Critical Studies in Television*. He is currently editing *Exploring Television Acting* with Tom Cantrell.

Acknowledgements

We would like to thank the actors whose words form the basis of this book. All were enthusiastic about this area and encouraging in their support of our research. They generously gave up their time and allowed their words to be published. Without them there would be no book. Thanks also go to our colleagues in the Department of Theatre, Film and Television at the University of York and in the School of Media, Arts and Design at the University of Westminster. We have been supported in this research by the care and wisdom of our publishers at Palgrave, in particular Jenni Burnell in the book's early stages, and Clarissa Sutherland who saw it through to publication. We would also like to thank colleagues who have offered their time and expertise over the past few years. Thanks to Dr Kristyn Gorton, Prof. Andrew Tudor, Prof. Andrew Higson, Prof. Duncan Petrie, Prof. Stephen Lacey, Dr Simone Knox, Prof. Michael Cordner, Prof. Judith Buchanan, Dr Tom Cornford, Dr Doug Kern, Dr Ollie Jones, Dr Nik Morris, Dr Mark Smith, Dr Karen Quigley, Conor Wilkinson and Dr Derek Paget. Thanks also to Rory Oliver for his contributions as research assistant.

Tom would like to extend personal thanks to Robert Waiting, Richard and Caroline Waiting, Lily and Jonny Vincent, to Brian, Janice, John and Richard Pinkstone, and to his family – Richard, Rosie and Rachel Cantrell – for their support, and to Anna, for being brilliant.

Christopher would personally like to give thanks to Ged Maguire, Jane Thorburn, Rob Benfield and Rosie Thomas for their support and warm welcome to the University of Westminster. Thanks also to Rinella Cere, Mark Leader, Chris Goldie and Louise Cope for being good comrades through thick and thin, to Patrick Wichert for doing all he could to help, to Isabel Ruiz-Mora for the smiles, to Kathryn Reaney and Keith Radley for the music, to Patricia Hogg for the bacon sandwiches and unwavering belief, and to Charlotte, for everything.

1

Acting in British Television: A General Introduction

This is a book about the experiences and approaches of British television actors. Given the book's title, an opening statement such as this could appear self-evident. However, in the context of broader academic traditions in investigating screen acting, it is an important opening statement to make. There already exists an abundance of articles, chapters, edited collections and monographs studying screen acting, but not necessarily the methods and insights of the screen actor. Whilst such work on screen acting originates within the field of film studies and remains focused predominantly on the cinematic, this is where we shall begin, as the prevailing critical philosophies and analytical approaches of this body of work play a significant and continued role in shaping subsequent academic investigations and understandings of television acting.

Touchstone examples of screen acting research for film, such as James Naremore's *Acting in the Cinema* (1988) or Andrew Klevan's *Film Performance: From Achievement to Appreciation* (2005), whilst offering richly detailed analyses of textual case studies tend to neglect the perspectives and processes of actors themselves in realising their contributions to the end performance texts that we see on screen. Indeed, there exists a long-standing critical tendency within screen acting research to prioritise the analysis of end performance products over an understanding of the professional or artistic processes on the part of the actor. This is no surprise, given the highly visible and accessible status of end text as performance artefact, versus the more problematically obscured or even invisible nature of many of the acting processes behind such end texts. Given the time constraints on television drama production in particular, as the following chapters shall go on to evidence, these acting processes are often highly personal to the individual actor and sit outside formalised rehearsal time, as opposed to shared rehearsal periods that constitute part of some (but by no means all) official production schedules. There are undoubtedly, therefore, methodological challenges involved in delving behind what we see on screen in order to better understand acting process as well as end product. Nevertheless, since a holistic understanding of screen acting is our aim, these are challenges that we must address.

In *Reframing Screen Performance* (2008), a noteworthy study in stressing the limitations to the prevailing practices of textual analysis in understanding screen acting, Cynthia Baron and Sharon Marie Carnicke note that

> [t]he mediated status of performance elements has led observers to elide the training, experience, and creativity that actors bring … Often overlooked is the bank of knowledge and experience that actors draw on to produce the gestures, expressions, and intonations that collaborate and combine with other cinematic elements to create meaning. (2008, 17)

Baron and Carnicke's resultant assertion that 'both academics and journalists … identify film performance with almost anything other than actors' labor and agency' (2008, 17) remains a persistent truth in the study and discussion of screen acting in general. The particularities of the screen actor's work often become overshadowed by the more visible 'authorial' status of the director, writer, producer or televisual 'showrunner' hyphenate, or conflated with the more easily discernible formal components of the finished performance text, such as framing, editing, lighting, costume and set design, for example, as parallel/intersecting performative elements. Tellingly, prominent essay collections with a cinematic focus, such as Lesley Stern and George Kouvaros's *Falling for You:*

Essays on Cinema and Performance (1999) and Cynthia Baron, Diane Carson and Frank P. Tomasulo's *More than a Method: Trends and Traditions in Contemporary Film* (2004), are inclined to foreground the director in framing their investigations of screen acting. More recently, Claudia Springer and Julie Levinson's *Acting* (2015) offers welcome new material on screen acting and includes interview data from the actors themselves, but still views film acting chiefly through the lens of broader technological, industrial and aesthetic shifts within the medium over the last century. Although it is indisputable that such factors inevitably influence (whilst also being influenced by) the work of the screen actor, it is important that they do not work to mask the individual creative contributions that the actor makes to the larger mechanisms of production, in terms of their training, experience, perspectives, skills and practices of character preparation and execution. Thus, whilst acknowledging that screen actors are by no means the sole creative agents behind screen performance and thus not the only authorities on screen acting, to overlook the distinctiveness of the actor's artistic input leads to an incomplete picture at best.

The evolution of 'star/celebrity studies' as a fertile offshoot of performance studies in film and subsequently television,[1] building on Richard Dyer's early contributions with *Stars* (1979) and *Heavenly Bodies: Film Stars and Society* (1986), could be interpreted as an affirmation of the individual agency of the screen actor. However, in practice, the impressively diverse range of interests and perspectives in contemporary star/celebrity studies, accommodating not only screen actors but also musicians, comedians, sports figures, television presenters, 'reality' show participants and online cultural commentators, amongst many others, works to expand the conceptual sight-lines for what constitutes 'performance' even further. This is aligned with Richard Schechner's inclusive approach to performance studies, beyond just 'theatre, dance, music and performance art', to encompass 'a broad spectrum of activities including at the very least the performing arts, rituals, healing, sports, popular entertainments, and performance in everyday life' (2004, 7). Whilst admirably ambitious, and indeed necessary for the long-term relevance of the field, such inclusivity of investigation does little to help pull the working methods and experiences of the screen actor into more precise focus.

What is Television Acting?

If the artistic perspectives and approaches of screen actors, in a collective sense, remain positioned on the periphery of the critical and conceptual spotlight, then the work of the television actor is even further in shadow. John Caughie, in his seminal chapter on the subject of television acting, 'What Do Actors Do When They Act?' (2000), stresses the conspicuous 'absence of theoretically informed critical writing about [television] acting', noting that whilst there is 'a considerable body of writing about film stardom, and some about television personalities ... there is very little attention to reading the actor' (2000, 162). There have been a number of valuable chapters/articles that begin to address this absence since the initial publication of Caughie's chapter, particularly in recent years, from television scholars such as Roberta Pearson (2010), Trevor Rawlins (2010), Lucy Fife Donaldson (2012), Douglas McNaughton (2014) and Richard Hewett (2013, 2014 and 2015).[2] Moreover, there have been two illuminating UK-based symposia investigating television acting specifically; the first, organised by the authors, *Playing the Small Screen* (University of York, July 2012), and the second, organised by Simone Knox and Stephen Lacey, *Acting on Television* (University of Reading, April 2016).[3] In addition, since 2015, Knox has co-authored a blog strand for *CSTonline.tv*, titled 'What Actors Do', with Gary Cassidy.[4] As evidenced by such recent activity, and as the authors argue elsewhere (Cantrell and Hogg 2016), there remains much work to be done to reach substantive answers to the question first posed by Caughie over a decade-and-a-half ago regarding what television actors actually do when they act. This book aims to make a significant contribution to arriving at those answers.

With the industrial motor of production on television dramas seemingly faster than ever before, alongside continuing broader trends towards what has been termed the 'soapification' (Nelson 1997, 30) or 'soapisation' (Ellis 2007, 104) of television drama, with increasingly non-finite, ongoing 'flexi-narrative' (Nelson 1997) structures prevailing, it is easy to dismiss television actors as being little more than replaceable cogs within the production machine which must and will motor forward at all costs, with or without the ongoing involvement of the individual actor.

Moreover, the ever more limited space for formalised rehearsal within the production schedules of long-form television drama appears to further compound this sense of a lack of space for exploration or agency on the part of the actor within these creative processes, echoing Caughie's description of the common conception of the television actor as 'a movable piece in the chess games of creativity and artistic innovation' (2000, 166). However, little to no formally scheduled rehearsal time for actors does not logically entail little to no preparation or thought on the part of the actor. As television director Sophie Lifschutz notes in relation to her work on the British soap opera *EastEnders* (BBC 1985–):

> [A]ctors often come to the set with their own pre-formed ideas about how their characters would handle certain situations … it's important to trust the actor and be open to what they bring to the floor, because, whilst I have my eye on the structure of the scene, they often know their character much better than a director ever could. (2014)

Supporting this, Baron and Carnicke reflect on comparable production conditions in a cinematic context, highlighting that such conditions necessitate 'more independent preparation than that required for stage performances', and that '[c]ompressed rehearsal time requires players to come to the set or location fully prepared, with a good understanding of their characters and a readiness to adjust that understanding to the director's vision as needed' (2008, 236). Therefore, what happens *before* filming begins must also be acknowledged as contributing to the final 'shape' of what is seen on screen. Yet, because these contributing elements often cannot be readily discerned (either in the presence of tangible rehearsal time within production schedules or in the ultimate composition of the text), they are all-too-easily overlooked.

Indeed, whilst its meaning may appear clear at a simplistic level, 'television acting' resists easy definition. Perhaps the most common-sense understanding of 'television acting' is 'what the actor does in front of a camera'. However, as the lessons of preceding screen acting studies tell us, this proposed definition fails to account sufficiently for the various preparatory processes which an actor may work through in advance of arriving at their mark ready for shooting. As Caughie notes, acting is 'very difficult to nail down analytically' and 'tests the limits of critical language' (2000, 162, 170), whilst Marvin Carlson has identified that analysis of acting has been viewed as a 'troubling distraction' in screen studies (1996, 82). Reflecting this, existing academic explorations of television acting collectively evidence ambiguity and discord in precisely identifying their object of study. As a launching point for addressing such ambiguities, as we have suggested previously (Cantrell and Hogg 2016), a working distinction can be made between 'television acting' and 'television performance'. For our purposes, 'acting' refers specifically to the actor's portrayal of a character within a dramatic context, whilst 'performance' extends more broadly to other forms of performative involvement within television production – of the sort suggested by Schechner's (2004, 7) more inclusive definition – such as presenting game shows or appearing in reality-based programmes, for instance. Textual 'performance' also extends to the inflection of an actor's work by other performative elements beyond the contributions of the actor themselves, such as costume, lighting, framing and editing. Such a semantic distinction is valuable when considered in light of the broader trends of previous screen acting analysis outlined above, in which the particular contributions of the actor are regularly elided with other adjacent modes of 'performance'. Elisions of this kind appear regularly in journalistic appraisals of television acting. For instance, in an article for the *The Guardian* titled 'Happy Valley TV Review – Sarah Lancashire Gives Her Best Performance' (3 January 2014), Mark Lawson frames his review of Lancashire's 'performance' almost entirely through noting the repeated use of close shots of her 'bloodied face' and discussing the merits of the script provided by writer Sally Wainwright, as opposed to reflecting upon what Lancashire actually offers up as an actor portraying a character within that story.

There are key drivers behind these tendencies towards critical conflation in relation to the work of the television actor. It is worth emphasising that such adjacent performative elements *do* undoubtedly inflect the work of the screen actor considerably, and therefore certainly merit recognition in the analysis of television acting. Our contention, rather, is that these elements should not conceal the work of the television actor. The framing of the actor, camera movements and the editing process, for example, are all production components which can be readily observed and considered by the researcher through watching the finished television text, perhaps proving better suited to television studies' now well-established parameters of interest and the 'quasi-scientific language of its analytic procedures' (Caughie 2000, 163). The actor's methods of preparation and the physical, verbal and psychological nuances behind their work, by contrast, prove harder to demarcate and examine with comparable clarity and precision.

Moreover, as Hewett (2015, 74) stresses in his valuable examination of the changing historical determinants of television acting, there is an 'analytical trap' waiting for those who aim to understand the work of the television actor through the lens of the end text in isolation. Hewett mobilises this argument through examples of the attempted analysis of acting from earlier periods in British television history which, when appraised textually and without any consideration of 'conditioning factors' such as (very different) technological, artistic and cultural performance contexts, often results unfairly in the dismissal of the work of such actors as 'embarrassing relic[s] of yesteryear'. Hewett's point is equally applicable to the study of contemporary television acting: the 'conditioning factors' driving and shaping the end performance text must also be examined and accounted for in understanding television acting, with the preparatory processes and technical approaches of the television actor constituting a significant factor in the mix. Without such an analytical awareness, the contributions of the television actor will forever be subsumed under the far more visible formal, aesthetic and/or narrative mechanics of the end text.

The question of precisely what television actors do when they act is a significant one not only for television scholarship but also for actor training institutions. As mentioned above, in 2012, the authors organised a symposium at the University of York which brought together television actors, actor-trainers and academics (and those who combine these roles) to discuss this very question. A number of high-profile British drama schools were represented by staff who lead or contribute to the screen training components of their programmes, including the Royal Academy of Dramatic Art (RADA), the London Academy of Music and Dramatic Art (LAMDA), the Royal Central School of Speech and Drama, Guildford School of Acting and Bristol Old Vic Theatre School. It became clear through round table discussions, presentations and subsequent conversations that all of these institutions have recently redesigned or are currently redesigning their training approaches for television, reflecting the fact that the specific demands of television acting, and how training institutions should best prepare their students for this work, are presently high on the agenda.

The actor trainers who spoke at the symposium were continuing to design innovative new programmes of training. Moreover, it was evident that such programmes were being constructed with an aim to move beyond the more well-established technical acting classes for television, in place in various forms at RADA, for example, since the 1950s in an attempt to meet the needs of a then relatively new performance medium.[5] These traditional technical classes, with their focus on becoming familiar with a studio environment and the industrial processes of making television, may have prepared actors for the day-to-day practicalities of working in the medium but left most of the more fundamental questions of character construction and narrative development largely untouched. Indeed, there is a growing awareness within a training context that television acting requires more than particular technical proficiencies but also tailored strategies for character and story. One of the primary intentions of this book is to provide a resource which might assist the theoretical underpinning of these developments in actor training for television drama. When designing courses on acting for the stage, actor-trainers can choose from a rich range of potential models of character construction and development. By contrast, the relative lack of detailed television acting testimony or 'process research' noted above means that designing new syllabuses to prepare actors for the specific challenges of television acting is a difficult undertaking. This book aims to assist in tackling these challenges.

Approach and Structure

In realising this book's key intention to position front-and-centre the television actor, sharing their creative and professional perspectives on the processes behind their television work, the dominant element of this research is original actor interview material. The book contains a total of

16 full-length interviews with British television actors, ensuring diversity in the age, gender, ethnicity and professional experiences of those actors who contributed.

We have employed a semi-structured interview approach, which allows us to make direct comparisons between interviews, whilst, crucially, being able to pursue each actor's own interests and most pressing concerns fully. A core cluster of topics for discussion thus offers continuity across all of the interviews, particularly in relation to the specificities of preparation and execution for television acting and the influence of various 'conditioning factors' such as technological and genre contexts on the individual work of the television actor, and also to any connections that can be made between the lessons of formal actor training and the realities of professional work in television. Indeed, because of the aforementioned importance of training as an area of investigation, the range of actor participants selected was determined in no small part by the desire to gain perspectives from television actors who had trained at different institutions and during different periods in the historical development of British television drama (from the 1950s through to the 2010s), and were therefore at very different stages in their television careers and consequently in their experiences of television work in its different forms. Beyond this, the actors were offered the space to express their work in their own words, with encouragement to move past the sorts of anecdotal details which are prevalent in journalistic actor interviews, to instead access detailed reflections upon televisual technique and experience. In recognising the national and cultural particularities of actor training and television production contexts (both historical and contemporary), the book maintains an investigative focus upon British actors, and British television drama specifically, as a foundation upon which subsequent work could then build in the future.

As Christine Cornea notes, '[R]eference to genre has certainly become pivotal in contemporary television's delivery and niche marketing practices', meaning that 'questions around genre and performance are now more vital than ever.' (2010, 9–11) Following Cornea's lead in acknowledging the significance of genre as a powerful 'conditioning factor' influencing screen acting, from production through to critical reception, the book's actor interviews are ordered and framed through the consideration of key popular genres in twenty-first century British television drama production: soap opera, police and medical procedural drama, comedy and period drama. The authors are by no means ignorant of the theoretical complexities surrounding genre as a concept, or of the ever-evolving and hybridising nature of television genres as mutable 'cultural categories' (Mittell 2004). Nevertheless, 'genre' means something tangible both to those who make television and to those who consume it, and therefore it invites investigation in connection to the work of television actors. Indeed, as continued academic discourses regarding the 'soapisation' (Ellis 2007, 104) of contemporary television drama attest, notions of genre are inextricably linked to the ways in which we conceptualise and appraise televisual form and content. We have focused our research on these four genres in particular as they are highly prevalent forms of production in the context of British television fiction, and between them make up the majority of programmes employing actors on British television. They are well-established, familiar and recognisable forms for actors and for audiences, and as such come with particular expectations which will be explored via the actor interviews here. We are aware that other genres, such as science fiction, fantasy and fact-based drama are also increasingly popular features of the contemporary television landscape, but none have become as synonymous with television acting as our selected genres.[6] We hope that this research suggests a useful methodological model for approaching other genres of contemporary television drama production within future research.

Rather than falling into Hewett's (2015, 74) 'analytical trap' of prioritising end texts over production contexts and processes, the primary intention behind selecting particular genres and specific textual case studies is to provide a framework of reference to support the actor interviewees in explaining more abstracted notions of approach and technique, through connection to concrete examples. In other words, end texts and the genres in which they can be situated are employed here as tools to facilitate the detailed examination of the actor's work, not to obscure it, and throughout the book we signpost the reader to useful end-text examples of the actor's work. Each of Chapters 2 to 5 is introduced by an overview of the existing critical conceptions and debates relating to the genre in question, particularly those relevant to acting and performance. Chapter introductions are followed by the actor interviews themselves, before thematic patterns are then traced and analysed across the interview content.

In this way, we hope that the range of actor experiences and perspectives shared in this book makes for illuminating reading, and that cross-genre analysis and comparison allow the reader to map similarities and differences in actor approach across the popular genres that constitute the mainstay of the contemporary British actor's work. Organising by genre also allows the reader with generic interests to easily locate the relevant interview content and analysis. To this end, we have presented the actors' interviews in full. We are very aware that our own research interests may not be shared by all readers, and presenting this new interview material allows others to analyse it from a range of critical perspectives. The analytical sections of Chapters 2 to 5 have been constructed in such a way that they can be read, understood and used independently of the full interviews, should a reader's time be restricted. We are, however, indebted to the actors' keen critical and reflective capacity and would strongly urge readers to explore their interviews in full.

It would be foolish to aim to extrapolate this selection of individual British actor perspectives and to argue that they somehow speak for all actor experiences in contemporary television contexts. However, the interview data gathered can be purposefully utilised to begin to trace connections and patterns of experience and technique in terms of television acting from the actor perspective, which is meaningful and valuable in its own right, as a launching point from which to promote further investigation and understanding regarding the work of the television actor today.

References

Baron, C. and S.M. Carnicke (eds), 2008. *Reframing Screen Performance*. Ann Arbor: The University of Michigan Press.

Baron, C., D. Carson and F.P. Tomasulo (eds), 2004. *More than a Method: Trends and Traditions in Contemporary Film*. Michigan: Wayne State University Press.

Bennett, J., 2008. 'The Television Personality System: Televisual Stardom Revisited after Film Theory', *Screen*, 49:1, 32–50.

Bennett, J. and S. Holmes, 2010. 'The "Place" of Television in Celebrity Studies', *Celebrity Studies*, 1:1, 65–80.

Cantrell, T. and C. Hogg, 2016. 'Returning to an Old Question: What Do Television Actors Do When They Act?', *Critical Studies in Television*, 11:3, 283–298.

Cantrell, T. and M. Luckhurst, 2010. *Playing for Real: Actors on Playing Real People*. London: Palgrave Macmillan.

Carlson, M., 1996. *Performance: A Critical Introduction*. London: Routledge.

Caughie, J., 2000. 'What Do Actors Do When They Act?', in J. Bignell, S. Lacey and M. MacMurraugh-Kavanagh (eds), *British Television Drama: Past, Present and Future* (First Edition). London: Palgrave Macmillan, 162–174.

Cornea, C. (ed.), 2010. *Genre and Performance: Film and Television*. Manchester: Manchester University Press.

Dyer, R., 1979. *Stars*. London: BFI.

———1986. *Heavenly Bodies: Film Stars and Society*. London: Routledge.

Ellis, J., 2007. *TV FAQ: Uncommon Answers to Common Questions about TV*. London: I.B. Tauris.

Fife Donaldson, L., 2012. 'Camera and Performer: Energetic Engagement with *The Shield*', in J. Jacobs and S. Peacock (eds), *Television Aesthetics and Style*. London: Continuum Press, 209–218.

Hewett, R., 2013. 'Acting in the New World: Studio and Location Realism in *Survivors*', *Journal of British Cinema and Television*, 10:2, 321–339.

———2014. 'Spaces of Preparation: The Acton 'Hilton' and Changing Patterns of Television Drama Rehearsal', *The Historical Journal of Film, Radio and Television*, 34:3, 331–344.

———2015. 'The Changing Determinants of UK Television Acting', *Critical Studies in Television*, 10:1, 73–90.

———Forthcoming. *The Changing Spaces of Television Acting*. Manchester: Manchester University Press.

Klevan, A., 2005. *Film Performance: From Achievement to Appreciation*. London: Wallflower.

Lawson, M., 2014, 3 June. 'Happy Valley TV Review – Sarah Lancashire Gives Her Best Performance'. *The Guardian*. Accessed at: www.theguardian.com/tv-and-radio/2014/jun/03/happy-valley-end-of-series-tv-review-mark-lawson (last viewed: 1 May 2015).

Lifschutz, S., 2014. Interview with Authors, York, 27 June.

McNaughton, D., 2014. '"Constipated, Studio-bound, Wall-confined, Rigid": British Actors' Equity and BBC Television Drama, 1948–1972', *Journal of British Cinema and Television*, 11:1, 1–22.

Mittell, J., 2004. *Genre and Television: From Cop Shows to Cartoons in American Culture*. London: Routledge.

Murray, S., 2005. *Hitch your Antenna to the Stars: Early Television and Broadcast Fame*. London: Routledge.

Naremore, J., 1988. *Acting in the Cinema*. Berkeley: University of California Press.

Nelson, R., 1997. *TV Drama in Transition: Forms, Values and Cultural Change*. Houndsmills: Palgrave Macmillan.

Paget, D., 2010. *Acting with Facts: Actors Performing the Real in British Theatre and Television since 1990 (2007–2010)*. Project website. Accessed at: www. reading.ac.uk/ftt/research/ftt-actingwithfacts.aspx (last viewed: 11 December 2016).

Pearson, R., 2010. 'The Multiple Determinants of Television Acting', in C. Cornea (ed.), *Genre and Performance: Film and Television*. Manchester: Manchester University Press, 166–183.

Rawlins, T., 2010. 'Screen Acting and Performance Choices', *MeCCSA*, 3:2.

Schechner, R., 2004. 'Performance Studies: The Broad Spectrum Approach', in H. Bial (ed.), *The Performance Studies Reader* (2nd edition). London: Routledge, 7–9.

Springer, C. and J. Levinson (eds), 2015. *Acting*. London: I.B. Tauris.

Stern, L. and G. Kouvaros, 1999. *Falling for You: Essays on Cinema and Performance*. Sydney: Power Publications.

Notes

1 Notable examples of research considering television stardom/celebrity specifically include: Murray (2005), Bennett (2008) and Bennett and Holmes (2010).

2 Pearson's work offers a valuable examination of the force-field of production elements and concerns that impact upon television acting, focusing primarily upon the US production context. The subsequent research of both Hewett and McNaughton continues to develop this approach but with a predominantly historical British focus, drawing upon actor testimony to consider the significance of studio and location environments for the television actor. Fife Donaldson provides further insight into the creative conditions of televising acting, investigating the relationship between actor and camera in US cop drama. Rawlins – himself a trained actor and acting teacher – supplies a useful counter-balance to

the production-context focus of the above body of research, driving his analysis more from the perspective of the actor's training and strategies in relation to television. Hewett's forthcoming monograph, *The Changing Spaces of Television Acting* (Manchester University Press), also promises to be a valuable addition to this emergent body of actor-focused research.

3   Lacey and Knox's symposium, *Acting on Television: Analytical Methods and Approaches* (8 April 2016), featured a wide range of research into all aspects of acting and performance, and also included a keynote interview with actor Phil Davis. A special edition of *Critical Studies in Television*, featuring articles by presenters at the symposium, will be published in 2018.

4   Knox and Cassidy's blog is a series of short articles exploring a range of British and American television programmes. Using both stills and clips to analyse performance, this is a lively and engaging platform for this research.

5   Hewett (2015, 81) outlines the limited success of such early classes at RADA, from the perspective of actors subsequently working on television.

6   Acting approaches to fact-based work have been explored by Cantrell and Luckhurst (2010) and in Paget's AHRC project, Acting with Facts (Paget 2010).

2

Soap Opera

Introduction

Soap operas are the most widely watched fictional stories in Britain. They are the most long-running fictional television programmes, they have the highest output of any television drama, and are home to some of the most recognisable actors working on television. However, within academic study, soap operas still occupy contested ground. The genre has gained scholarly attention within television studies over the past 30 years with researchers such as Christine Geraghty (1991), Mary Ellen Brown (1990 and 1994), Robert Clyde Allen (1995), Charlotte Brunsdon (1997 and 2000), Dorothy Hobson (2003) and Trisha Dunleavy (2009) making key interventions. These works, which represent the cornerstones of research into soap opera, view the form through a sociological lens (with a particular focus on gender and class representation), or via reception studies and, in particular, the female viewer. A constant across all of these works has been the authors' repeated need to demonstrate that soap opera is a form of television which is actually worthy of study. As Lez Cooke notes:

[Soap operas] began to attract academic attention in the late 1970s and 1980s ... one of the intentions behind the academic revaluation of soap operas was to rescue the genre from its tarnished reputation as one of the cheapest and most denigrated of televisual forms. (2003, 81)

Indeed, Cooke's rallying-call over a decade ago that 'soap operas are a phenomenon which exist apart from the rest of television drama, and which need to be considered on their own terms and not as debased forms of television drama' (2003, 83) has only relatively recently been answered by new research. This chapter engages with this new material, and is designed to further demonstrate the value of detailed research into soap opera.

Despite being a genre that has been repeatedly overlooked – or, as Geraghty calls it, 'neglected' (2010, 82) – within academic discourse, the ongoing narrative structures of soap opera have clearly generated a strong magnetic pull for producers, commissioners and audiences alike. In a production environment in which risk aversion is key and loyal audiences are a necessity, genres which were once dominated by discrete plots have gravitated towards longer-form structures. Ellis calls this tendency the 'soapisation' of television drama (2007, 104), as we note in Chapter 1, whilst Geraghty notes that '[c]hanges in British television since the 1980s ... have seen serials, series and sit-coms adopt features of the soap narrative form' (2010, 84–85).

This 'soapisation' has been viewed with concern by commentators, raising fears that a wider employment of the narrative structures of soap is to the detriment of other forms of television:

> Whether you watch a series about medics, cops, firefighters, lawyers, customs officers, oil-rig workers, life boat crew or soldiers, what you end up seeing is not them doing the job that gives the show its basic premise. You see them falling in and out of love, committing adultery, having babies ... Personal life is privileged at the expense of questions of power, politics, economics ... series are mutating into soaps, in content if not in form. (Wilsher, 1997, 11, cited in Creeber 2004, 1)

Whilst identifying some of the strengths of long-form drama, which he suggests are 'intrinsically better suited to explore and dramatise the complexity of character psychology as a whole' (2004, 6), Creeber also finds evidence to 'support Wilsher's worse fears that all television drama is now mutating into soap opera' (2004, 11). It is thus true that soap continues to be viewed by researchers as a maligned form of television. Kilborn's observation, some 25 years ago, of the 'low esteem in which soaps are held' (1992, 10), still holds true today.

The actors included in this chapter certainly noted the negative attitudes towards soap opera, and of the work of soap actors in particular. Julie Hesmondhalgh said:

> People really don't understand that acting in soap is a discipline. No one seems interested in how actors work on soap, and they have prejudices about their work. I remember a well-respected actor coming in to work on the show [*Coronation Street*] and he was talking to me about the process, and he clearly thought that he was above it.

If acting on television is a neglected area, then any scholarly investigation into acting processes in soap opera is all but non-existent. There have been cursory nods to process, such as a passing suggestion of the influence of Method Acting on television work (see Butler 1995, 149), but it has not been until very recently that scholars have acknowledged that soap actors' craft is worthy of sustained and probing academic investigation (for example, see Hewett 2015). This is particularly apparent given that 20 years ago Butler noted:

> It is actors who incarnate the characters in soap opera narrative structures, providing character types for content analyses; and it is actors' bodies and gestures – as much as the dialog scripted for them or the actions plotted for them – in which viewers invest deep-seated emotions and long-standing empathies. (1995, 145)

The current focus on textual analysis not only underestimates the actor's creative involvement in the process of generating a performance, but also provides readers with only a partial understanding of the genre. This chapter is based on the contention that soaps offer some of the most uniquely televisual challenges to actors, and thus identifying and analysing these features significantly extends our understanding of both acting processes and the televisual form.

The Case Studies

To explore these areas, this chapter includes four new interviews with actors from two case-study programmes, *Coronation Street* (ITV 1960–) and *EastEnders* (BBC 1985–). *Coronation Street* is ITV's flagship programme. Consistently popular with audiences, it tells the story of the inhabitants of the eponymous street in Weatherfield, a fictional Lancashire town. This chapter features interviews with Julie Hesmondhalgh, who played Hayley Cropper for 866 episodes from 1998–2014 and Graeme Hawley, who portrayed John Stape for 340 episodes from 2007–2011. *EastEnders* is the BBC's prime-time soap. Set in Walford, a fictional borough in East London, the soap focuses on the residents of Albert Square. This chapter includes interviews with Rachel Bright, who appeared as Poppy Meadow for 147 episodes from 2011–2014 and Gary Beadle, who played Paul Trueman in *EastEnders* for 328 episodes from 2001–2004.

In order to illustrate one of the challenges which defines acting in soap opera, it is useful to turn to Dunleavy's description of Ken Barlow in *Coronation Street*, played by William Roache:

> Ken Barlow has become one of the most enduring characters in television history, having amassed nearly 50 years of fictional existence to date [now 56 years]. Introduced as a young university graduate and former 'scholarship boy' in the debut *Coronation Street* episode, Barlow has enjoyed a lengthy and solid 'teaching' career in Weatherfield, amassed some 21 screen partners, and held more than eight 'addresses' in the same street. (2009, 112)

There are several acting challenges encapsulated in this remarkable biography which the actors interviewed in this chapter will go on explore, and which form the focus of the analysis at the end of the chapter. Firstly, very few actors play a character for such a long period of time. An actor on stage or on film might play a role for a few months, a television drama actor might play a role for several months to a few years, but there are very few actors who will play a character on television for decades, and continuously. Though shorter than Roache's portrayal, Julie Hesmondhalgh played Hayley Cropper for 16 years. How does this impact on an actor's work? How is this different from a much shorter relationship with a role? How does the public's association of the actor with the role affect their work? The four actors in this chapter have appeared in 1681 episodes between them. This chapter will thus focus on the experiences of actors playing characters over a long period of time, whilst acknowledging that the experience would be very different for an actor appearing in only one or two episodes.

An additional challenge which Dunleavy's pen portrait gestures towards is the fact that Ken Barlow's biography was not mapped out when the character was first created. How does the actor experience an unknown future for her/his character? This is different from the vast majority of roles that the actors take on. Most narrative structures in plays, films and traditional television dramas are discrete and actors can read the entire script and view their character's journey through it. Did this have a bearing on their experience? Finally, reflecting the preoccupations of the soap genre, Dunleavy points to Ken Barlow's personal life. How does this focus on the personal, on relationships, and on their character's home life, affect the actor's work?

This chapter is designed to provide the first detailed analysis of actors' work on soap opera, and will focus on their processes rather than their performance. As well as bringing this material to light for the first time, and analysing the shared experiences and concerns that the actors raise, the aim of this chapter is to reinforce a sense of respect for the actor's work in this 'neglected' form. Soap opera is a distinctive performative context which raises genre-specific questions of the actor's approach and prompts us to reconsider their work on a role.

Interviews

Julie Hesmondhalgh

London, 28 November 2014

Julie Hesmondhalgh trained at the London Academy of Music and Dramatic Art (LAMDA). She played Hayley Cropper in *Coronation Street* for 866 episodes between 1998 and 2014. Hayley was the first long-running transgender character to appear in a UK continuing drama, and Hesmondhalgh garnered significant critical praise for her portrayal including Best Serial Drama Performance at the 2014 National Television Awards and Best Actress at the 2014 British Soap Awards. Her 16 years on *Coronation Street* saw the development of Hayley's relationship with partner (and later husband) Roy Cropper, played by David Neilson. Raising the profile of a number of causes, her storylines traced the developing legislation for transgender marriage, for LGBT equality and, in her diagnosis of terminal pancreatic cancer, the complex debates surrounding the 'right to die' issue. Rather than take life-prolonging medication which brought with it risks of her losing her identity, and regressing to her earlier life as a man, Hayley took her own life.

Hayley is a very important character in the history of continuing drama and British drama more widely. How did you come about taking the role?

I hadn't done much TV when I got the audition and I hadn't been trained in television. I had the most minimal television training at LAMDA. LAMDA now has a brilliant television acting department, but when I was there it wasn't considered a big part of our training. I'd done a Catherine Cookson mini-series [*The Dwelling Place*: ITV 1994] and a couple of episodes of *The Bill* [ITV 1984–2010]. I had a real epiphany whilst I was working on *The Bill*. I was playing quite a small part, a doctor at the bedside of a grieving parent. Something happened to me during that process. We had a really good director and I remember that he gave space to the actress playing the grieving mum to have a moment to get herself in the right emotional state to do the scene. It struck me that everyone is here working, but they are all doing different jobs – putting down the tracks for the dolly, setting up the lights, focusing the cameras, the actress is getting herself in the right emotional state – and in the middle of it was me: I'm here with my few lines and I'm ready and I'm trained to do this. I'm completely capable of doing it. I'm a cog in this big wheel which is producing this programme. The programme rolls on and on and I'm just one small cog within it. I know some actors find that intimidating but I found it freeing. Something shifted in my head in that moment. Prior to that experience I hadn't been getting much television work. After that I got every audition that I went for. It was a real epiphany. The skill is allowing yourself psychological space in the flurry of activity around you. That's the hardest thing but also the thing that I really enjoy. There is something that I find really exhilarating about it.

I was asked to audition for *Coronation Street* when I was doing a play in Manchester. I was really excited to be asked because I'm from Accrington, which is a small industrial town where everybody watches it. I went for the audition and all I knew in advance was that the character's name was Hayley and that she was fun. I thought right, I need to be fun, so I decided to wear a leopard-skin coat – heavily inspired by Bet Lynch. The casting director explained that the part was going to be quite controversial. She told me, awkwardly, that it was a transsexual part (as people said then). She said that she was going to be a love interest for Roy Cropper. This was completely unexpected, and she asked me to come back the next week to meet the producer.

I went to Frontline Books, a radical bookshop in Manchester, as they had books on transsexualism. I have been involved in LGBT charities and politics so it wasn't something that shocked me, but it was something that I wanted to know more about. However, the available literature was quite radical and political and not exactly what was required for the role on *Coronation Street*. It fast became clear that I had to approach the role as a person rather than as an issue.

My initial thoughts were completely out of line with the writers' plans for the character. They initially saw the character as a joke. Hayley was to be part of a series of disastrous dates for Roy and some of the writers clearly thought that it would be amusing for him to go on a date with a transsexual. Thankfully (although I found out subsequently), this was never expressed to me at the time and so it was never part of my agenda for her. So, I went back the next week and I met the producer. I just said a few lines to camera, and before I left the building, they offered it to me. Although it was only a short contract at this stage, it was very different in my mind. I don't know why, but I knew, this was it, I was in. I could really do something with this character. I felt really confident about it.

Though there have been transgender characters in British television drama before your portrayal, playing the role in a prime-time soap, with a wide and varied audience base, is a considerable responsibility. Was this in your mind as you began work on the role?

I have a real belief in television's ability to change things. I had seen it happen in *Brookside* and *EastEnders* – how the public perception of things could change through the storylines. I really saw *Coronation Street* as an engine for social change, I had a real belief and determination with that.

So I was shocked when the trans community were very anti-Hayley and against me playing it. They had identified that it was planned as a joke. However, it became very clear that I was taking it seriously, and that I was playing her as a real person. She was very much part of the Corrie world.

So I started working on the role, and the research that I did was very perfunctory. It would have been a completely different story on so many levels now. For a start, I would not be cast as Hayley. They would cast a transgender person. In fact, I'm working on a series, *Cucumber* [C4 2015], by Russell T Davies and he has written a part played by a transgender woman, Bethany Black. We have a scene together and it feels a bit like passing on the mantle – from the old to the new. That was a real honour.

The issues raised by her gender shaped the character's trajectory through the storylines, but over the course of many years she came to be defined not by her gender, but by the warmth and the heart of the character. She transcends the issues that she arrived with on the Street.

Over the course of the 16 years of my involvement, the laws surrounding transgender people changed so much. Corrie got a lot of praise for the sensitive way in which they dealt with these issues and challenges in the storylines that they wrote for Hayley, particularly from the trans community. She was central to the Weatherfield community. That's the most amazing thing that it did, I think. This could only have been achieved through the longevity of the character. You can't do it in a three-part series. It's because it lasted 16 years. People knew her. She was somebody that they actually knew.

As my involvement went on, as has been well documented, the writing team got more interested in gay and lesbian storylines, and more sympathetic in their depictions of LGBT characters. These stories were more responsibly written. It became owned by the programme, rather than getting stuck with a particular storyline. Through Hayley and Roy's relationship they were able to explore the issues surrounding marriage [Roy and Hayley were married in 1999, but the marriage was not legally recognised. As a result of a change in the law, they were legally married in 2010].

It is a credit to the skill of the writers that they were able to pull the original story back into the plot through Hayley's battle with cancer. Hayley was concerned that the medication she needed to prolong her life might result in her becoming confused about her identity, and regressing back to her earlier life as a male. I thought that was a real coup. It was amazing – it was like somebody had mapped out a 16-year story arc. It was so specific to her. She felt that because her childhood was so terrible, if she regressed to that she would experience it again. I couldn't have dreamt of a more fitting conclusion to that character. When I decided to leave *Coronation Street*, I knew that the writers would decide that Hayley had to die, as that was the only way in which they would part me and Roy. Any other story would have been a betrayal of everything that we had built up. She had said everything that she wanted to say through this medium, and that's why I wanted to go.

It also meant that I got involved in other activist and profile-raising groups. There was the pancreatic cancer storyline, which had a huge campaign behind it. At that stage I didn't know anything about pancreatic cancer, but suddenly stories about it were everywhere. Simon Hoggart and Roger Lloyd Pack both died of the cancer around this time. So I joined the campaign to raise awareness about this illness. There was also the 'right to die' issue which I was asked to comment on. It was a real responsibility and was completely beyond anything that I could have ever hoped for.

Did you have discussions with writers about the storylines that they were constructing for Hayley?

No, as far as the storylines were concerned, I never had any say in it. *Coronation Street* is very writer-led in the way that some of the other soaps aren't. They are a powerful force. As a cast we do meet them (which is not the case on all soaps) and we have parties together so there is a strong bond there. When you get a script through you can tell that they understand the character and what you are trying to do with it. I also found that the writers responded to the performance that you gave. If they saw that you were good at certain things, they'd pick them out and develop them as part of your character. They enjoy writing comic scenes for the strong comic actors, for example. This results in scripts which feel tailored for you and your character. I can immediately see how to perform them. It is interesting working on a project where you don't know the ending – you don't know the character's arc. It can be a good thing. You don't try and play the ending from the beginning.

It is very rare that you get a script and you feel that there is something in it that doesn't fit naturally with your character. David [Neilson] had it a few times, where the writers might slightly over-write for him. The process is that you are meant to go upstairs to the script editor to request any changes or to discuss the script. Because I was a good girl I would do that. But David would just change it. But there is a really healthy respect between him and the writers and he wouldn't change it unless it really needed work. He would just discuss it with the director on the studio floor. For me, in the last year there were just a couple of times when I felt that I didn't like a line, or that it didn't fit with Hayley's current emotional state. So I would go and discuss these with the script editor. You feel more confident in doing this as you become more experienced in your portrayal of the character.

You can, however, get whole storylines that you don't like. I hated the storyline with my son. I love the actor who played him, but I wish that that storyline hadn't happened. When I found out that they were writing scenes about Hayley having a child when she was a man it felt like a betrayal to me. I was cross about that. It is very clear that Roy and Hayley were both virgins. There was a whole set of episodes about that, and from the transition of them being friends to being lovers. It was very beautifully and delicately done, and then a writer comes along with a new plotline which means that the circumstance that I played as true wasn't true. She was lying to him, and I have nothing to do with that decision. Sometimes you have to build a new past so everything that you thought was a fact was not true. You have to find a way to incorporate that. I found that hard. You do feel protective, particularly when you're playing a character like Hayley.

Is the creative hierarchy in soap a problem or is it helpful?

That's a very interesting question. Within the cast the hierarchy comes from respect and longevity. I could have refused to say a particular line. I do have that power. But I can't imagine myself ever being in the position where it would come to that. But, obviously, this power isn't a creative control, it is more the fact that I could withdraw my services. I could be wrong here, but I feel in television generally there is a sense of keeping the actors happy, keeping them pacified.

Becoming a voice for these issues is a significant responsibility.

You can get a bit carried away with that thought, but I was only doing what was written for me. But yes, it was a huge privilege. It went from a story in a fictional drama into the broadsheet arena – it became news. It was only towards the end of my involvement on *Coronation Street* that I started to do television appearances, and to talk about the issues raised in Hayley's story. It had a particular effect on my sense of worth as an actor, and especially as a soap actor. It is something I am incredibly proud of, but some people had, and still have preconceptions. This is particularly true of people who haven't seen *Coronation Street* and Hayley's story, and who are sniffy about it. It wasn't just a daft story. It had meaning for people.

Coronation Street brings with it a level of fame, but it is much easier for me because for years I was not recognised at all. It was the wig that allowed me this anonymity. I wasn't going to have a wig, but I cut my hair too short before we started recording, so I needed one. That haircut probably changed the last 16 years of my life! I could see how difficult it was for some of the other actors. I escaped that. Another reason was that I never appeared on any television shows as myself until the discussions around pancreatic cancer. I've kept myself completely separate from that world.

People really don't understand that acting in soap is a discipline. No one seems interested in how actors work on soap, and they have prejudices about their work. I remember a well-respected actor coming in to work on the show and he was talking to me about the process, and he clearly thought that he was above it. I said to him that this is a style, in the same way that there is a style to Restoration comedy, but that the style is difficult – it is a skill to develop. It is really hard to get round actors getting on set and doing what they think is 'Coronation Street acting'. I probably did, I was probably a bit broad at first. But you learn to moderate it, to pick up the style. But some people come in and they play everything huge. You feel like saying you don't have to do that – the camera is just there. But similarly, you have people who come in and do a film-style, naturalistic performance, but it's not that either. It is brighter than that, it is more vivid. It is in the balance between those two things and that's a really tricky area to negotiate. You can't come in and do naturalism because it looks dead on the screen. It's got to be slightly heightened but it is very individual, it's different from the other soaps; in fact each soap has its own style, and they really do vary.

There are specific challenges of continuing drama that seem to go unacknowledged. On other dramas that I've worked on, actors get so much help, such as beautiful lighting and sound. If you watch any ungraded TV drama, it looks very poor. It really looks awful before it has gone through the post-production process. But when it is all put together: the image, sound, music, the dubbing, the grading, it becomes a completely different thing – it looks wonderful. In soap the ungraded thing is pretty much what you end up with. You have three cameras, it is edited almost on the spot, there is no music, the lighting is harsh and the colours are bright, there is no rehearsal, you have 20 scenes with a lot of repetition and a lot of exposition. That is your challenge as an actor, and tackling this challenge is where the discipline, the craft, the skill of the actor comes in.

You mentioned the style of Coronation Street. *How was this passed on? Are there conversations between cast members about the style?*

It's difficult if you have done other work and you are used to being directed. Because there is no rehearsal – you just have line run, camera rehearsal, rehearsal, shoot – there is very little time. However, filming multi camera really helps, it means that apart from hitting your mark you don't have to worry so much about continuity. It is particularly helpful when you are doing emotional scenes, and you need to maintain the flow of action. It isn't really a show on which you get much direction on your acting. In fact, it is slightly odd when you get a director who comes in and wants to work on your character. When I went back into theatre, I thought that when I was being directed it must have been because I was doing something wrong.

There is, however, certainly mentoring within the cast. Alan Halsall, who plays Tyrone Dobbs, talks enthusiastically about how Bill Tarmey [who played Jack Duckworth from 1976–2010, and who was Tyrone's surrogate father when Tyrone entered *Coronation Street* in 1998] took him under his wing when he first started. Bill saw that he was talented. He was only about 13 when he started and he could've gone either way but Bill wanted to help him become a really good professional actor. Alan always knew his lines, was always the first person on set and always pleasant to work with. This is partly because Bill talked to him about the industry and about his work on the soap. I tried to play my part in helping new actors. In our Equity [the trade union for actors] group we put together a welcome pack for new cast members. It was designed to help people through the maze of the first few weeks. It explains where things were, who people were, who to go to if you needed help, how to read the schedule.

A lot of the character work sounds as if it is private and I wondered whether the process was lonely from this point of view?

The recording and the experience of working on *Coronation Street* wasn't lonely as you are constantly working as part of a team, but yes, you had to take a great responsibility for your performance – this couldn't be developed, as it would be in theatre, by working with other people. I wouldn't do much work on character at home because this was someone who I knew so well. Writers and directors come and go but the character is yours and so you feel protective. Your character belongs to you. It is your responsibility.

Did you find that your experience changed depending on different directors?

Yes, some directors were particularly interested in the shots. Hayley and Roy's flat was filmed single camera – well, it was multi camera, but shot on single camera – so the cameras wouldn't be able to focus in during it, they would have to do a long-, a mid-, and a close-up shot and so that would take a lot longer. Some directors are much better with actors than others. Some just don't understand acting and the process of it. They give you really unhelpful notes. But the best ones get invited back again and again. It's always a bit nerve-wracking when you get a new director and they are working on a big story of yours. You can find that you get defensive when a director asks you to try playing something in a different way, but you do have to be generous here and more often than not you can learn something about the character by trying this. But the main issue is the speed of turnaround which means that you don't want to jeopardise your instinctive response to the scene.

Could you describe a typical week on Coronation Street?

When I started working on *Coronation Street* there were three episodes transmitted each week. You'd get a hard copy of the complete scripts for the [next] week's episodes on the Thursday. The production office would be full of piles of scripts. On Sunday you would do the location work. When you got your episode scripts, there would be some coloured ones, they are what they call the PSC scenes [Portable Single Camera], along with your studio scripts. When I first started, Hayley worked in the supermarket, so we would do all the PSC scenes in the supermarket on the Sunday and a bit on the Monday. On the Tuesday, the whole cast would come in and you would block the whole set of episodes for the week. So you would go round with the director, set to set, in order, through the three episodes and you would block it. You would start to learn it as you were doing that. Tuesday afternoon you would normally have off and then you would record it on Wednesday, Thursday, and Friday. However, things changed dramatically whilst I was there, and by the time that I left, you'd be filming 15 episodes consecutively. So every week you would be pre-shooting a block of five episodes, you would be shooting a block of five episodes and that would go over three weeks. In a busy week you would be working 12-hour days. You'd be going from studio to studio, from block to block. It is really, really full on, and during all this, the scripts for five or six episodes would arrive each Thursday.

As you can imagine, when you get the huge pile of scripts, most actors would just tear out their scenes and then put them in shooting (rather than chronological) order. But I think one of the problems with this is that they wouldn't get the context of a scene as they had removed the scenes which they didn't appear in. I decided that I would always read the whole episode, not just my scenes. This was easier when we were recording three episodes rather than six! Some of the other actors found this hilarious; they couldn't believe that I was still reading the whole thing. I set myself this challenge – and it really was a challenge – this was a huge pile of scripts that arrived in the middle of an already formidable schedule. I found that this had real advantages, as sometimes a writer would construct a motif that runs through the episode. The script might have a line that taken individually makes no sense but, within the context of an episode, holds the scenes together. An example would be at the end of the scene the director would ask me to reach over to the phone. It wouldn't make any sense for the scene that you are in, but the next scene begins with someone picking up the phone, so you have a visual chime between the two scenes. Without reading across the episode, this would be lost on you. That was a big thing for me, but there was only a few of us who always read them.

You've mentioned that there is no time for rehearsal. How did you experience this challenge?

This is a really interesting thing, in theatre you rehearse and re-rehearse something and you hone it and develop it, but with television work, if you repeat it, you lose it. You can't keep doing it. The 'rehearsal' for me came in the form of the years that David and I spent working together. This isn't to say that we found each other's work predictable. David, in particular, would always surprise me. He has a very different process from me. I'm a really good line learner and have them absolutely down before we started recording. But David is much more organic and instinctive, but somehow it works when we are together. However, because you work together for so long, some conversations don't need to be had. There is a fantastic atmosphere working on *Coronation Street*; the cast and crew are very close.

Hayley's final scene was amazing – we just did it once. Some of it was so brilliantly written that I would read it and immediately know how to play it. They had written my character for years and knew her so well, and those final scenes were just right. For my last scene, in which Hayley ends her life, there was an understanding with the director that we wouldn't really discuss it before we recorded it. We wouldn't discuss the shape of the scene, we just did a line run but even then I found it very difficult, because it felt like it might break it, to step outside it. Luckily for me in those final scenes they made sure that everything was in place so that it happened smoothly, and so that I wouldn't be required to do it again. They created a sombre, almost holy atmosphere on set.

There can't be many actors in Britain who have lived with a character for that long.

One of the hardest things for me to talk about and to describe is the sense of the loss of Hayley. She was this person who sat between me and the fiction. Yes I miss the people, but I see my friends from the show, and I do miss the working environment, but most of all I miss Hayley. This person who sat separately from me. When I see recordings I get upset that she is not part of my life any more. I lived this whole experience with all of her friends, her community, her ups and her downs. It was a dual journey between me as an actor and as the character, so when I worked on the final few weeks it was both me and Hayley saying goodbye.

Graeme Hawley

Interview via Skype, 17 September 2015

Graeme Hawley trained at Manchester Metropolitan University. He played John Stape on *Coronation Street* in 340 episodes from 2007 to 2011. Originally introduced as a teacher and former boyfriend of Fiz Brown (Jennie McAlpine), in four separate periods in the drama John Stape's behaviour became increasingly extreme, and the character was at the centre of some of *Coronation Street*'s most dramatic storylines. Stape became a kidnapper and then murderer who, after a stint in prison and on the run, finally died in a crash following a car chase at the climax of the storyline.

How did you get involved with Coronation Street *and what were you told about your character when you started?*

I was told very little about the character when I started. The producers tend not to give you a lot of information when introducing a character.

I suppose that's because they don't have an arc at that stage – as it's a continuing drama, they develop plotlines over a long period. They do have an idea about where it might go but they don't want to impart too much of that to you initially because they're not certain if that story will develop in the way that they planned it. I was given very basic character information when I started: he's a teacher, and his backstory: that he was a boyfriend of Fiz many years ago but they lost touch. I was then told quite soon after I started on the show that there was the idea that he would have an affair with Rosie Webster [played by Helen Flanagan] but I wasn't made aware of that when I went for the job. In some ways this could be seen as a little naughty on their part as, although it wasn't quite a paedophile storyline, it was quite a dubious choice on the part of my character, and therefore likely to be a contentious storyline. I wouldn't have changed my mind at all in terms of doing it but I think, as an actor, you have to be aware of those sorts of things, especially in a soap opera context, which we all know is important in popular public consciousness. You do have to consider what the public reaction might be to particular storylines. You might even have to consider the impact on your career. The role might raise your profile, but you have to think about how it might impact on your career and your continued association with that particular role. It can be a dilemma. But they were never questions for me at that time and I loved *Coronation Street*; I always have done. I had been on *Emmerdale* [ITV 1972–] previously – I'd done about a year on that – so I thought I knew what to expect. I understood how the machine worked but I also thought I understood the exposure of a role of that kind, in terms of getting recognised and so on, but *Coronation Street* was another level entirely. It's so big, particularly if you live in the North. So it has a big impact on your career and your life.

How did things develop from the information you were initially given? What was their process for telling you how things would evolve?

A common experience of acting in continuing drama is that you are never able to play an arc, because you never know where the ending is. However, *Coronation Street*, for me, was a slightly different experience, as I kept playing out endings. When I was first introduced, I had a chat with the producer and he said, 'This is what we're going to do: you're going to have an affair with Rosie Webster, we're going to play it out over six to nine months, and what we think we're going to build to is a reveal on Christmas Day, where everyone will find out. You're going to be the villain, and I'm afraid that'll be it. You'll be gone and you won't be back.' So I was OK with that – that's the arc, and we played that out over nine months. I then left and I thought that was it. Literally two months later I got a call and was told that they were considering another storyline to bring my character back. I went in, met the producer again and he said, 'We're going to play this storyline in which he comes back, he manages to get Fiz back, but then his grandmother dies and he goes to a very dark place, and eventually he ends up kidnapping Rosie Webster and keeping her locked up. It'll be a really big storyline and we'll play it out over several months. You'll end up getting caught, you'll go to jail and that will be the end of you.' So, again, brilliant! I had a clear arc that was played out over another nine months. But then I was about to leave and they introduced another idea. The producers wanted him to go to prison but to keep visiting him in prison over the next few months. They wanted to try that out and they planned that he might come out of prison in a year and there was the potential for them to have the character on the Street again. So that was great. I was told I'd be working on *Coronation Street* once a month to film my prison scenes, but aside from that I could take some theatre work. We did that for a year, playing out the prison storyline, and the character was eventually released from prison. It was very soon after this that the producers approached me about another big storyline – my character wants to get back into teaching, he can't because of his conviction, so he steals someone's identity, and people will start 'accidentally' dying! I was very fortunate with this – they were able to give me a rough arc for that big storyline. I was told that this storyline would be huge and that it would be a slow-burner, playing out over about 18 months to two years. They did say, 'At the end of it, this time, you definitely have to go! You'll have to die!' So as much as I might say that you don't have an arc, I did, all the way through. It was like playing a four-act play over four years. In that sense, I probably had a different experience from most actors going into *Coronation Street* and I think that was very helpful to me because I was never playing 'keep me in the show'. I never had the responsibility to keep the interest alive in the character because I was always playing out these endings.

Would these story conversations take place with the writers and producers?

You would periodically meet the producer and then they would outline what would happen next. You would never really meet the writers professionally. You would see them socially, and they would talk to you in those social contexts about character ideas and get your input. But that would always be off-the-record rather than an official two-way process. Certainly for me, and I think for most actors on the show, the relationships exist only in that way. I never particularly felt as though I could suggest anything major, and I don't mean that in a negative way – it just didn't feel to me as though it was part of the remit of my job.

How was the experience of playing your character over such an extended period? Was it markedly different from the other acting contexts you've experienced?

Yes, and it was a joyous thing for me. As a lot of actors do, I forever finish plays and short-term television jobs where you go in and play a character and then leave the job, and then four weeks later wake up in the early hours of the morning and think, 'Ah – I've just worked out who he is, but it's gone now. I can't go back and do it again.' You are regularly left with questions about the play and your character when you've finished the project. So the brilliant thing about playing a character for four years is that, by the end, I could have written a novel about John Stape – I knew him so well. And a lot of that stuff is private, stuff that never really influences or manifests itself in the stories, but I knew it. This closely connects with the perception of a lack of rehearsal time in television: later on, that was never an issue for me at all, because when I received a script I knew precisely how John would speak and behave in these situations, as I was so closely linked to the character. I knew everything about him. I knew his attitudes, beliefs and his thought processes. Another brilliant thing about working in this context is that you have the history. You never had to ask questions about your backstory – you'd played out your backstory over years. So you can just take the script, learn your lines and do it, because the work is already there. And that goes for fellow cast members too. You have those long-standing relationships as actors but also as characters. All that information and work is all there when you walk on set at ten in the morning. All you have to worry about is the nuts and bolts of the scene. Where do I go? What happens at this moment? When do I go into the kitchen? It's only those sorts of details that are left to negotiate. Everything else is just already there. And that's fantastic from an actor's perspective. The work that's gone before is the preparation. That's the great thing about soap – everyone shares that information, actors and crew, and – crucially – the audience carries that history too, and more! The audience know the history of a house long before my character inhabited it, down to the history of a stain on a carpet. Someone out there will have retained that information. I know only as much as John knows, in that context, but the viewers can know far beyond that. That's what I think is incredible about it as a genre – an audience can carry that history with them. The production team, actors, writers, directors, crew – everyone can carry that collective history, or parts of it. You inhabit that fully fleshed-out world, working on the show but also watching it.

Would you ever have conversations with fellow actors about scenes outside the formal production environment?

Yes. You always take responsibility to run lines together, for example, or more complicated conversations about details. Jennie and I would talk all the time about how we were going to play a scene and what might be coming next. A lot of the time you're guessing about future scenes because you only have scripts for the next few weeks in advance, but we'd discuss where it might go and why. Once you get more comfortable and clever with it you can also discuss, as actors, where you might want to try to lead the writers. What do you want to show on screen to try to nudge the stories along in a certain direction? In that sense, it is a two-way process. It's not a formalised thing, but it's an intuitive relationship or process involving various forces at play together. I don't think that's necessarily the experience of all writers or actors – but certainly I felt that there were certain things that I could do in order to lead them down a path which they would hopefully follow and run with. But that relationship and that work happens on screen rather than in an office or a rehearsal room.

Did you have any contact with Jennie McAlpine to prepare that relationship in the very beginning?

I did a screen test with her and that was the first time I had ever met her before we started working together. There was no preparation beforehand. We were lucky that from the moment of that screen test we hit it off and got on very well, which is probably why I got the job. Within about ten minutes of being in the room you could tell it worked and they picked up on that straight away. But nothing formal.

When you started on Coronation Street, *did you get a sense of a particular 'style' to the show in terms of the acting?*

It was useful to have done *Emmerdale* before. I'd gone into *Emmerdale* to play a detective for about ten episodes which went well, so they then wanted to bring back my character for another storyline. With those sorts of roles, you're always serving another plot. So I'd done that a couple of times, and they were interested to bring him into the show more – the character had a girlfriend and then a daughter and so I came in more regularly. Partly because of the way that had happened and because of my naivety regarding soap at that time, and partly because there wasn't initially much flesh on the bones of that character to work with – he was just a police officer coming in for a related storyline – I just thought I'd play it straight and see how it went. I felt that my work was a little bland and that there wasn't much personality there. I finally ended up finishing on *Emmerdale* because a play I'd done previously was going to New York and I really wanted to do that. As a result of having done that, I went into *Coronation Street* with that information, knowing that I had to offer something up here, to find a hook and offer something interesting with the character. John Stape was a more interesting prospect because, even though there wasn't much to go on in the beginning, he was already a more fully formed character from the start. I definitely started to offer more because I was then familiar with the process and

I'd observed really good actors on *Emmerdale* and seen how they offered things. I also knew *Coronation Street* well enough to know who the actors in that show were who were doing great things with their characters and so I went in thinking I need to approach it like that. If I'm going to do this show, these people will be my blueprint, the actors to study and look at what they're doing. People like Julie Hesmondhalgh, David Neilson and Jennie McAlpine. It seemed to me that what they offered were well-rounded characters with quirks that hooked your interest. You have to make the writers want to write for you. They sit and write for the programme day after day – they want interesting characters and you have to inspire them. That is a big job for the actor in a soap opera context.

Were there particular directors that followed your storylines or did you work with a range of different directors?

It was a range but there were directors who would work on certain storylines. You would tend to do four or five blocks of filming on the trot, so if your storyline was central during that period, you'd work with a particular director a lot. Although there are many directors coming and going on the show, there's a hard core who are there regularly, and so you develop a relationship with them. With the best directors, you develop a shorthand: they know the character and the way you work, and you know the way they work, and you can predict how much input you will get from them.

Could you elaborate on what makes a 'good' director in this context?

As long as I knew what I was going to get from the director, it didn't feel to me as though there was one kind of director that is 'good' in television terms. I think it's more about knowing what you'll get. Some directors you'll get very little input from. They will just leave you to do your thing. But if you know them and know that they trust you and vice versa, you know that's the way it's going to be. That can be really great and freeing because you know that they'll take care of it technically and if they ask you to do something different, you know they're asking for the right reason – because you trust they know what they're doing, and they're not going to make you look stupid. Then there are other directors who will really go into detail with you about pulling out moments and they're also great to work with in their way. I suppose the only bad directors are the ones in that middle ground where you don't have that trust and you're not quite sure where they're going technically and they're trying to give you notes which aren't particularly helpful. But if the trust is there and you know what you're going to get then it's great.

The dynamic can be very different from theatre. In theatre, a director will say to you, 'I think he's like this, he has that', and you'll go, 'Oh yeah, I hadn't really thought about that.' Whereas that doesn't happen so much in a continuing drama as you do tend to be more in command of that information. If, in a play or a film, an actor says, 'My character wouldn't do that,' it can often be because the actor is blocking in some way, because any person is capable of doing anything in that context. Whereas, in a soap opera, an actor saying 'My character wouldn't do that' is probably right, because they know the character better than anyone. You understand the character's morals, their soul, if you've done the job right up until that point. You will know what a character is capable of and what they aren't.

Did the experience of the show feel like an ensemble, in terms of the day-to-day production?

Yes, I very much felt like part of a company on the show, maybe more than with any other show I've done. Part of that is to do with the length of time I was involved. My memories of the job are based on the whole experience. I possibly wouldn't have felt the same had I only been there for a few months as originally intended. But I really did feel like part of an ensemble and that it was our show, and that extended beyond fellow actors to the crew also. The crew and the cast are very close on *Coronation Street*. Again, it's about trust and working together to achieve something, and so you become very accepting of other people's quirks because you're all in it together. When you're busy, you're spending 12 or 13 hours a day together. It is a punishing schedule. In the first couple of years of my marriage, I spent more time with Jennie McAlpine than I did with my real wife!

When you received the script, how did you approach working on it, particularly as the turnover is so quick?

The way I approached every script on *Coronation Street* was the same. You get a block of five episodes. I would read the block, just read it all, because I need to know the context for myself, even if I'm just involved a little bit. Not everybody does that but I needed to, because I wanted to know the overall pace and where my stories and scenes would sit within that. You get a better sense of the rhythm from that. For me, that probably comes from my theatre background and experience. I would never be able to go in and rehearse a scene having not read the play, as I wouldn't know where it sat in the story. I also needed all the given circumstances. What if somebody talks about me in the café two episodes before something else happened? I needed all that information, personally. So I would read the block and then separate the script and just put my scenes together. I'd mark up the script very briefly – where I'd come from before and where I was going next. I'd then learn it very roughly, and then work day to day. The night before I'd go back to it, drill it, be very clear about where I've been and where I'm going and what's happening in the scene in terms of the wider story arc. That's how I approached the scripts every week. By the end, because of increased filming, it was very time consuming. I would spend whichever day over the weekend that I had off going through the scripts in between trying to spend some time with the family. I know some people do that for 30 years but it was never in my mind that I could sustain that.

You are also doing some teaching now relating to screen acting work. Which 'lessons' have you brought from your own television experience?

A key lesson is to dispel this myth that you have to try to be small on camera, which is absolute rubbish. It has nothing to do with size of performance. It's all to do with the level of intensity and the connection with the language. When an audience is sitting 30 feet away in a theatre you can lie to them. You can't lie to a camera that's six inches away from you. It's about drilling that into acting students and getting them to search for whatever their truth is within that, but then to be able to find character on top of that, and I think the only way you do that is through practice and watching yourself back. That's how I learnt. What puzzles me about drama schools is that actor training is still 80 to 90 per cent theatre. For the majority of drama students coming out of drama schools today, the first job they do will be a television job, the second job they do will be a television job, and the third job they do will be a television job! They'll do one play a year for the first five years, if they're lucky. And so they've had virtually no training in this art form that is going to earn them their living. Although I absolutely agree that the principles of acting are the principles of acting, the only way to be comfortable in front of a camera is to be in front of a camera. That's not to do with different principles, it's to do with experience. That's the great thing about soap as a training ground. You stand in front of a camera every day and then in two weeks, because of the turnaround, you can watch it and see what worked and what didn't. In that sense I look at *Emmerdale* and *Coronation Street* as my equivalent of repertory theatre. That's where I learnt from my mistakes and learnt what to change. It is great that those sorts of conversations about training in relation to television are now starting to happen.

Rachel Bright

London, 7 June 2015

Rachel Bright trained at Birmingham School of Acting. She played Poppy Meadow in *EastEnders* from 2011 to 2014. After two short periods on the programme, Poppy was introduced as a regular character, and Rachel recorded 147 episodes in total. Poppy's storylines were often comic, and revolved around her friendship with Jodie Gold (played by Kylie Babbington) and their romantic relationships.

How did you first become involved in EastEnders?

I first became involved when I attended a group audition. At this stage it wasn't for Poppy Meadow. They run general casting sessions when they are thinking about bringing a new family into the drama. They use group auditions to test the water, so they bring in a group of actors. They try you in different combinations and pair people up, to see how you work together and how a new family might work. In fact, I didn't hear anything back after this first group audition, as they decided that they weren't looking for a girl for this particular family.

However, I then got a call to play Poppy in two episodes. I recorded these two episodes and I didn't really think anything more of it when I had done them. I assumed that was the end of my involvement. A bit later on I came back for a short stint, and again I thought that this was just a very short run, as the storylines that I had did not seem to be designed to run for a long time; there wasn't a lot of foundation to them. I thought that maybe they needed a lighter storyline for a short time. I was very happy to come in and out and to be that 'light' they needed. My involvement during this period was under a number of different executive producers. It was clear that they had different ideas about the tone of the drama and thus storylines such as mine came in and out depending on who was executive producing the show. It didn't feel like a personal decision, it just depended on their outlook on the show, and what they wanted. So my longest stint was with an exec that enjoyed having a bit more comedy in the show.

Carey Andrews, the writer who wrote my early scenes, continued to be one of the main writers for scenes involving Poppy when she became a regular character. Because Carey 'gave birth' to the character, they allowed her to follow Poppy's storylines. I had quite a lot of contact with her, which was very helpful. In the first instance this was partly to say thanks and to ask her some questions about the character. Although there are so many writers, and they get given certain episodes to write, I often found that the episodes in which my storylines featured heavily would be written by the same group of writers. They knew these characters so well, and so were given these particular episodes.

When you first worked on the show, it sounds as if you didn't know a lot about the character. Did this change when you joined the show as a regular character?

Yes, absolutely. When I first joined the drama there weren't any detailed discussions about the character. My characterisation was very much on the back of what I had done in the audition. I was lucky though, as on set in my first scenes I had a really good director. There are a range of directors, some are very interested in and focused on acting, and some are more interested in the overall choice of shots. I had a really good acting director for those first scenes. She would make some interesting acting suggestions, she'd suggest trying the scene in different ways, she would take what I was doing instinctively and build her suggestions on the back of this. Some directors completely trust that you know your character and that you understand them – you get so many different directors coming in, and you are the one that knows your character. Therefore some directors would just let you work independently and would not make suggestions, whilst others would work closely with you on your performance choices. Some actors prefer one way, some the other. On a continuous drama like this though, the actors are the experts of their character.

In terms of learning more about my character, when I went back properly, for a three-month stint, I had a meeting with the exec producer, the writer who invented Poppy and a couple of the head storyliners (the storyline producers). They gave me a pack which included information about character traits – some very basic biographical information such as where she is from and a basic questionnaire-style list of facts about her. I also had a hot-seating session as Poppy. They asked loads of questions and I could either answer in the character or for the character. So I responded instinctively to the questions that they were asking, based on both my own understanding of the character as I had performed her in the first episodes, and also the information that I had received in the pack. By the time I had this meeting, I knew that I was going to play Poppy for quite a while, so I had had time to think about her and to make some decisions about her characteristics. It was really interesting that some of the facts that I invented about her in that hot-seating session then were incorporated into the scripts and storylines that I was given. This information influenced how they wrote her. It was great – I received a script and every so often a piece of information that I gave in the hot-seating would appear.

So some of the character decisions were yours – it wasn't a matter of just receiving a script?

That's right, though I suppose because this came so early in the process and I didn't know Poppy as well as I did later on, some of my early decisions I looked back on and thought, no, that wasn't right about her. But it was a really nice personal thing, when I saw the script and some of my thoughts had been incorporated. There is a two-way process with the writers on *EastEnders*, and you do have an input. Another way that this functions is that everyone – the execs, writers, and actors in the green room – have a live-stream of everything that is being filmed so you can see how far ahead they are in the scene running order and the writers can also listen then. And they certainly pick up on things. I don't want to take full credit for it, but when I came back as a regular character, myself and Ricky Norwood [who plays Fatboy] found ourselves next to each other at a wedding and we were messing about a bit and having a good time at the wedding and the writers must have picked up on us doing this because the more we did it, the more they wrote scenes in which we'd mess around and have fun. They are very intuitive, they see little things such as the way you might say something, the way that you had interpreted it and they will push that element of your character.

If ever you have ideas for things, you can talk to the writers about it. You could email about it or speak in person. It wouldn't always be taken on, because obviously they would have their own plans for the storylines. I suppose this makes sense, as you are the one who is living with the character through everything and can see how things might develop. This frequently happened with cast members – main storylines would be developed from our discussions. For me, though my suggestions were smaller, often they were incorporated. But if a storyline develops from a conversation with an actor, they will often take a long time to work through, because of course they already have plans.

There were other times when a script came down from the offices upstairs and there was something that was wrong in it. An issue that I came up against was the question of where she was from. When I first was on the show, I mentioned in the episode that I was from Shepherd's Bush. Several episodes later and I had received scripts in which she mentioned that she was from two different places. The first time I thought that we could probably get away with it because it had only been mentioned once very briefly in my first ever episode. But then it changed again and I thought we can't reinvent it – for me but more for the audience. They know everything, and they notice inconsistencies like this. I remember discussing this issue with June Brown [who plays Dot Branning]. I told her that we need to make a decision about this as I feel stupid saying these different places – would Poppy not remember?! You see, as I only came in as a temporary character, Poppy was developing so all the details of my character weren't finalised at the outset. June told me a story about a teacup or something very small and insignificant – one of the props in the kitchen – and this particular prop was always used in Pauline Fowler's [played by Wendy Richard] house. For some reason it had made its way into the Brannings' house, and so Dot would use it, and people wrote in to say 'that teacup is definitely not from that house'. So the viewers of *EastEnders* really spot these things. I had a duty to people who love *EastEnders* and Poppy rather than for me.

How did you go about discussing possible changes to the script?

The cast and writers were in different parts of the building. That wasn't ideal, because sometimes it can feel a bit like them and us. It certainly wasn't a bad feeling but it meant that you can't just happen to bump into them and have a chat. Each Monday, the script producer would be in the studio complex, so if we had any queries or concerns about the script we could raise it with them. They would note it down and talk to the writers about it. They were very clear that this had to be done before you got on set – if you spotted a problem you should raise it so that they had time to discuss it and change the actual script so that everybody on set has the correct information. Because everything is so quick they had to be as prepared as possible. This would work most of the time, but sometimes, because the scripts would change so often, you'd have missed them on the Monday and need something changed at the end of the week. This was a very open process though, if you read the script and felt that your character just wouldn't go down that road, you could raise your concerns.

So this wasn't just factual errors – it also applied to characterisation?

There are two answers to that really. The first example is if Poppy was having an argument with Fatboy, and I read it and I felt that she would take the blame more for that or she would not put it like that – those small conversational differences – that could be worked out quite quickly.

You would just call up the script editor and they would either agree and change it or come to a balance or they'd explain that they need you to do it that particular way because of a planned storyline or context that you didn't realise. As for bigger questions of character, you would have a meeting with the executive producer every three months. This was where you would find out where your stories were going and the longer-term plans for your character. They could tell you more of the specifics – where the character is heading. You wouldn't know exactly how they were going to get there, but at least you had an idea of the destination. This would be for the next few months at least. Of course, it would sometimes change because your storyline would be affected by the plans they had for other characters. This was different for more established characters but because my character slotted in around other storylines, Poppy's story was more subject to change. It was very helpful to have a sense of where my character was going. However, this can work both ways, I quite liked not knowing where my character was heading before I received the script, because that is more true to life. We don't know the future. You know what you want, but you don't know whether you will get there. I think that is true of the small day-to-day storylines but if they were going to give you a significant life event such as the birth of a child or a death of someone you knew, then knowing that in advance would be very helpful. Occasionally you don't have all the information on your character and sometimes, as an actor that can be difficult to get your head round. Usually, say on a film or in a play, you know the story from start to finish, and can decide how to play something, but on a continuing drama that is, obviously, not possible. As I said, this can be quite difficult, more difficult than I think some actors are given credit for – but it's a great skill to learn and something you need for such filming.

From the outside the structure of the storylines suggests a very strong ensemble across the cast. Did you feel this?

Yes I did, but this was something that builds up as I became a more regular character. On the same day as my hot-seating meeting, I also had a meeting with costume and make-up. It was there that we talked about the look of the character and had some discussions about costume but it must've been a quiet day because I didn't see any of the other actors. On my first day they were filming my scene first. I just had a very quick introduction with the other character in the scene and then we started the line run, then the camera rehearsal, and then we recorded. But because I only thought I was doing two episodes I didn't expect to meet everyone. When I returned as a regular character, I met more and more people as I worked on different scenes. There was a green room where you meet the other actors and of course you chat to them in the dressing rooms. It is a very familial relationship, and even if you don't know somebody very well, there's a real sense of camaraderie. But naturally the people that you work with the most are the ones you get to know well, as you are working with them all day for six days a week sometimes. When I started, Kylie Babbington [who played Jodie Gold] and I would be called in together, we would go to make-up together, so we got to know each other really well. She'd been there for about a year and showed me the ropes. She was in the swing of how the process worked and it was really helpful to have someone to guide you through. This wasn't to do with the acting side of it but just understanding the process of production, the admin associated with it, such as understanding your schedule, who to go to if you have a problem, and even advice about the paparazzi and where it is best to go for lunch to avoid being photographed. With your work as an actor everybody worked in different ways, and how you approach the role is your own private concern.

Could tell me a bit more about the mechanics of it and what a typical week might look like?

Kylie took me up to the scheduling department where they have huge white boards that run along the walls. Your character has a number so you find your number and therefore you can work out which days of the week you are in. Although this sometimes changes, you can see roughly when your busy periods are going to be over the next two months. There are always two or three blocks of scripts (four episodes per block) that you are working on, so you are either doing a double-bank or a triple-bank. They would be different colours, so you might have three scenes for one bank and two scenes for the other bank. So you can get an overall view of the shape of your weeks and you can mentally prepare yourself for a very busy period by checking the schedule.

You would normally receive your script about two or three weeks before you filmed it. You would never learn that version of the script because the wording and the structure would probably change, but you would know what was going to happen to your character a few weeks before. I was lucky, I didn't get many amendments generally, just the odd word here and there. The different drafts would come in different colours so the second draft would be on purple and the final draft on pink. When you got on set, a familiar question would be 'Have you got the pink papers because those are the ones that we are using?' You see people's hearts sink when they came in with the white scripts and had learnt an earlier draft. Occasionally I found that scripts changed on the studio floor – we would record them as written and they would ask me to do it again and slightly change it. Usually if that happened they would talk to the script supervisor who would be on the cans. Sometimes, if there had been a particular difficulty with the script, the script supervisor would be there in the studio, and sometimes if it was their script being filmed, they might come down to watch it and to see how it was working.

When I first started, I read the entire episode, but long-term I found that this was impossible so I limited it to reading my scenes and the scenes of the people that I came into contact with. That way, I could find out, for example, if I was having an argument with somebody, what they then said to their friend about the argument. I'd read around myself – around Poppy's world – so that I understood the context. But I wouldn't read storylines that didn't involve me. Some storylines never crossed over to you, and I'd have no idea what was happening in a different part of the narrative. Nobody read the whole script as far as I know – there just wasn't time. Often last-minute amendments are just pushed underneath your dressing room door so you would arrive in the morning and be greeted by a pile of new scripts.

Could you tell me how the process of recording worked?

You'd get there, have a line run, or maybe two depending on what the scene was. You'd run this for the camera guys, then do a camera rehearsal, then the take. So by the time that you had shown the run to the camera crew, that is pretty much what you would stick to.

So what would a week which involves your storylines look like?

A really heavy week would be six days (they tried not to do Saturdays but they often had to) and the calls started at 7am and ended around 7pm. You'd often be filming different episodes in different studios. The episodes would usually be filmed over two weeks and the first week would be all of the exterior scenes, and the second week would be the interior ones. It was always out of sequence. Because of the exterior–interior order of filming you'd often film walking down the street and then up to your front door one week, and then a week later do the moment that you arrived inside your house. From an acting point of view, I found this very difficult. In response to this challenge, I made myself a folder in which I wrote a list of all the episode numbers and next to the episode numbers I would note the basic storyline of my character through each scene. That was really helpful so when we filmed out of order I would always know how this related to the other scenes and the impact it had on the character relationships. Costume also helped here as you would put a costume back on and it would remind you of the scene that you had worked on the previous week. That would also help to give you the context. I found that if I didn't list the episodes and scenes in this way I would miss things. Also, if you don't do this kind of preparation, it slows things down on set because you have to ask the director about the context. The director might not have been working on the previous block, and so they would have to ring up the script editor and the whole thing grinds to a halt. I didn't give myself too much detail with this, because once I had a context I would remember and it gave me enough room to play with the scene but I did need the facts straight, so as to go into this quick process of recording. Not everybody would have the same process, I remember Jake Wood [Max Branning] in his episodes would come with a script covered in annotations and notes. Other actors were amazingly good at remembering the episode numbers and as soon as they asked which episode they were working on they knew exactly the context of the scene. I don't know how they did this! It is important as an actor not to get lost in the industrial processes of making this work. You can easily feel lost and pressured by it. Frequently acting processes are not a priority, it is not that they don't support the actors but they have so many other concerns you don't get the time that you would get dedicated to acting in other performance contexts. This can make you lack confidence. When you've been there for a while you get used to the machine, but it's a shock when you first arrive. It really made me respect the actors – their ability to give a strong performance first time without the support and time that you normally get.

I feel so much more confident when I'm going to record with an annotated script that I can refer to, it might be basic but at least I have the facts of the scene to hand, and understand the context. The thing I've noticed more and more as I have become more experienced is that you do all this work, all of this preparation, and then you have to try and forget it when you record. Otherwise it starts to become unnatural. It is finding the balance between preparation so you feel supported and freedom to make the conversation and context feel natural. My frustration with the process is not that we need more rehearsal time but that it would be fun to be able to try things out in different ways when recording. As much as you say you want more rehearsal, what you really want is a recorded rehearsal to capture the moment that things happen for the first time. June Brown is very good at that. In scenes with her you never knew what was going to happen – she would keep it very free. When I first started working with her it was petrifying. I wanted to know that I had to make a certain move at a certain point, but within the limits of certain marks you had to hit, if she felt that something was going one way in the scene she would go with it and you'd be expected to go with it too. That's brilliant.

Did you feel that there was a style to acting in EastEnders?

I suppose there is, but I went in there basically wanting to be as truthful as possible. A lot of people feel, or want to believe, that these characters are real. You are in their living rooms most evenings and they think of you as the girl down the road. So whatever script I was given, or circumstance I was put in, I wanted it to feel real. I think that was the main aim of the actors I worked with, but within that everybody had their own process – their own approach to achieving it. It wasn't a united process. There was never any discussion about this. You wouldn't sit around and talk about acting. People would talk about how great they thought an actor was in a particular scene, but there is never a discussion about how to do it.

But people differed in variety of ways, some actors, for example, could learn a script just by glancing at it which is very useful when the turnaround is so quick. But some people are classically trained, and some have been working on the soap for decades and have had no formal training. Some were thrown into it without any preparation at all. When I joined, I was glued to my script and I was analysing it in the way that we'd been taught to do through my theatre training. But it got to the point where there was no time to do that. But some people have no idea about these processes and their approach is much more intuitive and self-learnt. You can tell the people who have the same background as you, people who have been to drama school. You could see it in their process and I could relate to what they were doing. If you discussed a scene with them you talk about the structure and the script in the same way. But when you are working on the scene with somebody with a background that is different from you, they talked about it in a completely different way. They would generally be less interested in discussing the scene as much as the immediate emotional response that the character was feeling. It was very interesting to use elements of both techniques.

Did you get any support or guidance about the fame that comes with performing on EastEnders?

Yes, there is a structure in place to support you. When you arrive as a new regular character, you have a meeting with the *EastEnders* Press Office and they talk to you about what you might encounter. They talk to you about your past, and things that might come out in the press. You can always go up and talk to people. We had a company manager who would look after the cast in this way. The fame was difficult though. You realise that on social media there are lots of people talking about your character and your performance, talking about you, and of course you get recognised. There is much more of a blur between the actor and character on soaps than there is on other dramas I think. You are seen more as that character and you aren't seen in other roles. So when people met me they would treat me as if I were Poppy. Not as an actress playing her, but as if Poppy was there.

Could you tell me a bit about your training?

I did the three-year acting course at Birmingham School of Acting. It was three years of theatre training really. We did a short film project that lasted a couple of weeks and we had a couple of lessons on it, but nothing more than that. I think that it has changed now – I graduated seven or eight years ago. I've mostly worked in television and considering that I've had no training at it, there have been times when it has been difficult. There are always crossovers and things like script analysis that you can take from one form to the other but the actual acting skills for television were not something that we looked at. So I had to learn on the job, learning through experience.

Gary Beadle

Telephone interview, 13 November 2015

Gary Beadle played Paul Trueman in *EastEnders* in 328 episodes between 2001 and 2004. Introduced into the already established Trueman family, Paul's early storylines focused on his relationship with his brother, Anthony, and his adoptive father, Patrick. Paul's storylines became increasingly focused on crime and drug dealing, and his final scene on *EastEnders* suggested that he was being driven away to his death by a hitman. Following his decision to leave the show, Beadle spoke publicly about his dissatisfaction with this storyline, and the racial stereotyping he felt was inherent within it.

How did you first get involved in EastEnders *and how much were you told about the character at the outset?*

As with most acting jobs, I auditioned for the part of Paul but I came along quite late in the running. I think they were down to the final two when I rocked up. I'd been away and initially I thought '*EastEnders*? You're having a laugh!' but the character looked really interesting and so I put my hat in the ring. I thought that the part was quite revolutionary for *EastEnders*. To be honest I've never been a fan of soaps because a lot of it seems too instant. I have a problem with the pace of it and the lack of rehearsal time and character building. That's one of the reasons I love theatre. *EastEnders* requires you to act more instinctively and to be able to do that week in week out and then go home. That's fine for many actors but it wasn't really my thing. I went in there and tried to create a fully rounded character and got really serious with it and they liked it. It did offer up something different, especially in terms of the community that I'm representing. Black families don't tend to hang around too long in *EastEnders* but with the Truemans the BBC got it right because they allowed us to get on with it and play things out a little more. Having said that, it was a more liberal time when I arrived in *EastEnders* – you had different controllers, associate producers and executives who were more attuned to thinking in those ways. But, basically, in auditioning and starting out on the show, I did it my way and they liked it so I entered into a contract for the role of Paul Trueman.

Paul's brother and mother had already been introduced before I arrived. The father figure hadn't arrived quite yet but there was a directive to get a really good, prominent black family in the show and so they really wanted to make that happen. They established a sort of Cain and Abel relationship between my character and his brother Anthony [Nicholas Bailey], which established this great friction which allowed other characters and the viewers to choose their allegiance. They were two brothers with the same background but with very different lives and life views, which went beyond the stereotypical norms of representing a black family in soap, and I think people liked that and got into that.

When I first joined they didn't tell me anything in terms of the backstory for the character. I had no idea about planned storylines – I just knew that I was going to be a member of this family. They described the basics of the character and I liked the character so I took it from there. For me it's all about the quality of the character and then you react to the storylines accordingly. Beyond that, to start with they gave very little away, really, apart from the essence of the character. So I decided just to go in there as a South-East Londoner because that's where I'm from and I know loads of guys like Paul Trueman. I put my own spin on it with the cigarette-smoking thing and the leather-jacket thing and the way he walks and talks. I was comfortable with that because that was a type of person I was already very familiar with from life – that characterisation represented a lot of black guys all over London.

Did you have any conversations with the producers or the writers about how storylines might develop for Paul?

I was given hints of the directions in which that character might go but the details of these things are kept top secret. With shows like *EastEnders* you can make a suggestion but that's all it is. The secret is in what you do – it's all about what you do with what you're given. I was given certain things in terms of the character and then they liked what I did with those things and so you then play to those strengths. For example, Charlie Brooks [who played Janine Butcher] and I had a screen chemistry and so from that I was able to suggest that we had a relationship and they made that happen. That was only possible because we'd already shown them that there was a chemistry and that could work. That's what they do on *EastEnders* – they try people together and if there's a chemistry they go with it in terms of the storylines, if not then they move on and try something else. It's all trial and error, and it can be fun exploring those possibilities. But then as time went on I did gain more control over the character in making changes to certain phrases in the script and things like that. In those days, because of that liberal atmosphere I mentioned earlier, you could suggest changes to lines and if they were cleared and they made sense and offered a greater authenticity, they'd allow it. They were great like that and then sadly things changed.

Would these sorts of creative suggestions be part of a formal process or was it more informal?

A bit of both. It's a big family at *EastEnders*. The writers and the actors don't really mix – they're largely kept separate. Things go through the executives, so you may suggest something and they'll say 'OK, we'll get back to you' and then they might eventually say 'No, we don't like it' or 'Sure, we'll take that on board.' Largely they like to keep direct contact between actors and writer to a minimum, although I knew a few and I did, at times, informally suggest stuff. For changes to the script there was a protocol – you couldn't just change it there on the studio floor, you had to tell them about a week in advance. So you would have to read the scripts early in the process to suggest things and then they'd have time to clear or reject changes in time to be up and running on the filming. Time is money so you have to be organised if you want to have some input.

How far in advance would you get the scripts and what sort of preparation would you do?

My experience at the time was that about three months ahead of things being aired you'd get the scripts but then you'd shoot a month after receiving the script. However, you're constantly prepping and filming stuff so that process is continuous. This is where I have a problem with television work of this kind in that it is too instant and doesn't allow for depth or complexity to be explored because of the turnaround on filming. Lines get said and information gets thrown about before you have a chance to really consider the lines. For me, that's one of the sad things about soap – you often get one-dimensional performances because actors aren't given the opportunity to really get under the surface of it. When I was on *EastEnders* there was no rehearsal. You'd get the script, you'd learn your lines, you'd run the scene maybe two or three times on set and then you'd shoot it. No messing about. This means you have to deal with it instinctively, you can't go 'Method' on it, because there's no time. As a result, things can come across a little wooden at times. I was fortunate with my character in that I'd been acting since I was a kid, from the age of about 7, and so I knew instinctively how to make that character believable and also what I wanted from the character, and when it stopped feeling right I left. In some ways I think it's best to go to soap later in your career, when you've done it all, and therefore have nothing to prove but you have a bank of experience to draw from. But if you're young and you go into it straight from school then it's a different thing – because nobody really rehearses, you pick up bad habits or you just coast along – you don't really think about what you're saying and you just become part of this repetitive process. I saw that creeping into my game and that was when I realised I had to get out. Even now in theatre I have to remind myself to explore and not be such a slave to the text and the punctuation. In *EastEnders* it's all about being a slave to the text – you immediately identify what information is required, what needs to be said. In that, I found myself getting quite stilted and it's hard to get out of that mindset once you're in it. It's not the fault of *EastEnders* – it's just the nature of the beast. That's why now I'm a great believer in the value of rehearsal and getting under the script to find out more and more information. It's then that you start to see these three-dimensional characters in good drama because it's been rehearsed. In the context of something like *EastEnders*, it's more about running through to remember your lines than rehearsing.

Did you feel any benefits to living with Paul as a character for a prolonged period over a number of years?

Yes. The benefits of working on something like *EastEnders* are about getting into the discipline of learning your lines and being on it and not dropping the ball. You can get a comparable discipline at drama school and if you haven't gone to drama school then soap is probably the next best thing for learning that. I never went to university or did anything like that so *EastEnders* became my higher education in that sense. I've got a lot to thank *EastEnders* for there's no doubt about it. It made me deal with the realities of the business. I know a lot of great actors who aren't in work and it also made me appreciate having something secure. For me, a key benefit was portraying a character that was liked, or at least familiar, to the public. That brings real challenges because it's like being in a goldfish bowl and you can feel very exposed, but I learnt how to deal with it and it gave me a sort of patience and composure with people which wasn't there as much before, regardless of what opinion they might have of you. I wouldn't have that patience and that level of social skill in dealing with the public if it wasn't for my time on *EastEnders*. Because you're on television in people's homes most days of the week, they feel that they know you and therefore can approach you and talk to you. You only realise once you start on a soap that you become public property. It can bring negative comments but it also brings some lovely comments and conversations with people who enjoy your work, so it's a journey that's worth it.

Is it useful for your acting process to be able to get to know fellow cast members over long periods?

Absolutely. A lot of actors go into *EastEnders* and lose a sense of who they are on that show, and then get spat out at the other end. Especially if you're young, it can be easy to lose your identity to the production machine. It's the young ones I worry most about. Most of the time these actors aren't formally coached about what to expect and they really should be. I have to say that I was fortunate to have a producer like John Yorke on the show who told me exactly how it was going to be in terms of preparing for the best and the worst of it all. I think that's another big responsibility when running a flagship show like *EastEnders* that has such a public impact – to also make sure that those young actors involved are prepared. But, yes, that environment makes it all the more important to have other actors around you who are sharing the same experience and you can learn from each other. And I have to say that I met some fantastic people working on *EastEnders*, both cast and crew. You learn some very useful things from those people along the way. I've probably highlighted more negatives than positives so far but 90 per cent of my time on that show was a positive experience. The experience was priceless. 2001–2004 in particular were really good times on *EastEnders* and I worked with some really talented actors, writers and directors who seriously upped my game and we had some real fun with it. It was a real melting pot of creativity. That's what I love about the BBC – that potential, that opportunity, which they still have. But things keep moving and changing and some people got lazy and then others with ambition left and went on to do other things, as of course they should. There comes a time when you look around and see all your old allies gone and you just think: 'Time to go.' I'm definitely a better actor for having been involved in *EastEnders*, and also probably a better person – I'm more intelligent and aware as a result and I don't think I could have got that anywhere else. I'm very proud and grateful for what I did with the character of Paul. I've taken that experience and it will always be worth something.

Was the social power of soap in generating public discussion around ideas and issues something that attracted you to EastEnders?

In all honesty, no – I never really thought about it that way. I was just attracted to the character and thought I could make the character work, and that could have been in a play or a short film as easily as it was in a soap. It's all about the character as far as I'm concerned so I was attracted by Paul Trueman and the potential there and the ways in which he was described and sold to me. The power and the scale of soap in the minds of the public was something that only really dawned on me later. I was probably quite naive going into it, really. In fact, the very reason I left *EastEnders* connects to the question you just asked about the impact that soap representations can have in the real world, and when I became fully aware of that and the direction in which my character was being pushed, that's when I knew it was time to go. When storylines for Paul started to move towards drug dealing in a negative way, I was dissatisfied with how it was handled. I'm all for representing issues relating to drugs but if things are going to move in that way for the character, you need to know the journey. You need to understand why. I don't mean that sort of behaviour can be justified but that, as a viewer, you should be entitled to an opportunity to understand how and why that character has ended up at that point. Otherwise, people just see the end product, the stereotype, the bad guy, and that's what I always wanted to avoid. At the start, they began to weave a really complex history for the Trueman family which helped a lot in understanding the characters and their actions – good or bad – at that point. But when it got to a point where there were all these negatives being introduced around my character but with no explanations, it became a problem. When young people are watching and they just see the stereotype of a drug dealer with no explanation, it's time to call it a day. It was beyond my control, and so the only thing I could do to take back control was to go upstairs and tell them that I wanted to leave. They asked me if I wanted to leave it open to return and I said no. As far as I was concerned it had become a simplistic drug dealer narrative and the only way that could end for me was to kill him. I didn't want young people to watch my character and take the message that someone could take drugs, deal drugs and just walk away with no consequence. They'd sent the character so far down the villainous drugs route that, for me, the only option left was for him to die. I felt that was more of a positive message than him leaving for a while, coming back and all is forgiven. I wasn't having it. The executives were very surprised at my response. In the end, Paul's exit was left ambiguous. It was as if they wanted to leave it open in case I changed my mind. I don't think that was the right choice – I wanted him explicitly dead, lesson learned. I would never go back again. My conscience is clear with that. But I did realise the power of the show in representing things to the British public particularly towards the end.

The power of any art form is that it can change the way that people think – a power that many politicians wish they could harness. That's why I'm an artist, to hopefully do something positive with that, and with any character I play – good or bad – I'm always committed to showing the full journey, the full story, rather than a stereotype. With this in mind, I think the BBC can always do more in terms of representing minorities and diversity in a fair, nuanced way in its dramas. It has to be about more than just ticking that box or pleasing that sponsor. The BBC has a responsibility which it needs to take seriously. It's as if the BBC thinks, 'We've done *Luther* [2010–2015], we've ticked that box, job done.' It's just not good enough. The BBC can do better – I know they can do better. There's a whole lost generation of kids who just don't see faces like their own on television, they don't see themselves living certain lifestyles, they only see themselves as negatives and they think they were losers before they were even born and that the odds were always against them. People need to see positive images of people like them. If they don't, it's easy for them to think they're invisible and they're worthless. And the BBC has a responsibility there, in terms of what it shows in dramas like *EastEnders*. When I was a kid there were so few black actors on television but I locked on to them and what they did, otherwise I would have been in trouble. There are some brilliant people working at the BBC but they just need to stand by their convictions a little bit more. Don't get me wrong, the BBC has given me more work than any other channel – I love the BBC unconditionally! I'm just saying they can always do more. Without the BBC, we'd be in real trouble!

Acting in Soap Opera

Soap opera as an 'engine for social change'

An important contextual aspect of these actors' experiences is the prime-time nature of the programmes, and the popularity of *Coronation Street* and *EastEnders* among the general public. According to ITV's figures, 10.6 million people watched Hesmondhalgh's final scenes as Hayley Cropper (Episode 8305. This scene, along with many others, can be found on the *Coronation Street* YouTube channel). At their peak in the mid-1980s, for their Christmas Day specials, both soaps reached maximum viewing figures of around 30 million – over half of the British population. Therefore, whilst the researchers cited in the introduction to this chapter are correct in identifying soap opera as a maligned form within academic studies, it is an incredibly popular form with the general public. This, as the interviews testify, had a significant effect upon the actors' work.

Research into soap has repeatedly noted the ways in which, due to its widespread popularity, it has been able to function as a high-profile platform to address societal issues and has often led the way on tackling sensitive subjects, or courted controversy in introducing challenging and contentious storylines (such as British television's first pre-watershed lesbian kiss on *Brookside* in 1994 (see Brady 2014)). The societal importance of soap was one of the key features of the actors' experiences in this chapter. One of the recurring motifs across the interviews was not only the actors' sense of responsibility in their portrayals, but also, particularly for Hesmondhalgh and Beadle, their clear desire to advance a social cause through their work. Beadle had particular aims when auditioning for *EastEnders*:

> I went in there and tried to create a fully rounded character and got really serious with it and they liked it. It did offer up something different, especially in terms of the community that I'm representing. Black families don't tend to hang around too long in *EastEnders* but with the Truemans the BBC got it right because they allowed us to get on with it and play things out a little more … [It] went beyond the stereotypical norms of representing a black family in soap, and I think people liked that and got into that.

However, it was not until after he left *EastEnders* that Beadle allowed himself to fully reflect on the social responsibility of the role. When talking about the 'big responsibility' of *EastEnders*, which has 'such a public impact', he states:

> The power and the scale of soap in the minds of the public was something that only really dawned on me later. I was probably quite naive going into it, really. In fact, the very reason I left *EastEnders* connects to … the impact that soap representations can have in the real world, and when I became fully aware of that and the direction in which my character was being pushed, that's when I knew it was time to go.

This chapter will return to the specifics of Beadle's concerns over the representation of his character, but it is clear that the perceived social responsibility weighs heavy in his reflection, and that he entered the soap wanting to use this high-profile platform to move beyond the 'stereotypical norms of representing a black family in a soap'. As he says, 'When I was a kid there were so few black actors on television but I locked on to them and what they did, otherwise I would have been in trouble.' Similarly, Hesmondhalgh was very clear about her aims when playing the first transgender character in a soap, 'I really saw *Coronation Street* as an engine for social change, I had a real belief and determination with that.' Both Beadle and Hesmondhalgh's comments provoke searching questions about the actor's agency in soap opera. This is a complex field to which we will return. However, it is clear that, whilst they noted the prejudice against soap opera, these actors were also aware of the power of the form.

Audience investment and soap acting

High viewing figures and the public's level of engagement with the case-study programmes meant that the actors were very aware of the investment from their audience and their intricate knowledge about the show. This was a common theme across all of the interviews in this chapter. Bright notes that this awareness generated a sense of responsibility, not just to the character and the story that she was telling, but also to the drama's audience: 'They know everything ... I had a duty to people who love *EastEnders* and Poppy rather than for me.' Similarly, Graeme Hawley recalled that:

> The audience know the history of a house long before my character inhabited it, down to the history of a stain on a carpet. Someone out there will have retained that information. I know only as much as John knows, in that context, but the viewers can know far beyond that. That's what I think is incredible about it as a genre – an audience can carry that history with them.

All of these actors understood that they were entering into a 'world' when they joined the casts of *EastEnders* and *Coronation Street*. These narrative worlds had internal logics, shared histories, and audience expectations, all of which affected their acting work.

As noted in the introduction to this chapter, it has been widely acknowledged that soap operas focus on the personal. The social issues which were at the forefront of the actors' experiences indicated above were explored through their characters' personal lives, with a particular focus on their family, close friends and neighbours. Higson has observed the move from the public to the private and from the political to the personal as a general trend within television (1986, 83), and his comments have been echoed by Creeber (2004, 12–13). Dunleavy has gone as far as to define soap opera specifically in relation to 'its focus on the personal lives of the characters ... a preoccupation with private over public events' (2009, 97–98). One manifestation of an audience's investment in the soap, and the almost exclusive focus on the personal lives of the characters, was the actors' experience of a blurred line between them and their role. Hawley, who, as John Stape, was involved in numerous sensitive storylines, describes the challenge associated with his work becoming part of the 'public consciousness':

> You do have to consider what the public reaction might be to particular storylines. You might even have to consider the impact on your career. The role might raise your profile, but you have to think about how it might impact on your career and your continued association with that particular role.

This blurring of the actor/character divide has already been identified by numerous scholars. For example, Marshall, using the example of US television series *The Sopranos* (HBO 1999–2007), stresses: 'Its serial power, where audiences connect for hours and hours, where the actor commits to weeks and weeks of shoots, and years and years of being the character … transforms the actor into a blended public person and the related *personnage*.' (Marshall 2014, unpaginated) Similarly, Kilborn also points to the amount of material, rather than the style or nature of the form, as being a key contributor to the association of the actor with the character. As the actors are 'literally so often in the public eye … the distinction between their personal identity as an actor or actress and that of the character they are playing tends to become progressively more blurred' (1992, 65). However, the actors in this chapter pointed not only to the amount of screen time as a contributor to this blurring of actor and role, but also to the fact that their work permeated the viewer's *private* space several times a week. Bright remarks that:

> You are in their living rooms most evenings and they think of you as the girl down the road … There is much more of a blur between the actor and character on soaps than there is on other dramas I think. You are seen more as that character and you aren't seen in other roles.

Beadle shares the same experience, stating: 'Because you're on television in people's homes most days of the week, they feel that they know you and therefore can approach you and talk to you. You only realise once you start on a soap that you become public property.'

Bright's identification that 'you aren't seen in other roles' is also noteworthy. All of these actors are recognisable because of their work on these programmes, and though they worked widely on television before they took on their roles, they were not well-known television actors. Jeremy Butler has noted the lack of association with other roles as being a key component in an audience's blurring of soap actor and role:

> The soap opera viewer has comparatively little contact with actor promotion/publicity. He/she has usually not seen an actor in a role other than the present one … The idea of 'star vehicle' holds no currency in soap opera. (1995, 147)

Butler's point, though perhaps true 20 years ago, is not the case now. Soap opera, if not a 'star vehicle', has certainly become associated with casting choices which deliberately reference an actor's celebrity status or past roles (what Jordan has called a 'background resonance' (1981, 197–8)). For example, Danny Dyer, Kym Marsh, Timothy West and Les Dennis have all been high-profile additions to the casts of *EastEnders* and *Coronation Street* in recent years. Similarly, the proliferation, in print and online media of soap news, interviews and gossip, has meant the actors are much more involved in the promotion and publicity of the programme than was the case in 1995 (see Baym 2000). However, Butler's comments about the viewer's lack of contact with the actor in a previous role hold true for the actors included in this chapter. The resultant lack of intertextuality means that the actor's association with their role is arguably even closer.

The absence of intertextuality in soap acting is a key factor in the denigration of the actor's work on soap, as it can lead to what Butler (1995, 151) and Baron and Carnicke (2008, 31) have called an 'invisibility' of craft in performance. Without the capacity to compare characterisation and performance choices with another drama, the viewer cannot judge either the actor's departure from their own mannerisms and vocal idiosyncrasies or their range as an actor. This is exacerbated by the naturalistic aesthetic of soap, as Baron and Carnicke explain:

> When audiences encounter naturalistic performances ... [they] tend to overlook the crafted dimension of acting. The performance elements that have been crafted and carefully selected for inclusion in the film seem somehow inevitable and thus become a transparent window through which fictional characters are viewed. The conventions of naturalism require acting choices that emphasise the illusion of characters. Such performance elements are meant to disappear by calling attention neither to themselves nor to the skill of the actor. (2008, 182)

Soap's reliance on naturalism has been noted by several scholars, including Dunleavy, who observes that 'stylistically, the continuing soap demonstrates that the early aesthetic of theatrical "naturalism" has never entirely disappeared from studio-shot TV drama, its frequent close-ups continuing to exploit television's characteristic potentials for intimacy'

(2009, 21). The actor's skill within this naturalistic medium, without the reference points of contrasting roles for the viewer, can thus often be obscured.

Notwithstanding Hawley's concern about how portraying a character in a contentious storyline can, due to a 'continued association with that particular role', negatively affect an actor's casting in the future, it is arguable that actors often gain kudos and critical acclaim for their work after they have left a soap (take, for example, Sarah Lancashire and Suranne Jones, both of whom have enjoyed considerable critical success in their work after *Coronation Street*). Only at this point are viewers able to judge the actor's ability to portray different people and, crucially, to recognise the character as distinct from the actor. It is thus with hindsight that Baron and Carnicke's 'illusion' is broken, which calls attention 'to the skill of the actor'.

Actors in soap are therefore faced with a complex combination of factors. The actors included in this chapter were very aware of the social responsibility of their work, but also of the potential for their portrayals to be a driver for social change. Soap's focus on the personal, emotional and social lives of its characters, along with the blurring between actor and role, mean that the experience of acting in these programmes was qualitatively different from other roles that these actors had played.

Narrative flux

One of the central structural principles of soap is a lack of resolution for storylines, as Kilborn neatly identifies:

> Whereas other types of narrative fiction are working their way towards some suitable or satisfactory ending ... for soaps there can be no such act of closure. No clearly defined moment of resolution can ever be attained. They are forever projecting us – and the lives of their fictional characters – into the future. (1992, 36)

This lack of a discrete structure, or what Dunleavy has called a 'consistent evasion of narrative closure' (2009, 21), is one of the unique properties of long-running television drama. This was certainly the experience of the actors in this chapter, none of whom were given a long-term narrative plan for the character when they began their work. In fact, in all cases the initial plans for the characters, as far as they were explained to the actors, were fundamentally adapted as the storylines unfolded. For example, Hayley Patterson was introduced as a 'comic' example of Roy Cropper's unsuccessful quest for love; though John Stape was always designed to be a villain, there was no mention of him being a murderer when Hawley was cast; and neither was there any suggestion that Paul Trueman would become involved in drug dealing. It is, however, useful to consider how the actors in this chapter felt about the information that they had received, and how this affected their approaches to character building.

Image 1   Julie Hesmondhalgh's first appearance as Hayley in *Coronation Street*

Bright experienced a different process from the other actors in this chapter. She received an information pack and had a subsequent hot-seating session when Poppy Meadow became a regular member of the cast of *EastEnders*. Bright recalled that:

> They gave me a pack which included information about character traits – some very basic biographical information such as where she is from and

a basic questionnaire-style list of facts about her. I also had a hot-seating session as Poppy. They asked loads of questions and I could either answer in the character or for the character. So I responded instinctively to the questions that they were asking, based on both my own understanding of the character as I had performed her in the first episodes, and also the information that I had received in the pack.

This process, conducted after Bright had recorded only two episodes as Poppy, clearly relied heavily on Bright's own imagination and instincts about the character. This afforded Bright the opportunity to personalise her portrayal, though she was aware that these instinctive decisions were not always the most fitting as she became more familiar with her role: 'I suppose because this came so early in the process and I didn't know Poppy as well as I did later on, some of my early decisions I looked back on and thought, no, that wasn't right about her.' Embodying the character and improvising as her early in Bright's involvement was clearly a useful process, not only for the actor, but also for the writers who were able to use this material in their development of storylines for Poppy, 'It was really interesting that some of the facts that I invented about her in that hot-seating session then were incorporated into the scripts and storylines that I was given.'

There is a fundamental question to consider here, which is whether the actors found it helpful to know future plans for their characters, and the destination of their current storylines. We had started this research assuming that, as it is common practice on most stage and screen projects, actors would have found such information to be helpful in their work, and that a lack of information would be limiting. To some extent this was borne out in our research, and it is clear that the working processes to which Bright alludes were designed to allow some conversation to take place between actor and script editor/writers. The existence of these processes suggests that sharing future plans was privileged by the producers of *EastEnders*, and that they understood this to be of help to the actor. Bright comments that:

You would have a meeting with the executive producer every three months. This was where you would find out where your stories were going and the longer-term plans for your character. They could tell you more of the specifics – where the character is heading. You wouldn't know exactly how they were going to get there, but at least you had an idea of the destination. This would be for the next few months at least ... It was very helpful to have a sense of where my character was going.

However, it was certainly not the case that all the actors found that the more they knew about the destination of the character, the more this advantaged their acting work. Both Bright and Hesmondhalgh noted that the state of 'not-knowing' was more true to life. Bright continues:

[T]his can work both ways, I quite liked not knowing where my character was heading before I received the script, because that is more true to life. We don't know the future. You know what you want, but you don't know whether you will get there.

Similarly, Hesmondhalgh states that '[i]t is interesting working on a project where you don't know the ending – you don't know the character's arc. It can be a good thing. You don't try and play the ending from the beginning'. By contrast, Hawley was given a series of arcs in his portrayal of John Stape. In his interview, it became clear that this was an element that he found very helpful, and where Hesmondhalgh identifies the value of not playing the ending, for him it was quite the opposite; it allowed him to navigate the storyline with a strong sense of narrative progression:

A common experience of acting in continuing drama is that you are never able to play an arc, because you never know where the ending is. However, *Coronation Street*, for me, was a slightly different experience, as I kept playing out endings ... I was very fortunate with this ... It was like playing a four-act play over four years.

Clearly, the actors differed on this, and it is not a simple fact that a lack of information about the character's progression was to the detriment of the actor's process. This is a condition for actors which is a result of the structural properties of continuing drama, and is exclusive to forms that favour narrative flux over resolution.

'Living with the character': the lived experience of the character's past

If not knowing the future of a character is unusual in an actor's work, then so too is gaining a lived experience of their past. From these interviews, we would argue that whilst most actors had little information about their characters' futures, this was offset by the fact that the actors physically enacted many of their characters' significant life experiences. Richard Hewett has recently pointed to this feature of the television actor's work:

> The only temporal advantage available today is that open to actors working on long-running series such as soaps, which, while depriving them of the luxury of a full table read, at least allows regular cast members more time to inhabit their characters than would be available in a finite serial or single drama. This arguably gives performers the time to collaborate with scriptwriters and directors familiar with their working methods, enabling leads in long-running series to 'own' their characters in a way that guest incoming actors or those starring in shorter series cannot. (2015, 76–77)

We will return to the relationship with the writer that Hewett introduces, but it is evident across these interviews that the actors were able to 'own' their characters. Much of this ownership comes from the lived experience of playing the character. As the interviews here evidence, the six-day-a-week, 12-hour filming schedule means that the actor is on set, in costume, for the vast majority of their time. As Hawley joked, '[Y]ou're spending 12 or 13 hours a day together … In the first couple of years of my marriage, I spent more time with Jennie McAlpine than I did with my real wife!' This sustained engagement with the character certainly became 'ownership' for Hawley, who states that:

> I could have written a novel about John Stape – I knew him so well. And a lot of that stuff is private, stuff that never really influences or manifests itself in the stories, but I knew it … I knew everything about him. I knew his attitudes, beliefs and his thought processes.

This prolonged engagement with the role meant that many of the events that are referenced in the programmes, such as marriages, separations, and children growing up, are lived experiences for the actors. Stories with discrete narrative forms, such as in theatre and film, place emphasis upon the actor's ability to imagine the history and background of their character. Indeed, a significant body of actor-training techniques is based on developing this imaginative capacity in actors. Here, however, the actors have physically enacted these events.

In this sense, the received wisdom that the quick turnaround of soap deprivileges the actor to an extent not found in other forms is called into question. The formidable filming schedule and lack of a long-term character arc might be a challenge for some actors here, but the experience of playing these characters over years, and of spending hours working with fictional family members, proves to be a real value of the form in performative terms. Both Bright and Hesmondhalgh call this 'living with' the character. Hesmondhalgh recalls that

> One of the hardest things for me to talk about and to describe is the sense of the loss of Hayley. She was this person who sat between me and the fiction … I lived this whole experience with all of her friends, her community, her ups and her downs.

This intensely close relationship, though perhaps most keenly felt by Hesmondhalgh, was a shared experience across the interviews in this chapter. The level of engagement with a character as she or he develops across the duration of the actor's involvement raises questions about a complex relationship in soap opera: the actor and the writer.

Soap acting and writing the character

As Hewett notes, the actors' prolonged engagement with the character 'arguably gives performers the time to collaborate with scriptwriters and directors familiar with their working methods' (2015, 76–77). Whilst there has been some mention of directors in these interviews, and there is clearly more work to do to explore how actors and directors work together on soap, by far the most interesting relationship from these actors' perspectives was with the writers.

There are two distinct structures to consider here: the direct and indirect relationship between actor and writer. We have already encountered Bright's meetings with the executive producer every three months. On both *EastEnders* and *Coronation Street* the actors reported that the writers and casts were separate both in terms of physical location and organisational structure. Both programmes arranged informal, social events where they would meet, and the actors here noted that the conversations at these gatherings would occasionally shed light on the writers' plans for their character. However, the indirect links were at the forefront of the actors' experiences and it is these which thus demand the closest analysis.

Though they would rarely meet, the actors in both these case-study programmes clearly felt a connection with the writers. This manifested itself in a variety of ways, but was most frequently experienced as a sense that the writers were responding to the actors' contributions to the performances captured on camera. The writers would thus identify an actor's particular skills or their inclination towards certain emotional states for their characters. Bright, for example, explained how the writers responded to Poppy's scenes early in her involvement:

> [W]hen I came back as a regular character, myself and Ricky Norwood [who plays Fatboy] found ourselves next to each other at a wedding and we were messing about a bit and having a good time at the wedding and the writers must have picked up on us doing this because the more we did it, the more they wrote scenes in which we'd mess around and have fun.

It is also noteworthy that Carey Andrews, the writer who had introduced Poppy Meadow, tended to write Bright's high-profile storylines, suggesting again that there was a close affinity between the actor's and writer's work on the character. Therefore, though this was an indirect relationship, they certainly felt closely connected to the writers. It also meant that the relationship was based not on discussion or abstracted thoughts about the character's future, but by responding to screen evidence of the actor's work. Hobson underlines this link between actor and writer: '[W]hile writers create characters, after the actor has appeared in the part for any length of time, the writers pick up on the natural characteristics of the actor and incorporate them into the character.' (2003, 67) One of the issues with Hobson's identification is that basing this connection on the actor's 'natural characteristics' obscures the actor's agency, and underplays their acting skills to develop a role as distinct from themselves. In a form in which the industrial production methods move so quickly, the ability to respond to the actor's skills (rather than their 'natural characteristics') allows for this speed to be maintained whilst ensuring that they feel a connection with their character's depiction. However, as this chapter will go on to discuss (and as Bright experienced), actor–writer communication is often mediated by the programme's producers, who have their own agendas for narrative development.

The act of filming

This indirect relationship with the writers also had a bearing on the actors' experiences of filming. One of the distinctive features of working on the case-study soaps is the sheer amount of time that the actors spend in front of the cameras. The volume of material required to sustain four weekly episodes of *EastEnders* and five episodes of *Coronation Street* means that the production turnover was formidable for them. One by-product of this demand is that there was no time for rehearsal. Ostensibly, the mechanical process of line run, blocking rehearsal, camera rehearsal, and recording appears to reduce the actors' work to a series of physical actions and blocking moves. This prompts questions about where creativity sits within the process. If technically executing the scene as efficiently as possible takes priority in the production schedule, surely the actor's work is deprivileged? Our expectations had been that this tight turnaround and scheduling would have been universally unpopular with the actors. Though Beadle raises concerns about this in his interview, his view was not unanimous across the actors. Rather, this is where a lived experience of the character was invaluable for them. Hawley, in particular, is very clear about how this functioned for him:

> You never had to ask questions about your backstory – you'd played out your backstory over years ... All that information and work is all there when you walk on set at ten in the morning. All you have to worry about is the nuts and bolts of the scene. Where do I go? What happens at this

moment? When do I go into the kitchen? It's only those sorts of details that are left to negotiate. Everything else is just already there ... The work that's gone before is the preparation.

In light of Hawley's comments, we can understand that the blocking rehearsal merely provides the context for a scene which he felt had been tailored for him, and which revolved around a character that he understood intimately. His comments also prompt us to identify the difference between rehearsal and preparation. For Hawley, these are not the same thing. Though he may not have had rehearsal time, he could draw on years of preparation. It is the shared understanding between the actor and the writer that enables this speed of turnaround. As Hawley states: 'This closely connects with the perception of a lack of rehearsal time in television: later on, that was never an issue for me at all ... as I was so closely linked to the character.'

With these factors in mind, we can explore some of the ways in which the actor–director relationship functions. The actors in this chapter report that when working with experienced soap directors, they feel trusted with character questions and rarely would a director attempt to change an acting choice when the actor has played the character for years. Rather, the day-to-day importance of the director is to place those characters in a logical and plausible narrative context, as 'story technicians'. In addition, the director has an eye on the integrity of the narrative across the whole episode in ways in which the actor does not.[1] Therefore, as Hawley identifies, the backstory has been lived by the actor; they are the experts and custodians of the character. The director thus provides the context for these performances, but does not develop the character with the actor in ways which are familiar in other acting contexts.

Problematising the actor–writer relationship

In his interview, Hawley also suggests that the actor–writer relationship can become more complex than one based only on a close responsiveness to the actor's work. He comments that one of the great advantages of being given a character arc that stretched out over two years was that he 'was never playing "keep me in the show"'. Hawley goes on, 'I never had the responsibility to keep the interest alive in the character.' This problematises the actor–writer relationship, and suggests that, with little control over either their character arc or, indeed, the length of their contract, part of an actor's work is to make the writers want to write for their character. This element speaks to an important question about the actor's agency in these programmes. Despite becoming experts about their characters and often having specific aims about what they wanted to achieve with their depictions, despite becoming recognised by the public as them, and despite receiving episode scripts that were so responsive to their work that they felt that they had been tailored for them, none of these actors had any control over the length of their involvement, or how their character might change in the unfolding narrative. Though their public profile was high, and the programmes rely heavily on the actors to depict the lives of the characters, job security for these actors was very limited. This simultaneous sense of significant responsibility to their audience and powerlessness to control the narrative or duration of their involvement was brought into stark relief in Beadle's interview.

Image 2   Gary Beadle as Paul Trueman in *EastEnders*

Beadle's experience of powerlessness in *EastEnders* provides an example of the problems which can develop from the actor's lack of agency. We have heard about the way in which Beadle saw his role in *EastEnders* as an opportunity to go beyond 'the stereotypical norms of representing a black family in soap', and it is clear that, for a period, he felt that the producers and writers were of the same intent. However, this started to change, as Beadle remembers:

> When storylines for Paul started to move towards drug dealing in a negative way, I was dissatisfied with how it was handled. I'm all for representing issues relating to drugs but if things are going to move in that way for the character, you need to know the journey. You need to understand why. I don't mean that sort of behaviour can be justified but that, as a viewer, you should be entitled to an opportunity to understand how and why that character has ended up at that point. Otherwise, people just see the end product, the stereotype, the bad guy, and that's what I always wanted to avoid.

The particularly concerning aspect of this character development from the perspective of the actor's creative investment is that Beadle had very little power to do anything about it. Indeed, the only positive action he could take was to withdraw his services:

> It was beyond my control, and so the only thing I could do to take back control was to go upstairs and tell them that I wanted to leave … As far as I was concerned it had become a simplistic drug dealer narrative and the only way that could end for me was to kill him. I didn't want young people to watch my character and take the message that someone could take drugs, deal drugs and just walk away with no consequence.

His integrity as an actor was evidently compromised by this experience. Even here, he found his exit from the show to be more ambiguous than he would have liked, as the death which was promised by the hit-man storyline was not included in the episode, but rather suggested by his final scenes (clips from Beadle's final episode, aired on 23 December 2004, can be viewed on the *EastEnders* YouTube channel). Hesmondhalgh responded in a similar way to our question about the creative hierarchies in continuing drama, stating that the actors' 'power isn't a creative control, it is more the fact that I could withdraw my services'. Though Hesmondhalgh did not face the fundamental issues with her character's depiction which dominated Beadle's final months on *EastEnders*, the two interviews demonstrate that whilst both actors were led by a strong social sense of purpose, neither had ultimate control over their involvement.

There is a further structural property to soap acting which complicates the actor–writer relationship. Character backstories are frequently revised within soap operas, in order to better suit current narrative developments, in a process referred to as 'retro-active continuity changes' or, in fan discourses, 'retcons'. This feature of soap opera was universally seen to be problematic by the actors included in this chapter. Hesmondhalgh's example of the introduction of her son was one of her most frustrating experiences on *Coronation Street*:

> When I found out that they were writing scenes about Hayley having a child when she was a man it felt like a betrayal to me. … a writer comes along with a new plotline which means that the circumstance that I played as true wasn't true. She was lying to him [Roy], and I have nothing to do with that decision. Sometimes you have to build a new past so everything that you thought was a fact was not true. You have to find a way to incorporate that. I found that hard.

Narrative flux can thus apply to the past as well as the future. Clearly, here, the actor's work is fundamentally compromised. Hewett has also identified this challenge for actors in long-running drama, stating: 'the revelation of new character information in re-written scripts can also cause actors to regret performance choices already made and recorded on film' (2015, 80). The narrative technique of retro-active continuity change undermines the concept of 'lived experiences' and how these function in providing the actor with a lived (rather than invented) memory.

Conclusion

It is evident that the actors' position in the apparatus of these long-running dramas is more complicated than a simple belief that they are deprivileged would suggest. Whether it has been the 'invisibility' (Butler, 1995, 151; Baron and Carnicke 2008, 31) of performance, the quantity and speed of output, lack of rehearsal time, or the 'neglected' form in which they work, acting in soap has rarely been deemed worthy of study. This chapter has probed some of the common misconceptions about soap opera and, in viewing the production processes from the actor's point of view, we are able to identify some surprising features.

The lack of rehearsal time was much less of an issue than we had expected, and the actors' main challenges were a result of their lack of control over their long-term involvement, rather than the immediate performance context in which they found themselves. In fact, the actors in this chapter identified many aspects of soap which supported their work and allowed them a relationship with the character which is denied in other roles. The combination of the lived experience of the role and the writers' tailoring of the script to their portrayal was central to their ability to work quickly and confidently in front of the cameras. It was also this feature which proved to be so problematic when it was undermined. Either through retro-active continuity changes, or through narrative developments with which the actors disagreed, this compromised the actor's relationship with their character and destabilised their work.

At the heart of the actors' involvement is a paradox: they are simultaneously high status as they are the faces of these dramas and audiences invest in the stories that they are so central to telling; they are the constant feature in a production landscape where writers and directors come and go. However, at the same time, they lack any ability to control their character's destiny or their own involvement in the programme. As explored in this chapter, this simultaneous privileging and deprivileging of their work prompted the actors to find specific and hitherto unexplored strategies for character development, preparation and execution. These combine to make acting in soap opera a distinctive and unique experience for these actors.

It is important to note that these four actors, like the actors elsewhere in this book, self-selected to be interviewed about their acting work in soap opera. It is also noteworthy that all of these actors had finished appearing in the role that they discussed. This was inevitable given the working hours of soap actors; those currently appearing were too busy to be involved. Elsewhere in interviews included in this book and for our other research in this area, acting on soap continues to be a touchstone for actors when discussing how challenging television work can be.

Snobbery about the form is less common amongst actors than a combination of wonderment and concern about how actors manage in such exacting industrial conditions. This further suggests that these four actors might be unrepresentative in their broadly positive (although critically reflective) outlook on this form of television. However, as stated in the introduction to this chapter, soap continues to be a disparaged or overlooked genre of television within public and critical discourses of televisual 'value', particularly in terms of its acting. If this chapter goes some way towards identifying the specific processes of actors within soap, and acknowledging the skill and creativity with which they work, then we make no apology for focusing on actors who view soap as a uniquely televisual acting challenge, and one with significant opportunities as well as limitations.

References

Allen, R.C., 1995. *To Be Continued … Soap Operas from Around the World.* London: Routledge.

Baron, C. and S.M. Carnicke, 2008. *Reframing Screen Performance.* Ann Arbor: University of Michigan Press.

Baym, N., 2000. *Tune In, Log On: Soaps, Fandom, and Online Community.* London: Sage.

Brady, A., 2014. 'Heroic Kisses, Pseudo-events and Homosexual Propaganda', *Celebrity Studies,* 5:1–2, 83–86.

Brown, M.E., 1990. *Television and Women's Culture: The Politics of the Popular.* London: Sage Publications.

———1994. *Soap Opera and Women's Talk: The Pleasure of Resistance.* London: Sage Publications.

Brunsdon, C., 1997. *Screen Tastes: Soap Opera to Satellite Dishes.* London: BFI.

———2000. *The Feminist, the Housewife, and the Soap Opera.* Oxford: Clarendon Press.

Butler, J., 1995. 'I'm not a Doctor, But I Play one on TV', in R. Allen, *To Be Continued … Soap Operas from Around the World.* London: Routledge, 145–163.

Cooke, L., 2003. *British Television Drama: A History.* London: BFI.

Coronation Street YouTube Channel. Accessed at: www.youtube.com/user/corrie (last viewed: 1 February 2017).

Creeber, G., 2004. *Serial Television: Big Drama on the Small Screen*. London: BFI.

Dunleavy, T., 2009. *Television Drama: Form, Agency, Innovation*. Basingstoke: Palgrave.

EastEnders YouTube Channel. Accessed at: www.youtube.com/user/EastEnders (last viewed: 1 February 2017).

Ellis, J., 2007. *TV FAQ: Uncommon Answers to Common Questions about TV*. London: I.B. Tauris.

Geraghty, C., 1991. *Women and Soap Opera: a Study of Prime Time Soaps*. Cambridge: Polity Press.

———— 2010. 'Exhausted and Exhausting: Television Studies and British Soap Opera', *Critical Studies in Television*, 5:1, 82–96.

Hewett, R., 2015. 'The Changing Determinants of UK Television Acting', *Critical Studies in Television*, 10:1, 73–90.

Higson, A., 1986. '"Britain's Outstanding Contribution to the Film": The Documentary-Realist Tradition', in C. Barr (ed.), *All Our Yesterdays: 90 Years of British Film*. London: BFI.

Hobson, D., 2003. *Soap Opera*. Cambridge: Polity.

Jordan, M., 1981. 'Realism and Convention', in R. Dyer, *Coronation Street*. London: BFI.

Kilborn, R., 1992. *Television Soaps*. London: Batsford Cultural Studies.

Lifschutz, S., 2014. Interview with Authors, York, 27 June.

Marshall, P.D., 2014. 'Seriality and Persona', *M/C Journal*, 17:3, unpaginated.

Wilsher, J.C., 1997. 'TV Series Drama: A Contradiction in Terms?', *The Author*, Spring, 11–12.

Notes

1   As *EastEnders* director Sophie Lifschutz stated, 'The way I see it is that I'm visiting director and they are continuing actors. It is not my role to come in and say it shouldn't be like this, I don't have a right to do that. I see myself as being in charge of the story, facilitating the story. Nobody else in the studio has an eye purely on the story. The camera team are fantastic and they can easily set up the shots without me. Actors know their story, they know where they are coming from and where they are going to, and everything – lighting, make-up, hair – runs like clockwork. But nobody is looking for story apart from me, so I need to follow the thread through of people's emotions, plot points, I'm looking for story from an acting and performance perspective.' (2014)

3

Police and Medical Drama

Introduction

Representations of policing and medicine dominate British television drama production. Twenty years ago, critic A.A. Gill had already identified what he saw as a saturation point in British police dramas, stating: 'Review television and you will meet more policemen than the Krays' (1996). Similarly, critic Jan Moir commented of hospital drama: '[T]here are so many medical [shows] … you will soon be able to conduct your own operations.' (1996) Showing no signs of abatement, British television's depictions of law enforcement and medicine have continued to proliferate since these comments were made, with David Stubbs noting of police drama that we continue to see 'a spread of variations on a very old and trusted format' (2015). As the tone of the above comments implies, critical accusations of overly formulaic, predictable repetition in police and medical dramas persist, with Peter Ansorge, former Head of Drama at Channel 4, memorably asserting that '[t]here are too many cop shows and they are becoming all the same. The same stories, the same lighting, same camerawork, same dead bodies' (cited in Brown 1996). Compounding this, albeit less pejoratively, John Yorke, also previously Head of Drama at Channel 4 and former Controller of BBC Drama Production, claims that genuine character change is the great illusion of long-form television drama: 'Characters have only one story, and all attempts to counter that are a lie … great and glorious ones if the lies are well told, but lies nonetheless.' Instead, Yorke argues, characters often 'find themselves in endlessly similar repetitive storylines, becoming paler shadows of their former selves' (2014, 184). Indeed, the associated challenges of such narrative repetition and perceived character stasis within these dramatic forms emerge as key concerns for actors across this chapter's interviews.

The pervasiveness of police and medical dramas endures in no small part because of the attractive narrative flexibility that these formats facilitate for television makers in an ever-increasingly competitive, risk-averse and commercially driven production environment. Back in 1985, Horace Newcomb noted the rise of 'cumulative narrative' (23) techniques within US television drama (in the first instance, specifically in relation to US detective drama), through which the traditional series structure (which prioritised episodic narrative resolution) was gradually being augmented and redefined by the inclusion of trans-episodic, hermeneutic elements which focused instead on characters and relationships. Previously, these ongoing, serialised attributes had been the province of daytime US soap opera, but the arrival of prime-time, evening soaps such as *Dallas* (CBS 1978–1991) saw these attributes permeating genre-based formats more broadly, particularly police and medical dramas. The resultant market success of such US texts (both in domestic and international contexts) saw these narrative strategies traverse the Atlantic for incorporation into European drama formats, with a resultant soap-like privileging of the 'personal' as noted by television dramatist J.C. Wilsher in a British context (Wilsher 1997, 11, cited in Creeber 2004, 1). In line with these aforementioned trends towards what has since been termed 'soapisation' (Ellis 2007, 104), with 'flexi-narrative' (Nelson 1997) structures resultantly predominating in British television drama production, police and medical dramas offer highly adaptable narrative precincts within which interwoven storylines of various lengths can be spun out indefinitely if a format proves successful with audiences. Moreover, following the soap model, the adaptability of these precincts often extends even to the characters who populate them, with regular characters becoming replaceable once the world of the drama is established sufficiently to withstand such change and renewal is required. As this chapter's interviews evidence, such format adaptability, which can be perceived as disposability from an actor perspective, can impact upon the work of actors in these dramas in a variety of ways.

The long-standing success of police and medical dramas on British television can also be attributed in part to the appealing mythical oppositions that they provide, at their foundation, for viewers. As has been considered extensively elsewhere (touchstone examples include: Fiske 1988; Tulloch 1990; Jacobs 2003), beneath the surface-level characters and storylines of these dramas exist fundamental structural binaries between good and evil, life and death, order and chaos, with police and medical protagonists often acting as the anomalous figures straddling the boundaries of such narrative oppositions in order to face our worst collective fears and to restore balance and order. The repetition of these mythical deep-structures, in the guise of stories about the everyday work of detectives and doctors, provides an almost ritualistic catharsis for viewers. Recognising this process in a literary context, Jonathan Culler postulates that there is something profoundly satisfying about the shape of the traditional detective narrative, with its pattern of deduction, solution and final reinstatement of stability in response to an initial social disruption:

> The detective story is a particularly good example of the force of genre conventions: the assumption that characters are psychologically intelligible, that the crime has a solution which will eventually be revealed, that the relevant evidence will be given but that the solution will be of some complexity, are all essential to the enjoyment. (1975, 148)

Similarly, whilst the surface details change, every time a television detective apprehends a criminal or a television doctor saves a patient, there is a repetitive yet gratifying essential narrative process – of inciting problem, skilled response and ultimate resolution – which must first be followed. As this chapter's interviews indicate, such ritualistic narrative deep-structures and mythic character archetypes, although clearly pleasing to audiences, can test an actor's capacity to find sustained psychological credibility in character actions or in more long-term character development.

Above such deep-level narrative structures is a social realist aesthetic which has proved an enduring feature of both police and medical drama on British television throughout the last 60 years. As David Buxton acknowledges of the early genre approaches of the mid-twentieth century, 'In Great Britain … the police series proudly waved the banner of realism' (1990, 120), with James Chapman supporting this in stating that 'early police series … drew upon the conventions of the documentary-drama to offer realistic accounts of police work' (2009, 11). Similarly, Jason Jacobs highlights that the British Medical Association provided advisors who would check through the scripts of the earliest hospital dramas for medical accuracy (2008, 34). Indeed, aims of verisimilitude were prominent in depictions of both policing and medicine on British television from the start, very much in keeping with the broader social realist preoccupations of British new wave cinema and 'kitchen sink' drama at that time. Whilst increasingly stylised production values and melodramatic content have intervened somewhat in determining the direction of these genres over the decades that followed, those early aims of verisimilitude left an indelible mark on production to this day, evidenced by the continued popularity of 'procedural' forms of both police and medical drama interested in incorporating authentic representations of the day-to-day professional practicalities of such work into their narratives. Without delving too deeply into the rich and complex histories of these genres and the similarly rich and complex associated academic studies, these lasting concerns of verisimilitude have a continued bearing upon the concerns of actors working within these forms. As this chapter's interviews attest, unlike the precincts of soap opera, the precincts of police and medical dramas are often highly professionalised, necessitating a level of fluency in the professional language and procedures of these precincts on the part of the actor, if their work within these dramatic worlds is to seem credible. However, there are always limits to realism in the creation of engaging drama, and this fact is also borne out in the insights of our actor interviewees regarding the unequal power dynamic between authenticity and effective storytelling, in which accuracy is desirable but must sometimes be sacrificed for the sake of entertainment.

Connected both to the mythic and the realist dimensions of police and medical dramas, much has been made within existing scholarship of the significance of these forms as discursive sites for 'working through' (Ellis 2002) evolving social understandings and resultant issues and existential concerns. Supporting this, Charlotte Brunsdon asserts that police drama 'works over and worries at the anxieties and exclusions of contemporary citizenship, of being British and living here, now' (2000, 197), whilst Jacobs sees medical drama of the 1990s onwards as a mirror on the 'intensification of the medicalisation of everyday life', playing out storylines connecting to important social debates and fears around topics such as euthanasia and HIV (2008, 36). Within the analysis of these discursive practices, there is a particularly rich vein of research relating to evolving discourses of gender in British police drama (e.g. Brunsdon 2000; Jermyn 2003; Creeber 2004; Sydney-Smith 2009), as both examining and influencing the disintegration of traditional masculinity and the redefinition of femininity through the lens of such narratives. Indeed, both police and medical representations on British television have taken markedly more critical turns over the last few decades, focusing increasingly upon the institutional failings, prejudices, inequalities and corruptions of both law enforcement and national healthcare, and with detective and medical protagonists becoming ever-more fallible and emotionally and psychologically flawed. As this chapter's interviews indicate, these more socially discursive aspects to the genres deliver dramatic opportunities but also representational responsibilities for actors, in 'working through' increasingly complex notions of justice, gender, ethnicity, health and disability, amongst other themes, for contemporary audiences.

Interestingly, actors have been at the forefront of such genre innovations in the British context. Television dramatist Lynda La Plante, for example, has revealed in interview that she created DCI Jane Tennison (played famously by Helen Mirren), the protagonist of the critically acclaimed and much-studied gender revisionist police drama *Prime Suspect* (ITV 1991–2006), in no small part because of her experiences earlier in life as a bit-part actor for police shows, in which the best role she could hope for was as a WPC or a prostitute: 'You could play Ophelia at the Royal Shakespeare, or star as Hedda Gabler at the National, and when you went up for a television part they would … invite you to read the two-line part of a prostitute.' (cited in Day-Lewis 1998, 81) Thus, it was an actor's experience of gendered inequalities of opportunity in the casting of traditional police dramas that determined La Plante to offer 'something better' (cited in Day-Lewis 1998, 81) with *Prime Suspect*.

Equally, actors are key to the often less-than-innovative commercial drivers behind these popular television genres. Relying upon a small casting pool of pre-established, 'bankable' names to lead dramas and casting to type to minimise production risk are common branding strategies for both police and medical shows on British television. ITV, for instance, regularly develops drama concepts primarily as vehicles for (often pre-contracted) 'star' actors, who carry with them a 'background resonance' (Jordan 1981, 197–8) from their previous screen roles, offering a familiarity which appeals to audiences but also limits the potential for exploring new dramatic directions and performative opportunities within these genre formats. Two of this chapter's actor interviewees who can both be said to occupy such 'star' status – John Hannah and Ken Stott – reflect upon the consequences of these commercial drivers for their work.

Police Drama Case Study: *Rebus* (STV, 2000–2007)

Based upon Scottish author Ian Rankin's popular series of crime novels following the investigations of DI John Rebus in and around Edinburgh, STV's *Rebus* adaptations offer a rich example of both the opportunities and the limitations for actors leading police drama formats within a commercially focused production environment. Following the considerable international success of ITV's *Inspector Morse* (1987–2000), adapted from the novels of Colin Dexter and starring perhaps the most iconic male actor in the history of British police drama, John Thaw, it is of little surprise that STV – ITV's Scottish affiliate – was receptive to implementing a comparable production strategy in a Scottish context with *Rebus*. Not only did *Inspector Morse* harness the significant popular 'background resonances' of its star to bolster public appeal, it also effectively merged the genre components of traditional police drama with the historical beauty of Oxford, offering a detective-heritage hybrid which proved an attractive commodity to audiences both at home and overseas. The clear aesthetic and cultural attributes of Edinburgh offered the possibility of similarly successful hybridity for *Rebus*, as did the casting of John Hannah as the eponymous detective, a Scottish actor who had become a popular face on film and television during the 1990s, with roles in highly successful British-based but internationally distributed films such as *Four Weddings and a Funeral* (dir. Mike Newell 1994) and *Sliding Doors* (dir. Peter Howitt 1998), along with a lead part in the earlier STV forensic detective drama *McCallum* (1995–1998).

However, *Rebus* followed a more unsteady and ultimately less successful production path than *Inspector Morse*. Series One, starring Hannah, was produced by the actor's own production company, Clerkenwell Films, first airing from 2000 to 2001 (but with the final episode postponed indefinitely following the 9/11 attacks, not airing until 2004 as part of a rerun of Series One on ITV3). With the departure of Hannah after the first series and a substantial production hiatus, STV eventually reactivated in-house production on *Rebus* in 2005 for a further three series, first airing from 2006 to 2007 and starring Ken Stott, another 'bankable' Scot, having previously starred in successful British police dramas *The Vice* (ITV 1999–2003) and *Messiah* (BBC 2001–2008). For Stott's *Rebus* episodes, substantial format modifications of both structure and style were made to the initial production model offered by Clerkenwell Films, moving from 120-minute to 60-minute story running-times (including commercial breaks) and adopting a notably more conventional-realist approach to character and story presentation, far closer in line with STV's flagship police drama, *Taggart* (1983–2010). In 2008, following Stott's decision to leave the show, the cancellation of *Rebus* was announced (Holmwood 2008). Since then, STV has intimated that *Rebus* is planned to return (*scotsman.com* 2011). However, in 2012, Rankin confirmed that he had reclaimed the rights to his creation, having not been happy with the later STV adaptations of his stories (Dingwall 2012). This chapter's interviews with both John Hannah and Ken Stott address their work on *Rebus*.

Medical Drama Case Study: *Holby City* (BBC, 1999–)

Created as a format spin-off from the popular BBC medical drama *Casualty* (1986–), after 19 series and over 800 hour-long weekly episodes, *Holby City* has become a staple example of the medical genre on British television in its own right, with high intensity production demands placed upon its regular cast and crew through 50 weeks of the year (Redwood 2003).

Set in the same fictional hospital as *Casualty*, *Holby City* moves beyond the boundaries of the Emergency Department to depict the more general professional and personal dramas of a core ensemble of doctors, nurses, surgeons, hospital managers and ancillary medical workers operating across a number of different wards within Holby City Hospital. The show was launched in 1999 with a cast of 11 actors in central, recurring roles, all of whom have now left. Indeed, in line with the aforementioned adaptability of the precincts of medical drama, many actors have entered into and departed from *Holby City* over almost two decades of continuous production. As a proximate rule, the show maintains a core cast of around 15 actors at any one time, regularly refreshing storylines with character entrances and exits. From the start, *Holby City* has adopted a casting strategy which combines little-known actors with highly 'resonant' pre-established screen faces such as Jane Asher, Robert Powell and Art Malik. The success of such approaches in casting and production has been borne out in the show's enduring popularity with audiences, along with critical recognition, nominated for over 100 television awards since 1999 and winning ten, including a British Academy Television Award for Best Continuing Drama and four Screen Nation Awards.

However, the melodramatic tendencies of *Holby City* which hold a clear appeal for many viewers have also invited criticism, particularly around issues of realism and medical accuracy. *The Independent* critic Tom Sutcliffe (2009), for instance, declared it 'astonishing' that any of the show's patients survive, with medical staff 'so busy looking stricken or lovelorn at each other', signposting broader criticisms of the steady pervasion of 'personal', soap-like narrative attributes and emphases across a wide spectrum of popular television genres, as identified in Chapter 2. On the other hand, *Holby City* maintains production strategies more aligned with the social realist – even socially progressive – traditions of the genre. As this chapter's interviews go on to explore, the production employs medical advisors to offer scripting and performative input on medical terminology, procedural accuracy and health service hierarchies and politics. Moreover, actors are taught to emulate a variety of medical skills, from basic injections to complex open heart surgery, with many cast members spending research days shadowing real medical activities. At a less pragmatic and more symbolic level, inclusivity of casting has been a priority for *Holby City*, recognised by Channel 4's 2008 review of British television's representation of ethnicities as a positive example of diverse programming (*news.bbc.co.uk* 2008). Alongside this, the show has made equally progressive developments in its representations of disability in a professional medical setting, as evidenced by the interview material below. This chapter includes interviews with actors Paul Henshall and Niamh Walsh, both of whom have played regular characters on *Holby City*.

Interviews

John Hannah

Telephone interview, 26 November 2015

Having graduated from the Royal Scottish Academy of Music and Drama in the late 1970s, Hannah has since gone on to high-profile leading roles across theatre, film and television. His 'breakthrough' screen performance was as Matthew in the romantic British comedy *Four Weddings and a Funeral*, subsequently moving into various leading television roles in shows such as the crime thriller *Cold Blood* (ITV 2005–2008), the legal drama *New Street Law* (BBC 2006–2007), and, more recently, Charlie Brooker's detective parody *A Touch of Cloth* (Sky 2012–). This interview focuses upon Hannah's lead performance in the forensic detective drama *McCallum*, followed by his portrayal of DI Rebus.

You've worked extensively in theatre, film and television. Do you prepare in different ways for the different media contexts in which you work?

The process is totally different in that in theatre you have a rehearsal period. I was going to say 'a longer rehearsal period' but in fact just '*a* rehearsal period' is something that is markedly present in theatre in a way which it isn't in film and certainly isn't in television. I've never seen the benefits in terms of what some older actors have talked about in relation to lengthy rehearsal for film because often, in my experience, the best-laid plans of all of us can go awry when it comes to actually filming.

I remember spending a day on *Four Weddings and a Funeral* rehearsing the scene just before Simon Callow's character dies, and then on the day we had just 15 minutes left to shoot the scene and we ended up having to shoot it in a doorway and part of a room because that was the part that had been lit. So there's a practical reality that comes into play. I think what's fantastic about Mike Newell, and all good directors, really, is that you can have plans and you can – with the best will in the world – want to do things in a certain way, but on the day you have to be adaptable when things don't go to plan, and be able to process other options.

Theatre is a much more planned process. You rehearse it and you take away choices systematically. You might explore avenues in rehearsals but then ultimately close them off because you realise that they're not contributing to the story or helping with the direction the production is aiming to take. You do that in a much more spontaneous way with film and definitely with television. There's very limited scope for formal television rehearsal today. That hasn't always been the case in television, however – I remember 20 years ago, when I started, the director would clear the floor and allow the actors to investigate the scene, albeit fairly brief, and then get in the heads of departments to figure out how to shoot it. Whereas a lot of the time now, because it's so fast, the director has more or less already made their mind up about blocking the scene, with requests to move on particular lines, which a lot of actors resent. However, many younger actors, especially given the status of soap opera as a major training ground, see this as the norm, with people working incredibly quickly. They don't have the time to explore things and try things out. Also, a lot of the time, people are cast now because there's so much about them that is similar to what is required of the character in the script. Less and less do you see actors being given opportunities to stretch themselves.

However, there's clearly a logic to finding connections between actor and character, physically and psychologically. Personally I've never found it helpful or necessary to disguise myself physically to access the truth of a character. I remember Jack Nicholson once saying: 'An actor is entitled to believe that they have at least 75 per cent in common with the character they are playing.' I'm probably paraphrasing slightly there but that central idea has always resonated with me. I've always tried to find the truth of the character for me in the moment rather than find a character that comes solely from the material or from some physical transformation. I respond to the material – if I've read something and I like it then I figure that I am going to have something in common with that character, perhaps because I've gone through some similar experiences or thought processes. If I can identify with the character then there's no point or need to make them fatter or to walk with a limp or talk with a stutter, because there's already a connection of feeling or experience within me.

Do you find there are particular challenges to approaching character in long-running television drama, in which often you don't know the full journey of your character from the outset?

I've done a number of television dramas that ran for long periods. The *Rebus* adaptations [with Hannah involved from 2000 to 2001], for example, stemmed from me enjoying reading Ian Rankin's books and wanting to do something with that material, but I didn't have any idea from the outset of how long that would go on for. However, I had assumed that if you worked on long-running dramas of that kind that you would have a much greater chance to develop a character and to understand a character across a much larger arc. Also, it offers the opportunity for a character arc which is more like life, where you don't know what the end is. In reality, I was entirely wrong about that because the very nature of television is that something is being sold – a brand – something that is recognisable as a cop show, a medical show, a legal show or whatever. Once that brand is established in a long-running show, there is no real desire for that character to develop. What I have found instead is that you are encouraged to go through the same journey again and again. With something like the adaptation of Rebus, there may be elements to the stories or the character that you really like but that can't be incorporated because of the nature of television, and because things have to be packaged in these burger-sized pieces of product that can be sold and consumed. Therefore, you end up being repetitive in the journey and in what is required of the character. The executives involved aren't much interested in character development – they want the same thing that proved popular the last time. For me, that's when it becomes predictable, less challenging and less interesting and enjoyable as a result.

To offer a further example, when I was involved in the forensic detective drama *McCallum*, playing McCallum, it became clear that Scottish Television as a company were focused upon the continued viability of their shows as entertainment brands above all other creative concerns about the dramas, which is understandable, I suppose, from their perspective as a business. If you think about *Taggart*, for instance, that continued to be sold as an entertainment brand long after the demise of Taggart as the detective protagonist, with various other cops taking his place. Because I've always been wary of committing to long-running shows, I argued from the beginning on *McCallum* that it should be called something else because I couldn't guarantee how long I would be doing it. However, STV stuck with the title of *McCallum*, and eventually I left, but they were left with an established brand, on which they'd already spent money marketing and attracting viewers. So – as with *Taggart* – they attempted to continue the show with another lead character and another lead actor, because it was the brand rather than the lead character and his journey that was ultimately important to them. Perhaps learning from the lessons of these previous brands, it's less common to see police or legal or medical dramas named after their leads these days, because what's desired by the producers is brand flexibility to keep these shows going even if the lead actor decides they're done. Look at *Silent Witness* [BBC, 1996–], which continues to have a tremendous run because of that flexibility of character and cast. And casting is often about who is felt to be a safe bet with their audience at any given time. The problem is that these sorts of emphases on marketing, branding and brand safety make it more difficult for someone to come along and say, 'Here's a really interesting story offering something different,' because that's a risk.

Having played a number of lead characters in the detective genre on television, do you actively try to work against some of the more repetitive and obvious genre stereotypes in your performances?

Fairly quickly you realise that nothing is new in the purest sense in television drama. Things are always playing off other things to some extent, which is true of all drama really, but there has to be something about the character which is interesting for you as an actor and not just a set of clichés. With *McCallum*, for example, I did feel that there was enough which was sufficiently interesting in the character for me to play with. Beyond that, you are working within a box, to a large extent, in these genre shows, and it's very difficult to break out of that box in any major way. It's a myth that actors can completely reinvent the wheel within these genres – you just bring yourself to the character and to the stories and sometimes that combination of elements works to generate something fresh. All of these jobs come these days with an option, with a possibility to make it a long-term arrangement if it is popular, and the reason why many actors avoid these sorts of dramas is because they recognise them as products with rigid parameters for what you can hope to do with your character.

How much background research do you do for these sorts of roles? Is it helpful?

It is helpful for me to do background research, to an extent. For example, for *McCallum*, I went to a coroner's court to get a feel for the language of forensic pathology, and I did a bit of general medical research to get a sense of the world of forensics and pathology. Beyond that, it's more a case of talking to the writer about their perspective on your character and the choices your character has made. For me, talking to the writer is the most helpful way to make those sorts of imaginative leaps. I think what's most important is that you construct a background for yourself so that you can feel there's a framework of meaning and feeling there for when you're playing that character in the moment of a scene. Much of that may never come out in the drama explicitly but it's there for you as an actor.

How does the creative process work for actors in practical terms on a show like McCallum*? When do you get to see the scripts in advance of shooting, for example?*

There isn't enough money invested up front to see very much at the start with regards to the long-term development of your character in script form. What you'll have at the outset is possibly a rough outline or an arc indicating where your character might be going. You'll be shooting Episodes 1 and 2 and simultaneously the scripts for Episodes 3 and 4 will be getting the final polish. You'd then get those scripts one or two weeks before you start shooting on them, and the scripts for Episodes 5 and 6 are still in the process of being written. The time frame depends also on whether or not it's a single writer or a writing team working on the scripts, which is more along the lines of the US system. However, the US system doesn't really offer much lead-in time either. I did a US series where it took about eight days to shoot one episode whilst the second episode's script was still being polished and the scripts beyond that only had a rough outline. It always seems a bit seat-of-your-pants, really! And, as ever, it comes back to money: there's a reluctance to invest too much money up-front and then, once things get moving on a production, time is always of the essence. So you're generally forced by those conditions as an actor to work in the present tense rather than planning too far ahead.

Does filming scenes out of continuity have an impact on your sense of character and story?

At the level of each episode, generally in my experience I've worked on one episode at a time rather than jumbling up episodes. My time on the legal drama *New Street Law* became more challenging because people wanted to change things and do reshoots and so we had to do pick-ups from other episodes but that hasn't been a typical thing for me.

I think the worst thing early on for me was when I had big pauses in my career. You might do a television job and then have a break until another job comes up, perhaps in theatre, which requires a different mindset. So then you do that for a few months before going back to filming, which means you then have to go back to getting comfortable with the camera and that can be difficult, which is why I think practice on camera is so important for actors going into television. The most difficult part of any job is starting. Once you've been doing it for a couple of weeks, particular scenes might be more of a challenge but in general terms you are in command of that character and that environment. Perhaps this is partly why many television actors stay with characters for so long, because it's comfortable and you know your character and your environment, whereas for other actors that familiarity or predictability becomes a problem.

If you think about any screen story, there are probably only about three important scenes for the actor, important in the sense that these scenes themselves have an internal journey in terms of a character's emotional standpoint or point of view. In these important scenes those things are affected and in the process the character becomes a different person. So you deal with those scenes and their journeys internally. The rest of the time, you're working on the bread and butter rather than the filling of the sandwich. You are doing the things that construct the character and the life of that character, or enable the story. This is particularly true of detective dramas where, as the lead, you're often on the same investigative journey as the viewer, and you're following that journey as they do, without any major emotional consequence for your character. Take, for example, a scene where you're going to visit the family of a victim to gain information. You're getting out the car, you're walking up the path, you're knocking on the door, you're drinking a cup of tea in the living room and you're asking some questions. There's no emotional journey there for your character – it's more the journey of the investigation. And that's part of the 75 per cent of the character that can be you – there's no real demand upon you in those scenes as an actor, other than making sure you can put one leg in front of the other! Although I shouldn't dismiss these practicalities so quickly – often drinking a cup of tea on camera can become a logistical nightmare! There's an art to the practical details too, for sure. It's often best not to think about it. And that relates to the idea of being in the moment which I think is so important – if you step out of that moment mentally and start analysing it then you're in trouble.

Of course, you are aware that there's a construction around you that takes away reality and that you're pretending to be real. Given what I've mentioned already about the fast pace of production and the writing process, and therefore the lack of sacredness around the script in television today, as it's always a working document, that can be valuable to an actor in keeping things alive and as real as possible in the moment. Where I can, I often resist learning scripts too precisely and paraphrase within parameters, as that helps to keep the script lively and keeps me thinking in that moment. This is in contrast to theatre, where you might have been in a play for three months and you may be in the middle of giving some speech of great emotional profundity and yet at the same time wondering where you'll go for dinner afterwards! It becomes so routine but it can be terrifying because suddenly you're thinking: 'What did I just say?! Did I say the line or did I share my mental shopping list for tomorrow?!' It's rather bizarre what can happen in long-running theatre productions. For television, repeating the same lines seems to me to be fairly static and dead and so I try to keep things lively. I try to keep a sense of spontaneity and improvisation in my television work rather than overlearning scripts. Of course, there's always the danger in this approach that you might screw up and paraphrase a line in such a way which just gives it a slightly different colour of meaning which might have story consequences later on. But you have the script editor and the director to keep an eye on that. Overall, for me, it's a valuable thing in making characters appear spontaneous and real in the moment.

Presumably those emotional and psychological points of empathy or understanding with your character become all the more important when using this sort of technique then?

Yes. I mean, going back to *McCallum*, the 75 per cent of me that was in there was also about recognising issues that the character was going through, and the writers were recognising an ability for me to relate to those issues. I think it was also an age that I was at when I was looking at myself and posing questions about who I was and where I was going, and all of those questions were also there for my character, which kept it interesting for me whilst I was still on that journey myself. I suppose, at some stage, you then grow up a little bit and start to find answers to those questions for yourself and therefore feel frustrated that the character isn't also growing up but is instead, in the repetitive way that I mentioned previously, covering the same emotional ground over and over. After a while, that gets tiring.

The character of Rebus was also a very complex one in emotional and psychological terms. As you were also an executive producer in that process of adapting the Ian Rankin novels for television, did that facilitate something different in shaping the character and your performance?

Initially, I hadn't wanted to play Rebus myself. I was really responding to my interest in the books and I think I started with the eighth of Rankin's Rebus books, *Black and Blue* [1997], in which the character was older than I was, and I didn't particularly see myself as being right for that character. However, I'd started a production company alongside Murray Ferguson [Clerkenwell Films] and I really wanted to adapt the stories for television. Scottish Television had the adaptation rights and they were keen for us to do it as a company but they were pretty adamant that they wanted me to play Rebus. This brings us back to the importance of branding and marketing as a creative factor. I suppose they saw me as a hot property at that time because of *Four Weddings and a Funeral* and then *Sliding Doors* and things like that, and so things are put your way that you might not otherwise be seen as being an obvious choice for. I'd initially wanted Peter Mullan to do it, an amazing actor who'd recently won a Best Actor award at Cannes, but Scottish Television didn't want that and were sitting on the rights. So I went back and read some of the earlier novels and also spoke with Ian Rankin. At the time I was in my late 30s and Ian said that was the age the character was at when he created him. Ian said he was happy for me to play the character and we hung out for a bit and chatted about the material and I gradually came around to the idea. I'd already connected to the material as a reader and then I got my head around taking on the part.

Because we started with an adaptation of the eighth novel, I could use the information of the earlier novels to construct a backstory for my performance in my head. As an actor, I've always disliked the idea of using the material as a vehicle to stardom or whatever you want to call it. Instead, I aim to do justice to the material and to serve the material and what it's trying to say as best as I can. So having a series of books that Ian had spent years creating was a fantastic resource. There was already a very long, detailed arc for the character that was still unfinished but had a logic of continuity, and which offered up a character that was already three-dimensional, with his quirks and contradictions. That's what can sometimes feel lacking in short-burst television dramas – the lack of space to introduce contradictions or complexities of character, because those contradictions are very human and very real. That's what I enjoyed most about Rebus as a character – his contradictions. We did try to bring in those complexities as much as possible but ultimately what was required was another television cop show, as opposed to a realisation of these novels, which is largely why in the end I only did four stories. Another factor was that I had other work I wanted to do and I simply wasn't available, and Scottish Television simply wouldn't wait! They wanted to keep the motor going on it. It's back to this idea of a brand, a product.

Do you find that changes in writers or directors on a long-running show can impact your work as an actor?

I think writers can be conscious of the fact that changes in the writing team can affect the actor's work but, in the context of long-running dramas, after a while the actor becomes the main custodian of their character and writers and directors are aware that actors already know their characters very well. Once you have that stability in your role, bringing a new writer or director in may in fact offer a slightly different, fresh voice that you like and can work with, within the framework of what you've already established for your character. Also, as an actor, if you connect with a writer that can be so valuable. And it's often so casual as opposed to a formal part of the process. You can be having coffee with that person and talking about stuff going on in your head, some ideas, some images, which can inadvertently inform the work of that writer. So, changes in a creative team can actually bring in new perspectives and skills which might open up a character in ways you hadn't thought about before, and this is often brought out through conversations. That personal connection amongst the creative team is essential. The problem is time. Often, you're busy filming so you don't see the writers. In the US, if you're filming at a studio, you're often all together, so between scenes you can go and see the writers and talk. Whereas, in the UK, you're more often nowhere near where the writer is working. Equally, speaking with the editor can be useful – in the US that often happens on the same site but in the UK you're more dispersed. You might see the editor every once in a while at lunch but that dialogue isn't a sustained part of the production process, which would be useful from an actor's point of view. In television drama, as in any dramatic form, the best work comes through effective communication and collaboration with others involved in the creative process. There needs to be more of that in television.

Ken Stott

London, 14 December 2015

After attending Mountview Academy of Theatre Arts in the 1970s, Stott worked extensively in theatre but with early supporting roles in television dramas such as *Secret Army* (BBC 1977–1979) and *The Singing Detective* (BBC 1986). Lead television roles followed in the 1990s and 2000s, most prominently in the popular detective dramas *The Vice*, *Messiah* and *Rebus*. In this interview, Stott reflects on the changing professional landscape of British television acting, with a particular focus on the nature of his work as a lead actor in detective drama.

Did your training at Mountview offer any preparation for your television work?

In the early '70s, when you had your theatre training, you read Stanislavski and then that was pretty much it. You had to become a member of the union and that did offer you at least the opportunity to get two years of experience before you did television or film because you simply weren't allowed to as a provisional member. It also could not be West End theatre, it had to be provincial. The reason for that, of course, is very sound: it sorts out those who really want to carry on with this and those who do not. You had to clock up those hours and days for two years, then you get your full membership and you were allowed into the profession in every aspect, which included television.

Now, if you are a kid straight out of drama school today, you can say that you aren't going to go to Stratford and carry a spear and observe how to do acting, you're just going to hang around for some television to come along. This is rather sad because they don't realise how good our profession was and could be. It meant that, as an actor, you arrived in television if you were lucky enough to get a job after your two years' apprenticeship and you really relied on your powers of observation to get you through. However, you had already honed your skills, your adaptability and your observational abilities in those two previous years. So, you were ready and you didn't take it for granted.

Do you think it was being involved in those regional productions that was your training ground and not drama school itself?

Sure. Drama school doesn't prepare you for the outside world or at least it didn't. What it can do, if you have good tutors, is it can give you a solid understanding of yourself and your relationship to acting. Your acting. The physicality of getting on stage. The business end of it. How to contact people. We were given no help of any kind, we fell off the edge of a cliff when we came out of drama school in those days.

So that was a route you did, a couple of years outside of London in rep and then moved in?

So I did the repertory route. There really was no other route, and for television, having had some experience behind you of acting meant that you had your armour when it then came to working in TV and film.

What were the most important things you learned on stage that fed into your subsequent television work?

Well I remember it being a very difficult start. I remember the pressure to not act, and people would say, 'Less is more, acting is doing less', and of course it's very easy, when you have little experience, to confuse less acting with less energy. So if you're going to kill somebody on screen then you still have to kill them, you have to put all of the energy in but you may have to do it in a very small environment.

How you deliver it is always the lie because, in theatre, if we are playing a scene, a two hander, and we're on a stage that is as wide as this room, and you're sitting in an armchair that is over there and I'm having a chat with you, the easiest way for me to communicate with you is to raise my voice and pitch it up until you can hear me over there. In theatre, this is complicated as you're turning what is supposed to be an intimate situation into something that really isn't. You're now in a huge room that is playing for all to see. What you must do is try to create with your voice an intimate relationship so the audience feel and understand that you're actually in an ordinary dining room as opposed to one that is 37 feet long. In television and film, different rules apply. That is the lie, you try to achieve a big performance in television but it has to be done in a small but focused and intense way.

It's actually hard to talk about because once you've been doing it for such a long time it's something that you think less and less about. For example, here's something I'll never forget, I was working with a young, inexperienced actor on a television project and she said, 'How do you learn all of your lines?' I said to her that I don't really learn them, I do but I don't. The following day she came in and she didn't really know what she was going to say. She got very upset because the director was a little upset and I said, 'This is my fault, I blame myself entirely.' I told her not to learn the lines but when I said that she shouldn't learn the lines I didn't mean don't learn them – I meant have a working knowledge of them because what you're going to do tomorrow is going to have to be real and in the moment and you don't have the time that you do in the theatre to rehearse. In the theatre, you have the luxury of the read-through which is a great stab, a glimpse of how wonderful it could be and then when you start the work and go right to the very beginning it sounds like shit. In the process of rehearsal you then reclaim the play. With television it's very different, you have to do something very immediate and it has to be real. That's why learning lines is like making a soufflé rather than basting this beast and putting it into the oven. I make it my business to try to preserve what the writer has delivered but to make it sound like it is being said for the first time. Even though you're suffering because you've only just got a grasp on it. Essentially, it's the same with theatre. The truth is required. Simple truth is usually best. First of all, one must serve the writing.

Were you aware that you were becoming increasingly associated as an actor with the genre of detective drama when doing shows such as The Vice, Messiah *and* Rebus?

Yes, I was aware of it and it worried me a little. By the time *Rebus* came along, I turned it down on numerous occasions because I'd already done *The Vice* which was something we were quite proud of. I had then done *Messiah* and I was already glad to be getting out of that because of the continuing nightmares of death and destruction. I just thought that I wasn't happy. If I had been asked this question maybe 20 years prior, 'Do you take your work home with you?', I would've said, 'Certainly not.' I would say I go down the pub and enjoy myself. However, by the time I got to *Messiah*, I was older and more experienced in life. Seeing and looking at dead bodies every day took its toll. I would look in the mirror and ask why I was so depressed. The answer is probably because I did too much work like this.

We used to laugh a lot during it because you had to have a gallows humour, it's required. In order to get through the day, we'd fiddle around with the props and stab each other with rubber knives because otherwise you would go insane. Nevertheless, it took its toll because as an actor you have to make a truthful response. I would also be asking myself the question: 'How many truthful responses to the first time you see a dead body are there in the lexicon?'

Do you feel that the nature of the detective roles that you've taken throughout your career has changed?

Yes. When I started with *The Vice*, I made a promise to myself that I was not going to impose a character but to use me. To come back to me. To always refer to myself. How would I react in that situation? What is my feeling towards this? That was very useful for me. I always had something I could rely on as the truth and also I never had to think about character before making a decision because in the moment I was me. How would I react? What would I do in that situation? All decisions, all attitudes apart from those that were absolutely clear in the writing, I was free to manipulate. Over ten years of doing this, with three different characters in police drama, the change that I recorded ended up really, I think, being a change in me. The change in me made it possible, because after *Messiah* and feeling that I've had to get out of this hell, there emerged a character that was quite suitable for *Rebus* in me. There was a man who'd seen a hell of a lot of stuff but survived.

So, particularly in The Vice, *did you have any conversations about the journey of the character or was it episode by episode? Your character went on quite a journey of transformation.*

I remember that towards the end, I had a conversation with the producer and I said, 'It's time to move on,' and we thought we'd try and come up with a storyline that was not simply just him getting stabbed during a raid or something.

It was almost a meltdown for that character, wasn't it? It wasn't just a get out, it was crafted.

That's right, we could've eked it out more. That was perfectly possible and I know that if I had wanted to then we could have done. We thought we'd bring matters to a head rather than bring it to a close. The character's strength was the fact that he was willing to compromise which I know sounds like a contradiction but it's true. I think I always felt that this was the strength of his character, that he was able to bend the law for the right, for the proper and just result.

Did it therefore seem less appealing to go onto Messiah *where the character development was not the same? It was based more on repetition than development.*

Well I wanted to know if I could do something that had a shock value and where I played a hard cop – although his background is his relationship at home and his relationship with his wife who is deaf – he's a tough cop. I thought it was interesting to play that. I was fully expecting to play it once and once only, then they said, 'Let's do more,' and then, 'We'll do another.' It was successful with audiences and so I got drawn back in but it became more of the same. Eventually, you feel that it's enough.

So, in that context, what was the process of you eventually taking on Rebus *after having previously turned it down?*

Honestly? Every time I went back home to Edinburgh people would say to me, 'Hey, are you going to play Rebus?' 'You should play Rebus.' 'Ah come on, come on. Play Rebus,' and you'd say you weren't going to play Rebus and they'd say, 'Ah come on, play Rebus, you'll be brilliant,' and the pressure became intolerable! So I did it and of course it was sheer enjoyment during that. I did that simply for the enjoyment and the enjoyment of course was that I was playing another part of myself which was somebody a little bit older who has seen quite a few things and it was enjoyable to play somebody who was always a step ahead.

Did you discuss anything with Ian Rankin?

No, I've never discussed anything with Ian Rankin. I had dinner with him on a couple of occasions and that was the extent. I read one of the books and was told not to bother reading any more because I was told they didn't want me to try and fit into what I thought Rebus should be from the novels. I read one and I realised from that that there was nothing that was going to stop me from being me in that role. Which, of course, as we just talked about, was the new me. The current me. Actors that are lucky enough to work all of the time have an opportunity to see and watch an arc develop in their work and the way that they work reflects what has happened in their lives. I wouldn't do that for other characters but I could do it for these three detective characters that I've played because the opportunity was there to do it and ultimately it's much easier to refer to yourself.

Also, you cannot afford to look at it in a linear way otherwise it's disastrous. Instead of building a character, as we would call it, I'm so against the idea of building, I'd rather like to think of it more as you being in an orchard and just plucking fruit from so many other trees and filling this basket in which you've got a huge mass of different, conflicting, somewhat in harmony, fruit.

Does character research for detective dramas become less significant the more of them that you do?

I've done some research. I did research in terms of how you deal with murder, how you deal with what it's like for you as a police officer to go into that situation. The emotion and emotional survival in that environment was important to me.

How does rehearsal function in your television work?

It is useful in acting terms because it is a last chance to fully formulate an opinion of how to play the scene. It is an opportunity to fully try it before going in front of a camera, to make sure that a scene works in its entirety and also to see what is possible in the geography of the scene with regards to the locations which you have not seen before until you arrive on the day. So the mistake is to rehearse the scene in front of a mirror or to sit in the bath on a morning imagining how it's going to look because you will be disappointed. What you must do is have flexibility. I don't so much see it in terms of words but flexibility in terms of stress and emphasis. Then there is the added joy of something just happening in that moment of rehearsal that turns it round and you think, 'Ah, let's play it like this.' The pressure, of course, is always time. There's always time in that you rehearse and then all interested parties will come onto the location to observe it when you run that scene, because prior to that has just been director and actors. So then there's a setting up of cameras and lights where you can think about what you're about to do, go back to do a camera rehearsal and then start to shoot. That is the structure which I live by, or rather what I've known and have enjoyed. I'm willing to do what anybody wants if it's going to get the right result, but that's the method that's employed.

Do you deal with the story as a whole or scene by scene?

It's absolutely essential to have read, understood and made pretty firm plans about the whole story. You need to know fully the effect that your character will have. The only change to this will be moment-to-moment inflections. You must always be aware of what happens before and what is about to happen because if you're not then you are in perdition and sadly so many actors, many of whom are there because they look very pretty or handsome, are in the situation where they have no idea or had no idea that they had a responsibility to do that. Or they were encouraged not to take responsibility which often happens. I've worked with an actress who told me that she didn't know how to read a script really. She said, 'I just come in and the director tells me what to do.' No agency of her own. How unsatisfying.

Do you have a notation process that you use for scripts, particularly if you're filming things out of continuity?

No, it's all in my head. If you have to write it down then I think you're in trouble because then I think you haven't really fully grasped it. If you have to keep referring to notes then I think you only have a tenuous grip.

From an actor's perspective, what makes a 'good' and 'bad' director for television?

It's an interesting question. I don't like working with directors who will accept anything. That makes you feel very lonely. I also don't like directors in television and film who see the actor as being there to serve their grand design. I prefer to think of it as a collaborative art form. Theatre is collaborative because of the simple fact that when you're on stage there's not much that the director can do about it. So he or she has to remember that when they open their mouth to discuss something in rehearsal. So as an actor you feel much more in control of what you do on stage because you know that. I swear most of my best work for camera has landed on the cutting room floor, I can think of a couple of films, more than two films, where I have just wondered 'why?' Why have they made these editorial choices and who made them? With film and television you can never really get to the bottom of the performance, because you can never tell what happens behind closed doors in the cutting room and you can't tell whether it's directorial or whether it's the producer. Where is the money coming from? When you get to understand that, you understand where the decisions are probably being taken.

Can you be over-directed?

Yes. There's got to be trust, you have to trust the actor. To know that they understand the progression of the character that he or she is playing. So a mutual understanding and a mutual respect is important. I think some directors don't trust that, but then we create the situation where we actively search out actors that aren't really actors. The art form of acting has been downgraded since the '70s when I started.

Is there a distinction that you recognise between an actor's director and a technical director?

Yes I do. Most actors' directors will say, 'Don't worry about continuity,' 'Forget about continuity.' I'm willing to forget it but one must remember as an actor that it is your duty to look after your continuity. Take, for example, drinking a glass of water. You learn to do it almost instinctively by making sure that when you do that you do it with the intention that took it to your lips and then it was a thought that made you put it down. Once you attach a thought to it, to the action, then it's easy to remember your continuity. If you don't you can suffer and you can end up doing it all day long. One of the worst things is when the script supervisor will come to me and say, 'Ken, just don't forget that you picked up the ... ' Oh don't tell me, don't tell me! If I'm told then all I can think about is this bloody glass. I don't want that information – it has to be instinctive.

As an actor, is a lot of the preparation you do for television work private in nature?

Yes. For example, in a situation where I need to become emotional. How we reach emotion is a difficult one. For me it doesn't happen organically, it doesn't happen in the moment because I am the character. I have to refer to my own little black box of secrets that I use to take me over the edge into what is required. Memories or images or associations that get to me and trigger those emotions.

If you could pass on any knowledge or insights to actors coming straight from drama school to television, what would be the key things you would pass on?

I would say, first and foremost, do not be afraid to ask questions and ask questions of experienced professionals in every department because by and large people respond well to being asked a question. By that I mean, what do you do? And why are you doing this? I would ask these questions because it's the only way you will learn and you have to learn very, very fast. Don't pretend that you know everything. Secondly, I'd remind them not to confuse action with movement. Don't confuse emotion for actual physicality because if you are asked to physically make it smaller then making it smaller cannot mean making it less intense. Making it smaller is probably the most used piece of direction given to young television actors. Do what you're doing, keep the action and the emotion but make the physical movement smaller. Don't let it be at the expense of what you've created.

Paul Henshall

Interview via Skype, 13 November 2015

Graduating from Manchester Metropolitan University's Theatre School in 2001, Henshall has since worked across comedy and drama in a number of television roles in shows such as *Playing the Field* (BBC 1998–2002), *Casualty*, *I'm with Stupid* (BBC 2006) and *Off Their Rockers* (ITV 2013–). As an actor with cerebral palsy, Henshall became the first wheelchair user in a regular role in BBC drama when he was cast as ambitious trainee doctor Dean West in *Holby City*. In this interview, Henshall considers his experiences working on *Holby City* from 2005 to 2007, during which time he appeared in 34 episodes.

How did you first get involved with Holby City?

I went down a fairly conventional training route in going to drama school and then entered a competition called BBC Talent which I won back in 2001. The competition's prize was getting a part in *Casualty* as a patient. On the back of that, the people at *Holby City* got in contact and asked whether I would be interested in taking part in a hot-seating session, and I agreed. So I went in and they gave me a brief, rough outline of the character that they had in mind and then they hot-seated me, with me improvising as this character. They then called me a week later and offered me a contract. At the outset, they didn't have much that was concrete about the character – they didn't even know for certain if they wanted the character to be male or female – but the character then seemed to be developed from some of the things I'd experimented with in the hot-seating session. I often respond better to improvisation as a casting process – I tend to feel more nervous in auditions when given a definite script – and so I think the initial set-up worked well for me and they saw a spark of something interesting for a character in the improvisation I offered.

Following the contract, we had various further discussions around the character and I was made familiar with the set, and I started working in the auditions for actors who were being considered to play the other medical student being introduced to the show. I went in and read with the different actors for the role and was a minor part of that selection process, which was interesting for me as an actor to see the other side of things in terms of casting.

Adam Best, who was cast as the other medical student, Matt Parker, and I also went to a real hospital to observe an operation, to watch how the surgeons behaved. I had to scrub up and put on the kit, and it was fascinating – the difference in the way people saw you and talked to you, just from wearing that uniform. I picked up a lot from that. Apparently every actor who joins *Holby City* has the opportunity to go and observe these practices within a real hospital.

Were there medical professionals and advisors around during the production process to inform your work?

We had real medical professionals who were around to advise us. However, it's drama, it's an edited version of life, so we took professional advice on board but ultimately the drama had to come first. We weren't aiming for hyper-real – we wanted something credible, but something that would entertain. Also, as with any of these shows, you have to go for a medical screening yourself before you start work, and even the doctor doing that was giving me advice on how to behave like a medical student in my role! So I was constantly absorbing from real medical professionals wherever possible, but in the end it has to be good drama.

How were the technical aspects of the story handled in a practical production sense, in getting to grips with medical language?

Well, we had the input of advisors and also at the back of the script there would always be a glossary of terms which they thought we might find difficult to understand. One was 'Scissors – used for cutting things.' I'm hoping that one was a joke! I was lucky in that my mum used to be a nurse so I could always ask her for clarification on things too.

There's a clear hierarchy of power and politics in the drama too. Was that something that was ever discussed in getting to grips with character relationships and the stories or was it just implicit in the script?

Well, it's there in the script – it's clear in the drama who the bosses are. Dean, as a medical student, was always being told off and getting stuff wrong! But also there were moments when he'd fight back. When the real doctor gave me my medical, they said: 'Make him arrogant, because medical students are always arrogant!' So I made Dean a bit cocky and he would argue back when he could. I suppose, to start with, he was just arrogant and not particularly likeable but gradually he became more caring with the patients, and I think that's something that I probably brought to it, to try to make him more rounded and to explore where that arrogance, or confidence, came from. The writers did follow that desire for more complexity and to show that, beneath the exterior, he does care. As an actor, you're constantly thinking 'Why? Where does this come from? Why is this character behaving in this way?' I research to the point where I think it will help me. If it's not going to help to push the character forward, then I don't need to know it.

What was the day-to-day process for production on Holby City?

It varies but we filmed on average six days a week and if they were getting behind then they might use Sundays as well. I was OK script-wise because I ended up with quite a bit of time to learn lines but others who had more screen time were learning constantly. It is tough for some in that sense but, as I was told by another cast member when I started, your brain gets used to taking the content into your short-term memory and you get quicker at the process. You can be there from seven or eight in the morning to seven or eight at night and there are times when you don't see daylight. For a time, my glimpse of daylight was going from the set to the canteen and that was it. I'm not complaining because it was a great experience but for those with children and young families it's a challenge, especially if your character is central to the storylines.

I remember that my first script was given to me on the Friday and then we started filming on the Monday. It wasn't always that fast but

I remember the first few episodes I did being like that. On the day, we would have a read through, block it, test run with the cameras and then go for it. That isn't always the way with television – I've been on other projects where we've rehearsed for four or five days and then gone in to film but that's a luxury reserved for single dramas, really. The first few weeks being on something like *Holby City* are stressful because you have to get acclimatised but I'm OK once I calm down in front of the camera and become comfortable enough to allow myself to think. I remember asking Robert Powell [who played Mark Williams] what he thought I should do with the character with regard to accent and so on and he advised that, with the lead time available, I should make the character as much like me as possible. You haven't got time to do lots of character work. In these sorts of shows you are playing a bigger version of yourself. Of course, there are ways that my character behaved that I would never mirror in my own life but in essence you are playing a version of yourself. It's you but you're also tapping into aspects of you that you wouldn't show in your own day-to-day life. For example, my character was a very confident person and I wouldn't describe myself as particularly confident. A lot of actors get into acting because they're shy and it's a form of expression for them. So my character was very different from me in some ways – his sarcasm, his cutting humour, which isn't me. I'm ridiculously polite most of the time, which Dean certainly wasn't. But a lot of actors would argue that all characters are elements of you, perhaps buried elements which don't surface in your real life, and it's about tapping into elements that suit the character at the time. We all have the possibility, the potential, to behave in any number of ways when responding to a situation, so it's about accessing those options. Some actors see it as putting on a mask but more and more I think it's about using yourself and knowing yourself. For me, that's when characters start to really emerge, because you didn't realise you could act like that or be like that and it comes to life.

You mentioned being comfortable with improvisation earlier. Is that an important skill for a television actor?

I don't think it's essential but it has been useful for me. Of course, all acting should look like it's happening then and there. Improvisation becomes valuable in something like *Holby City* because often you're working with people you've never met before and you've not had any rehearsal time, and so you're playing off what happens and what they do in that moment when the cameras roll. Then on the second take the director might ask you to try something a bit different. But because you haven't had weeks of rehearsal there's often this feeling of 'Let's see what happens', and that's valuable because it keeps things fresh. In theatre, you go out every night and try to understand it as though it's never happened before but the television process allows for that much more naturally. I suppose the trick is that you're trying to surprise yourself. You know what you want from the other character and you go in there to get it but the routes to that might take you by surprise. I think working with lots of new people in that way, that you've never worked with or even met before, and just going straight for it, keeps things alive and also makes you up your game, really. I was lucky in that I got to work with a lot of the guest actors and that means you can play off different styles and ways of working. It was interesting in that way. Doing multiple takes can diminish that freshness. Although it's also the case that, on occasion, if you do multiple takes of the same scene, you get tired and you stop trying so hard, and in fact that makes you better because you stop over-thinking it and you just let it be. That's when the interesting performance comes – when you stop doing and just let it happen. For me, when I was tired and felt I couldn't do it anymore, I'd often do the best take!

Did you have any conversations with the writers about your character?

Yes. Because my character wanted to be a surgeon, they asked me what I thought of that as an idea, and I responded by acknowledging that, as a disabled person, it wasn't going to be easy for him, and I felt that reality had to be there in the show. However, I also said that just because something seems unlikely it doesn't stop you wanting it and so we played with this idea of the character desperately wanting to make this work, against the odds. So we worked with that angle and the producers or writers would call me with questions about things along those lines. For example, they might ask why my character might be off work on a particular day, due to his disability. There were also occasions when I would change certain things in the script that didn't work for me from a disability angle. For example, one of the other characters was going to move in with my character for a while and the line was: 'Alright, as long as you give me right of way in the bathroom.' I thought that was a bit too clunky and on-the-nose and so I requested it be changed to: 'Alright, as long as you don't leave a ring around the bath.' I felt that was more human and more authentic. So there were odd things like that which I thought, as a disabled person, I ought to change but generally you do what's written, because that's the writer's job not mine. I was the first actor with a disability to be in that show and so I was in an unusual position in that they were at times being guided by me in what they should be doing and writing about. That's not the general rule for actors working on other characters. That could become frustrating for me sometimes because it was new ground for them and I felt the need to think hard about where stories could go and we talked about the nature of my disability, and whilst that could be a great creative opportunity, at times I felt the pressure of that. It's partly to do with my personality and my own insecurities coming through and my concern that they might run out of useful things for me to do for the story. It was all very new for long-running BBC dramas at the time, although since then more disabled actors have come through. At that time, there was still a desire to foreground the disability and now I think there's more of a desire to get beyond that and explore characters who may be disabled but it's not the main reason they're there. I do think progress has been made on that, although there's still some way to go. It's not a blame thing from my point of view, it's just the way in which characters like mine were being handled on television in that period.

Did you have conversations about the long-term journey of your character or was it handled more episode by episode?

It really was episode by episode. I was happy for them to take Dean where they wanted, but they do respond to what they see you doing on screen. I ended up with a lot of scenes with guest patients, trying to make them feel better emotionally, presumably because they'd seen me come across as caring on screen, and so they incorporated a lot of those scenes for my character as a result.

Did discussions take place amongst cast members during the production process about approaches to character and story?

I didn't happen that much in my experience. I think a lot of actors are reluctant to give advice not because they don't want to help but because they don't want to be seen as arrogant. They don't see that as their job, to coach other actors. So amongst actors we do have those sorts of discussions but generally only when asked, rather than spontaneously offering up advice which might be seen as arrogance. Although, I was working on the show with some truly wonderful actors like Robert Powell and Art Malik who are household names because they're good at what they do so I would take the opportunity to take advice whenever I was able.

Did different directors working on the show change the process for you?

Different directors would have slightly different approaches, of course. I think the biggest battle for all of them was with time, because we were working to tight schedules and didn't have much time to rehearse. In that environment, I suppose a director has to trust their actors, trust that they know their characters and that they know what they're doing. In shows like *Coronation Street* [ITV 1960–], some of these actors have been with their characters for 50 years, so the director often has to go in there and trust that they know their character, probably a lot better than the director themselves. In practical terms, some directors like to do more takes than others. It would have been interesting to see what some of those directors would have done with more time. In television, directing is more about how it looks, the visual, rather than thinking too hard about the performance. In that sense, for me, television is more a director's medium and theatre more an actor's medium. Having said that, we would be given character notes and I would be asked about how I felt my character would respond at certain moments, and when something worked that was unexpected the directors were very good at complimenting the actors. Generally, however, in these sorts of shows there's not a massive amount of subtext – it's mostly on the page. People often watch these programmes with one eye on the ironing and so things have to be clear in the sense of what's happening from moment to moment.

Did you do much television training whilst you were at Manchester Metropolitan University?

I think they do more now but there was very little when I was there. We did a couple of television projects but most of it was stage work, as I suppose that's where you're able to learn the foundational skills of voice and movement which you still need in television. You adapt those skills but the skills are still the same. For example, you still need to look after your voice, even though you're not having to be as vocally strong in television, because if you don't you'll still lose it, because of the tension. Also, all those things you learnt about character still apply for television – you just have to do them faster, a lot faster. It's not just about learning the lines and going for it – you have to make it your own, you have to understand it and connect with it and make it part of you, so it sounds like your words. All those things you do in theatre. My first television job was scary – a small part in *Playing the Field* – because I really was learning on the job. I think a lot of drama schools are now moving more towards television but it was largely theatre for me. One of the interesting things I was taught about television whilst training was to think of a wide shot as performing in a big theatre and a close-up as performing in an intimate venue. Another thing was that, although you're being watched by millions, on television you're performing for one person – the energy is for one. In theatre, it's bigger. I don't know if the difference between television and theatre is as pronounced as some might think but you do have the opportunity in television to focus things down.

Niamh Walsh

London, 27 November 2015

After completing her training at the London Academy of Music and Dramatic Art (LAMDA) in 2012 and appearing in a number of theatrical productions and short films, Walsh was cast in a visiting role for an episode of the popular medical drama *Casualty* in 2013. Subsequently, Walsh gained the regular role of bold and mischievous nurse Cara

Martinez in *Holby City*, in which she appeared for a total of 42 episodes from 2015 to 2016. This interview centres upon Walsh's experiences as a recently trained, early-career actor working on a long-running television production such as *Holby City*.

How did you gain your role in Holby City?

I graduated in 2012 from LAMDA. My first gig out of drama school was the month after I graduated, which was a guest part on *Casualty* – it was six days of filming. Liz Stoll and John Cannon cast both shows, so about two years later they got me in for a new regular character on *Holby City*. The information said the character spoke in RP [received pronunci-ation] so I did all of my accent work and was ready to go and, as always happens with me, I walk into the room and I'm asked if I'm Irish, and then they say, 'Oh, do it Irish!' That was with the casting directors but the second audition was with the casting directors and the producer, and the third audition was screen tests which is in BBC Studios in full hair and make-up and costume. So it really felt, as soon as I put that costume on, that it was the real deal. This is what I will look like if I get this job, this is how it will be. They get you on a set in a surgery and have you basically fiddle with the medical equipment. It was literally, 'We need to see that you can say lines and also be unwrapping a thing or putting in a cannula.' I think I genuinely took something out of a packet and then put it back in the packet, nothing medically sound at all, I was just saying 'Look, I can walk and talk and do this all at the same time!' Then they brought the executive producers down, which was terrifying. We had to go through the doors because, likewise, they have to see that you can do that, and I completely lost my lines. I skipped right ahead but the director, who was reading with me, luckily caught it. Then I found out I got it which was great and it was a year contract, with a six-month-break clause. I think that's for our benefit and their benefit. So if you don't like it you can jump ship, and if they don't like you they can get rid! I started in March and there's a three-month delay before broadcast. So it was weird because I had three months in which my whole life had changed but there was no evidence of that out in the world. Then of course it came out in June and all my family came over to watch my first episode.

It's interesting having seen it initially from the point of view of a guest artist, now being on *Holby* as a regular, because on *Casualty* you come in as a guest and you feel instantly like, 'These are the regulars, this is their job, this is their daily work.' It is such a well-oiled machine. I found with guest stars as well, it really works because they just slot in. It's not like making a film or new show where everyone is finding their feet and trying to work out what it will be. We already know very much what it is, it's a machine that will keep going on with or without you. You can come in and just do your job, you don't need to worry about the tone of the thing as a whole, you don't need to worry about what anyone else is doing because they are entirely comfortable with what they're doing. It's all there already. On *Casualty*, I'd learned all of my lines inside out and was quite nervous but I felt like the regulars were so casual. As a regular myself now on *Holby*, I realise that some of it is changed on the floor and you can be flexible.

Are you able to make any changes?

We get sent the scripts, normally a couple of weeks in advance, but that can change as well. At the moment we're filming Episode 24 and 25, which is a block. We haven't yet read the script for Episode 24, but we have had the script for Episode 25. So you'll be playing in a scene and referencing something you haven't yet read! (Though that is very rare.) So we get sent them, normally two weeks in advance, and we can ask for amends. We can say, 'I don't understand this' or, 'I'm not sure about that, could we change it?', and normally they'll send back an amended script. There are also little things on the day when, if you say it and it sounds like marbles in your mouth, you are able to change on the floor. We're talking tiny changes – phrasing rather than meaning. I should be absolutely clear about that, we never change the sense of what we say, but sometimes we do change how we say it. Any more than that is not my job. I'm not a writer and would never presume to think that I have a better instinct of how something should go than a writer, because it's not my job. But I do know my character. There's always a producer on the floor who small changes have to go through because there are some occasions where you can't use someone's name or you can't reference something. We're only allowed the word 'God' a specific number of times, for example. You get something like two 'Gods' per episode. So I've ad-libbed an 'Oh my God' and they've stopped and told me I can't have it, because we're already over the God quota. You can usually change phrasing, though it depends on the director. You learn very quickly who you can change things on the floor with and who likes more notice. By and large naturalism is at the heart of it so it really needs to sound as authentic as possible, whatever way you need to flip the words around, because the text isn't sacrosanct. It doesn't have a strict rhythm to it because it's not verse, so you can be more flexible. The most important thing is that you sound authentic. Having been there for six months, I now read scripts and can see they're starting to write in my voice. They're really tuning in and with all of the characters you can hear people writing for them specifically.

How much agency do you get in determining your character's path more long term? Do you discuss with writers and producers?

I haven't asked yet for anything. So far I've been told what's going on with me and I think largely that's how it works. I know that when people want to leave there is a discussion and it's very much a two-way conversation about how they will write their exit, but everything else pretty much comes from the top down. Any other way might get very messy, so they rightly make it clear that you don't get to choose.

How much were you told about your character on Holby *to start with?*

They send you a paragraph-long breakdown, as with most castings. For me, that summary actually hasn't really changed. I have read about times when they've written those breakdowns and then met the person and plans have changed completely, but my character is pretty much still who she was and what she is. They give you a little précis but there's a real ongoing dialogue with the producers about the storyline and about where you're going and what they think.

So what kind of thing is in that précis?

It's a load of adjectives. The one online is pretty much what I was sent, it says: 'Cara is feisty and strong-willed and a great nurse.' It's the kind of thing that you'd never see in a theatre script. You read a play and it's up to you to work all that out, it doesn't say she is neurotic or funny or strong or whatever but she is. You have to find that for yourself. It's different with continuing dramas because multiple writers write the script. They have to have a skeleton of the character so when they write they know what she's like and what she sounds like. There have to be some background guidelines because more than one writer has charge of the character.

Were you given a sense of what your storylines might be along with the précis of the character?

Yes. My big opening storyline was that my husband was an undercover cop, which I couldn't be told in the first audition. All I knew was she was madly in love with him, so I needed to play that. Then when I turned up, when I got the part, the big plot was this secret. No one knows she's married and in a few episodes' time he's going to turn up and there will be this huge revelation. Then because of the way it works and the way storylines go, about two episodes before he arrived, they changed it so in fact everyone knew I was married and I had just been lying about his job. I'd being playing it for two months that it was a huge secret, but that's just the nature of the beast. I worked myself up in knots about how I'd not shown that at all but actually it was a gift, as it just made Cara seem a much better liar! There's also a storyline cycle in long-running television, especially with something like *Holby*, whereby when you first enter something happens to your character and then in a year or so it will happen again, the thing will come back, or you'll have to deal with the repercussions of what came before. That's the nature of a drama like this.

After your audition, when you arrived, did you have a conversation with any fellow cast members?

No, I just went straight in. The first day I was doing some medical stuff, taking blood pressure (which I started out doing completely wrong, with the cuff on upside down), but thankfully nothing major. They really throw you in the deep end but it's the best way to learn, the best training

I could possibly imagine. I was also lucky because I went to LAMDA which I think has the best screen training in the country. I was really ready for the audition and even once I got on set I felt comfortable, because we had done so much screen and audition prep.

What about that complex medical world, are there production processes to get to grips with that?

We have medical advisors on set. There's always a medical professional, usually a nurse, to tell you how to pronounce that, how to do this, how long that would take. There are three regulars – you need regulars, because they understand the theatricality of it, that the medicine is key but at the end of the day we're telling a story. Also sometimes they're there to say, 'No, that's nonsense!' Actually when you're able to be really precise with the medical stuff then the whole thing lifts and is much better. We keep it as realistic as possible but we do all know that ultimately it's about the story not the medicine. The advisors are there for us but also are really helpful for the guests. A guest actor will have some problem, a hernia or whatever, and the advisors will point out that your breathing would get heavier and you'd feel the pain there and this is what happens to your body as your adrenaline reacts. It can really help because if you're sitting at home working on something you might not necessarily know the manifesting symptoms of food poisoning or lung cancer or an infected wound. I've seen whole performances really shift because one of our nurses has told someone that they have an elevated heart rate. The advisors are invaluable.

Is it a challenge as an actor to deal with all of the procedures and intricacies of the medical world whilst also playing the scenes?

It's hard to stop 'pretending' to do something and actually do it. What's great about *Holby City* is you can't pretend to do anything, because you are genuinely and practically interacting with the stuff. You're focused on doing it; you don't need to *play* concentrating on stitching someone because you actually are. Sure, it's a latex arm, but the action is the same. It's all really there because with HD TV, the special effects have to be impeccable.

Getting the timings right whilst doing these things is a real skill, isn't it?

Actually it was a steep learning curve for me in terms of continuity. They teach you about continuity at drama school obviously but I hadn't quite realised that it's a real compression of the rehearsal process. You need to make your choice and, once you've made your choice, you have to stick to it. If you decide that on that line you're going to pick this file up then so be it, forever and ever Amen. Once they've taken that first wide shot (and they start with the first wide, so you commit in that first shot) you can't really change your mind, you'll be repeating that for the close-ups. I very quickly learned to tie actions to words, quite theatrically, to a beat. If you're just randomly doing things you'll fail because you'll never be able to remember. You have to tie it in, so that you're not just arbitrarily moving and doing things, you need to hook it to something. Otherwise it'll cut badly, the editor and director will be stuck, and you'll look bad.

To return to your early involvement, did you do any personal character research before you started?

Holby sends you on placement to an actual hospital ward, which was invaluable for finding out the day-to-day realities of working in medicine. And my mum's a nurse, so a lot of my character research was based on her. My aunt as well, and some close friends of the family. I pretty much combed them for facts about their training and more general stuff about the daily work – how you deal with people dying, people at their most vulnerable, how you deal with difficult patients. Also the one thing you get to pick in your costume is your trainers and my mum had said nurses wear white shoes (it shows you have good hygiene if you can keep your shoes white) so it was really important to me to have these snowy white trainers. Luckily, costume were able to get me some!

In terms of your training, which is relatively recent, have you made any conscious connections between what you've learned whilst training and the character work you've been doing?

It's all there. How you create a character and how you break down text, for me at least, is the same no matter what you're doing. But you have to do it at hyper-speed. They're going to point the camera at you no matter what and if you haven't done the work, I reckon it will show – even more so than in the theatre because you haven't got four weeks to find it, you haven't really got any time to find it. It means the one difference for me is that I need more shorthands; whereas in theatre you can ease into something, with this I have certain on-switches. For instance, I always make sure that I know what somebody smells like. Scent for me is really useful. I have a specific perfume for Cara which is really handy because you're in it as soon as you put that on. It needs to be instant.

Does it make a difference that you don't know the future of the character?

That's funny, I've never thought about it. One of the tricky parts about theatre, I think, is playing not knowing. Lady Macbeth doesn't know she's going to go mad. So I guess we're lucky in that we literally don't know, I don't have to risk playing the end point because I'm finding it out along with everyone else!

When you are filming things out of sequence, how do you cope with that?

For me personally, I have to prep like crazy. I'm all about the highlighters and sticky notes. I make as much of a map in my brain as I can. I need to know, before we do every scene, where I've been and where I'm going. Also, often an episode will have an overarching theme and it really helps to know where you fit into that and what is going on in the world around you. We're lucky because we only do five scenes a day, so it's not too difficult to keep that in order. A friend of mine is in *Hollyoaks* [C4, 1995–] where they're doing 25 scenes a day and sometimes six episodes at a time and it can literally be, 'Do I know that you've killed this guy?' I have a lot of respect for anyone doing that.

Do you take your marked-up script to the studio floor and use it?

That's my Bible. My script becomes this totem because it's so ugly and written all over, this strange living thing that is important and cannot be duplicated. I always have it like a security blanket because it has my path in it. It's a real luxury that I only have to follow Cara, I only have to worry about my character. With script edits, we do have some influence because it's acknowledged that we're in the privileged position of only having one character's journey in our heads and having a very clear path.

Is the ensemble nature of the cast important on a long-running show like Holby City?

Big time. It's like any touring company or theatrical company except it's not over after three months, it's open-ended. It could be for the next 15 years. I think that the six-month-break clause at the beginning is also very much to find out who you are as a person because at some points you'll be working 12 hours a day, five days a week together. The crew often change round, there are regulars who come back, but with the actors it's just us, all the time. As with theatre, personal chemistry is hugely important.

What's the difference between a 'good' and 'bad' television director, from an actor's perspective?

As with anything, people differ hugely in style and it's so hard to say what's 'better' than anything else. Like with actors, people come up the ranks in different ways and everyone brings their personal take to it. For example, someone might have been a camera operator so would be very much about angles and how the shot is lit, and they might just leave you to it. Then there are people who've come in from theatre who might pause the whole shoot to talk to you about your motivation and give you notes. Mostly people fall somewhere in between. My preference is definitely more towards someone who's more concerned about performance, but then again it would be! And I genuinely believe that every really good director is, however that manifests.

Do you have a sense that there's a particular style to something like Holby City?

I came in and was determined that I wasn't going to over-act. You hear this rumour that people say, 'Oh God, these kids train and then they have no idea how to make it small for TV, they come in and it's too big', which I was so bent on not being, I wasn't going to be stagey. So I watch those first few episodes now and find I'm mumbling. I'm whispering, because I thought I had to make it 'small' for the TV. As we went on, I found it incredibly useful to watch the other actors. The level of experience and expertise on that set is incredible so in scenes I wasn't in, I would be sat at the back watching our regulars and guests. I realised very quickly that sure, it needs to be naturalistic, it needs to be believable, but more than that you need to be making choices and you need to be doing something. You need to find a sweet spot between doing something strong but in a way that is still authentic. That's what makes people want to watch. It's not observational drama; these are human relationships and actually I had gone way too far down the other end of the spectrum. So now I'm still trying to find a way of doing something bold and making a choice but in a way that's still believable. We had one actor come in and he was on set and, I confess, I couldn't see what was going on. He played it so small that I thought there was nothing there. Then it got broadcast and my God, everything he had been doing, it showed up on camera. It was all there, it was incredibly precise, it was all going on and it was very compelling.

So the style isn't just about scale, it's something less tangible?

Scale is a part of it, but not all. To think it's all about scale is misleading – that's what I thought it was. I thought it was the difference between big and small but actually it's not. I think the closest I can get is it's about energy rather than size. It's about conviction and energy, I think. And intensity. There's this amazing thing that happens on the studio floor which I didn't know about until *Holby*. When they say 'Turning' the whole room just goes silent – more than silent – all the air goes out of the room. There's such respect for the moment we start shooting. That's the intensity of it. I've never experienced anything like it before, the stakes just go up in that instant. It's all very friendly and casual but we're there to do a job and, once that camera is rolling, there's no messing around.

Acting in Police and Medical Drama

Creative agency

A prominent theme emerging across all of the above interviews is the complex, collaborative 'authorship'[1] at work over prolonged periods in the development of police and medical dramas on television. Actors are clearly conscious of limitations of agency within these processes but also experience a variety of creative opportunities, enabling them to be far more than the pawns 'in the chess games of creativity and artistic innovation' that Caughie highlights television actors as being so often perceived to be from the outside (2000, 166). At a most basic, pragmatic level, and as also suggested by the interviews of the preceding chapter, there are formalised 'amends' mechanisms within the production schedules of long-form television dramas through which actors can request changes to scripts. As Walsh states:

> We can say, 'I don't understand this' or, 'I'm not sure about that, could we change it?', and normally they'll send back an amended script. There are also little things on the day when, if you say it and it sounds like marbles in your mouth, you are able to change on the floor.

Thus, even for an early-career actor working within the well-established mechanics of a large, long-running ensemble production, there are channels of contribution open in relation to scripted content, particularly when clarifications and proposed modifications relate to the immediate practicalities and pressures of shooting a scene effectively and efficiently without 'marbles in [the] mouth'. Walsh connects this flexibility also to the strong naturalistic sensibilities still at work in the production of a medical drama like *Holby City*: '[I]t really needs to sound as authentic as possible, whatever way you need to flip the words around.' However, Walsh goes on to clarify with notable emphasis the parameters of such flexibility:

> We're talking tiny changes – phrasing rather than meaning. I should be absolutely clear about that, we never change the sense of what we say, but sometimes we do change how we say it. Any more than that is not my job.

I'm not a writer and would never presume to think that I have a better instinct of how something should go than a writer, because it's not my job. But I do know my character.

Here, Walsh stresses a respect for the particular agency of the television writer in terms of the construction of narrative and its associated patterns of meaning. Such respect is echoed across all of this chapter's interviews, regardless of actor status within a production, with Stott asserting, for instance, that his goal is always 'to try to preserve what the writer has delivered but to make it sound like it is being said for the first time … First of all, one must serve the writing'. Nevertheless, at the micro-level of phrasing, it is clear that both Walsh and Stott see their creative agency in relation to the script as highly legitimate when deciding upon how best to present their characters truthfully within the precise moment of a scene, in order to generate a sense of authenticity and spontaneity to the meaning intended by a writer. This seems particularly true of police and medical narrative contexts, in which regular exposition and use of professional terminology must be tempered by a sense of fluency and naturalness if it is to be believed.

Image 3   Ken Stott as DI John Rebus in *Rebus*

Indeed, it is evident in this chapter that this micro-level phrasing, and the ability to shape the utterances in the moment of recording, went beyond those charted in the soap opera chapter. Hannah sheds further light upon this when discussing his resistance to learning scripts too precisely, opting instead to 'paraphrase within parameters, as that helps to keep the script lively and keeps [him] thinking in that moment'. Henshall compounds this through his observation: 'It's not just about learning the lines and going for it – you have to make it your own, you have to understand it and connect with it and make it part of you, so it sounds like your words.' Such an approach marries also with Stott's aim to have only a 'working knowledge' of a script's phrasing for television, to keep his work more 'immediate' and therefore more 'real': 'That's why learning lines [for television] is like making a soufflé rather than basting this beast and putting it into the oven.' Therefore, 'presence' in the moment, and the resultant sense of sincerity that brings, is often deemed more important within these televisual contexts than strict adherence to the linguistic intricacies of a script. What is surprising is that this is not only the domain of high-profile actors, but also those at the start of their careers on screen.

Both Hannah and Stott explicitly contrast this process to theatrical work, during which time to learn the specific phrasing of a line takes on a greater significance. Indeed, across all of this chapter's interviews is a sense of the nature of the script in long-form television drama production as a perpetual 'working document' of authorial negotiation, as opposed to the more 'set' or even 'sacred' authored text that one might associate with theatre. For example, Hannah asserts that 'the lack of sacredness around the script in television … can be valuable to an actor in keeping things alive and as real as possible in the moment', with Walsh supporting that 'the text isn't sacrosanct. It doesn't have a strict rhythm to it because it's not verse, so you can be more flexible. The most important thing is that you sound authentic'. Interestingly, for Walsh, the script only achieves 'totem' status when it has been annotated by her in relation to her character, becoming a 'living thing that … cannot be duplicated'. Again, such 'totemic' significance is linked to the transient utility of the annotated script within the present moment of filming, as opposed to anything more enduring or inherent within the text itself.

Beyond the persistent hierarchies of perceived cultural value – 'it's not verse' – there are a number of other potential explanations for the status of the script as 'working document' in the production of long-form police and medical dramas on television. In a similar vein to soap, the most obvious explanation is the intensity behind many shooting schedules, during which actors will most likely be given multiple iterations of scripts and also move through (or between) one episode's script to another very quickly. This places practical time constraints on engagement with the phrasal minutiae of a script, whilst also establishing more symbolic limitations on a script's 'totemic' value, as no sooner has an actor familiarised themselves with one than it is time to begin work on the next. Moreover, because of limited space for formalised rehearsal and exploring performative possibilities as a production ensemble, it can be potentially detrimental as an actor to over-determine routes forward through personal work on scripted content; as Hannah suggests, 'on the day you have to be adaptable when things don't go to plan, and be able to process other options'. Equally, there is an awareness that 'authorship' becomes more collaborative in such working contexts, with actors establishing their stakes and then consolidating them by various means. Walsh, for example, highlights that the nature of *Holby City* entails that 'more than one writer has charge of the character', which – in a comparable fashion to the soap process – means actors often become the 'authorial' constant for their characters within a sea of production change, in which writers, directors and producers more regularly come and go. Indeed, Hannah supports the perspectives of both Walsh and the preceding chapter's soap interviewees in stating:

> [W]riters and directors are aware that actors already know their characters very well. Once you have that stability in your role, bringing a new writer or director in may in fact offer a slightly different, fresh voice that you like and can work with, within the framework of what you've already established for your character.

Hannah's comments indicate the complex nature of 'authorial' power dynamics in long-form television drama production, in which the actor regularly becomes a more stable creative agent than the writer or director. Of course, Hannah's status within the productions that he discusses, as leading player and – in the case of *Rebus* – also executive producer, means that his experiences of creative communication with writers and directors may not be as generalisable for the other actor interviewees. Interestingly, in deciding whether or not to play Rebus himself, Hannah ultimately deferred only to Rankin – the 'ur-author' of the character in literary form – for creative approval, reflecting adaptation studies' long-standing debates around the primacy of the 'source' text (see, for example, Cardwell 2002). Nevertheless, irrespective of star status, it is clear that interviewees felt an increasing 'authorial' stake in their characters during production, with writers adapting to write more in their particular 'voice' as time goes on, again echoing soap actor experiences. As Walsh states: '[I]t's acknowledged that we're in the privileged position of only having one character's journey in our heads and having a very clear path,' indicating links with aforementioned notions of actors as chief 'character custodians' within the ongoing mechanisms of long-form production. Walsh makes equally clear the limitations of such agency for the 'average' (i.e. non-producer) actor within larger discussions of long-term narrative development, however, with decisions coming very much 'from the top down': 'Any other way might get very messy, so they rightly make it clear that you don't get to choose'. Walsh articulates the sense of liberation that can come from an awareness of a broader, 'well-oiled' structure of creative control – 'It's a real luxury that … I only have to worry about my character' – but also acknowledges her ultimate disposability within such a production framework: '[I]t's a machine that will keep going on with or without you.' Similarly, Stott recognises the definitive control of production hierarchy and finance in determining what finally ends up on screen: 'I swear most of my best work for camera has landed on the cutting room floor … Where is the money coming from? When you get to understand that, you understand where the decisions are probably being taken.'

Yet, there are other instances in which 'authorial' agency in determining longer-term storylines, in addition to the truthfulness of a character in the moment, can be increased for the television actor. Henshall, for example, shares the ways in which his casting as the first wheelchair user to portray a regular character on *Holby City* led to enhanced creative agency but also anxieties. Henshall's initial hot-seating session generated the basic shape for his character and he was subsequently involved in the audition process to find an appropriate actor to work alongside him as a fellow medical student. Furthermore, Henshall's perspective within the production meant that producers and writers would solicit his input on the development of storylines and scripted content as well as character details:

> [T]he producers or writers would call me with questions ... I was in an unusual position in that they were at times being guided by me in what they should be doing and writing about ... That could become frustrating for me sometimes because it was new ground for them and I felt the need to think hard about where stories could go and we talked about the nature of my disability, and whilst that could be a great creative opportunity, at times I felt the pressure of that.

Henshall's experiences are a reflection of the naturalistic sensibilities and connected representational responsibilities that continue to act upon the development of stories within the medical genre. Henshall articulates an interesting resultant tension within the creative approach of the production team: positively seeking insights into his experiences as, for example, a wheelchair user to enhance the authenticity of character and story but, in so doing, also imposing a more intensified 'authorial burden' than is usual for a television actor, which resulted in feelings of increased creative pressure. Therefore, Henshall's reflections point towards the potential challenges or complexities of expanding the creative agency of the television actor beyond conventional parameters. Such 'authorial burden' could also be read within Hannah's descriptions of being both lead actor and producer on *Rebus*. Whilst Hannah's executive producer status afforded him increased access to writers which proved a clear positive in terms of effective creative communication, he also felt pressured to assume the starring role himself but with an awareness that he had intended for another actor to take this part within his initial vision for the adaptation as a producer. The resultant tensions arising from the double weight of these creative roles inevitably coloured Hannah's experiences on the project as an actor, perhaps contributing to his short tenure in the part.

Alongside these more exceptional circumstances, Henshall identifies a further route of creative agency through acting process in long-form television drama which echoes the comments of soap actors in the preceding chapter: what can be termed as 'leading' the writer through making conscious acting choices. Henshall notes that his desire to pierce beneath the exterior arrogance of his character to access inner sensitivity manifested itself in the way he handled caring scenes with patients, which in turn encouraged the writing team to pursue this path for the character: '[the writers] do respond to what they see you doing on screen. I ended up with a lot of scenes with guest patients, trying to make them feel better emotionally'. This is very much in line with a strategic approach of soap actors identified and elaborated upon by Graeme Hawley (Chapter 2):

> Once you get more comfortable and clever with it you can also discuss, as actors, where you might want to try to lead the writers. What do you want to show on screen to try to nudge the stories along in a certain direction? … I felt that there were certain things that I could do in order to lead them down a path which they would hopefully follow and run with.

'Leading' writers is an indicator of the tacit nature of much of the 'authorial' negotiation within long-form productions, in which creative relationships and collaborations are developed over time, although not always through direct contact but instead often through an actor's mediated response to the script and, in turn, a writer's mediated response to its realisation on screen. Ultimately, mutual respect amongst 'authorial' agents within these creative collaborations appears key to success.

Character stasis and narrative repetition

In no small part because of the aforementioned mythic and socially cathartic functions of police and medical dramas on television, stable character archetypes and the ritualistic repetition of narrative structures are commonplace features of these genres. Walsh, for example, observes the 'storyline cycle' of *Holby City*, 'whereby when you first enter something happens to your character and then in a year or so it will happen again … That's the nature of a drama like this'. Whilst such cyclical genre attributes may facilitate meanings and pleasures for audiences, they pose challenges for actors, as this chapter's interviews attest. Yorke's assertion that character change is the 'great and glorious' lie of television drama, and that '[d]rama demands that characters must change, but the audience by and large … insist they stay exactly the same' (2014, 184, 185), is at its most apt in relation to these genres in particular. Yorke's resultant question of how to 'create change in a world where … characters must always stay the same' (2014, 186) is a substantial dilemma, and indeed a frustration, articulated at various points in the interview data from the actor perspective. Hannah offers a memorable example of this when discussing the expectation versus the reality of character work in long-form television drama production, assuming 'a much greater chance to develop a character and to understand a character across a much larger arc' but discovering instead 'that you are encouraged to go through the same journey again and again': 'The executives involved aren't much interested in character development – they want the same thing that proved popular the last time.' Interestingly, in his portrayal of Rebus, Hannah reveals that he constructed his own psychological journey for the character by relating his screen work to Rankin's preceding novels: 'Because we started with an adaptation of the eighth novel, I could use the information of the earlier novels to construct a backstory for my performance in my head.' Therefore, in a production environment in which narrative repetition prevails, Hannah was still able to construct a sense of meaningful development for his character through an internalised backstory. Whilst this may not be readily discernible on screen, this private work, away from formalised spaces of rehearsal, enabled him personally to reconcile his work with the logic of character journey as opposed to the difficulties and frustrations of character stasis.

Image 4   John Hannah as DI John Rebus in *Rebus*

Within these repetitive narrative structures, Hannah also stresses the value of identifying the key scenes to each story in which a character is subject to genuine change:

> [T]hese scenes themselves have an internal journey in terms of a character's emotional standpoint or point of view. In these important scenes those things are affected and in the process the character becomes a different person. So you deal with those scenes and their journeys internally.

Hence, in locating such scenes and focusing upon the significance of their internal emotional journeys, Hannah suggests that an actor can still establish a micro-logic to the development of a character within a scene, even if at the macro-levels of the episode or the drama as a whole the character ultimately experiences no perceivable or enduring change. Hannah refers to the remaining narrative content as 'the bread and butter rather than the filling of the sandwich'; those scenes 'without any major emotional consequence for your character', which constitute a significant proportion of work on police drama in his experience:

> You're getting out the car, you're walking up the path, you're knocking on the door, you're drinking a cup of tea in the living room and you're asking

some questions. There's no emotional journey there for your character – it's more the journey of the investigation.

Although crucial for the mechanics of the narrative, Hannah argues that these generic elements should be invested with less significance for the actor, as they offer no opportunities for emotional transformation, only repetition and familiarity. For some actors, Hannah recognises that such familiarity can be comforting and even empowering but, often, ultimately dissatisfying:

> [Y]ou are in command of that character and that environment. Perhaps this is partly why many television actors stay with characters for so long … whereas for other actors that familiarity or predictability becomes a problem.

It appears that the higher the profile of the actor, the more pronounced the dilemmas and frustrations of repetition become. Actors struggle to find variety and change in their professional experiences due to encouragement to 'play to type' and therefore to provide audiences with another performative iteration of something that has already been deemed gratifying. Stott, for example, mentions the ways in which he felt pressure to play DI Rebus, from both producers and viewers, as a result of his existing status within the contexts of both the police genre and Edinburgh culture: 'Every time I went back home to Edinburgh people would say to me, "Hey, are you going to play Rebus?" "You should play Rebus."' Similarly, Hannah notes the force with which STV determined his lead role in his production company's *Rebus* adaptation, acknowledging: 'they saw me as a hot property at that time'. Not only had Hannah experienced recent cinematic career successes, he also had a track record with *McCallum* in leading crime dramas for STV: 'This brings us back to the importance of branding and marketing as a creative factor.'

Within such casting constraints, resulting often in offers of very similar roles, both Hannah and Stott stress the importance of finding correlations between aspects of the characters portrayed and themselves at different stages in their lives. For instance, Hannah states:

… I am going to have something in common with that character, perhaps because I've gone through some similar experiences or thought processes … there's already a connection of feeling or experience within me.

Referring to his work on *McCallum* specifically, Hannah elaborates:

I think it was also an age that I was at when I was looking at myself and posing questions about who I was and where I was going, and all of those questions were also there for my character, which kept it interesting for me whilst I was still on that journey myself.

The value of actor–character correlations of this kind is also expressed by Stott:

When I started with *The Vice*, I made a promise to myself that I was not going to impose a character but to use me. To come back to me. To always refer to myself. How would I react in that situation? What is my feeling towards this? That was very useful for me. I always had something I could rely on as the truth … Over ten years of doing this, with three different characters in police drama, the change that I recorded ended up really, I think, being a change in me.

Thus, operating within a narrative environment in which characters and storylines can become highly repetitive in nature, Hannah and Stott both access a sense of logical development in their work by relating the thoughts and actions of their characters to their own lived experiences at different stages on their personal journeys. Whilst such performative elements are private and may not always translate explicitly onto the screen, they act as an internal coping mechanism through which – often in the absence of any formalised structural change for their characters – actors are able to impose psychological change, and therefore truthfulness and meaning, upon their work. This process can operate effectively not only internally within an individual drama but also, as Stott suggests of his police drama work, across multiple roles within the span of an actor's career. Of course, both Hannah and Stott's experiences in this regard rely upon a rare luxury for television actors: choice. Although they both felt pressures to 'repeat' the successes of previous roles through assuming similar characters, within that their existing status enabled them to select projects which they deemed most suitable for them at that time. Thus, whilst character development within individual police and medical dramas is often limited, the ability to select roles within these genres across a career can afford a sense of development for an actor. This is particularly significant for actors as a coping response to the structural repetitiveness they perceive as inherent to these genres.

Moreover, actor–character correlation is strongly encouraged by the casting strategies of police and medical dramas, in which, as Hannah notes, '[P]eople are cast now because there's so much about them that is similar to what is required of the character in the script.' When cast, the intensity of production then continues to encourage such correlative approaches to a role, with Henshall recognising that associated time constraints mean '[y]ou haven't got time to do lots of character work', instead necessitating the presentation of a 'version of yourself':

[M]ore and more I think it's about using yourself and knowing yourself … Of course, there are ways that my character behaved that I would never mirror in my own life but in essence you are playing a version of yourself. It's you but you're also tapping into aspects of you that you wouldn't show in your own day-to-day life.

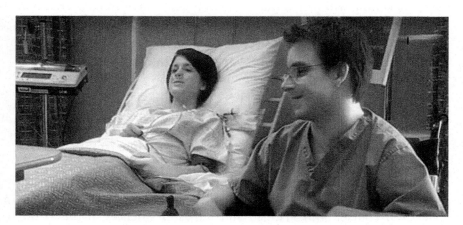

Image 5   Paul Henshall as medical student Dean West in *Holby City*

As Henshall's comments suggest, this is a far more complex process than simply 'playing yourself', an accusation frequently levelled at actors working in long-form television roles, often with the associated implication of a lack of thought or skill required for television work within popular genres such as police and medical drama. Rather, Henshall stresses this as a valuable technique, within the production conditions available, for accessing and utilising aspects of self, or possible versions of self, whether active or dormant in everyday life, to facilitate a general sense of character coherence over long narrative spans but also to generate moments of genuine revelation:

> We all have the possibility, the potential, to behave in any number of ways when responding to a situation, so it's about accessing those options … For me, that's when characters start to really emerge, because you didn't realise you could act like that or be like that and it comes to life.

It is noteworthy that the importance of actor–character association is emphasised more in relation to these case-study programmes than within the soap opera chapter, which is surprising given the duration of an actor's work on a role in soap. Arguably, the inherent repetitiveness of action and emotion is more pronounced for actors within police and medical narrative contexts, further necessitating a reliance upon self to impose internal coherence and truthfulness. There are obvious points of contact here with the various permutations of the American post-Stanislavskian 'Method' approach to actor training developed by the likes of Stella Adler, Sanford Meisner, Lee Strasberg and Uta Hagen. However, the breadth of the narrative canvas upon which the television actor potentially works, often sustaining, over years of production and many episodes/storylines, a broad character coherence both within and across projects, whilst also regularly creating instances of emotional sincerity and revelation, places a uniquely televisual inflection upon the nature of actor–character correlation as an approach and the ways in which it can operate. The experiences of actors within police and medical dramas in this regard are also distinct from the demands of soap opera, in that these processes often operate across multiple dramas and are intensified by the more explicitly repetitive nature of the narratives offered. Therefore, in having to repeatedly access appropriate emotional responses to very similar story beats (such as the discovery of a dead body in the police context), yet still imbue such story beats with a sense of authenticity and revelation, actors rely increasingly upon their own intuitive responses.

Alongside character coherence and believability, as Hannah recognises, some of the most satisfying television work comes when an actor is given the narrative span to introduce and explore more complex character contradictions:

> That's what can sometimes feel lacking in short-burst television dramas – the lack of space to introduce contradictions or complexities of character, because those contradictions are very human and very real. That's what I enjoyed most about Rebus as a character – his contradictions. We did try to bring in those complexities as much as possible but ultimately what was required was another television cop show ... which is largely why in the end I only did four stories.

Indeed, there are limits to the sustainability of correlative methods for the television actor within the long-term, cyclical narrative mechanics of police and medical dramas. Chiming with Henshall's notion of drawing from aspects or versions of self, Stott describes character development as being like 'plucking fruit' from an 'orchard' of potential characteristics, emotions, actions and responses. However, eventually, the orchard is left bare and cannot always effectively replenish itself: '[A]s an actor you have to make a truthful response. I would also be asking myself the question: "How many truthful responses to the first time you see a dead body are there in the lexicon?"' Similarly, Hannah says of his eventual departure from *McCallum*:

> [A]t some stage, you then grow up a little bit and start to find answers to those questions for yourself and therefore feel frustrated that the character isn't also growing up but is instead, in the repetitive way that I mentioned previously, covering the same emotional ground over and over. After a while, that gets tiring.

Hence, whilst a close emotional association with the role might aid the actor in finding an emotional link to the situation of the character, the repetitive structures of the form can, in time, limit the actor's capacity for fresh and intuitive responses to the situations in which they find characters. However, if structural repetition across the span of a single production might gradually diminish their capacity for imaginative response, over the span of a television career, making use of actor–character correlation can bring professional satisfaction, even in a creative environment in which character stasis and narrative repetition prevails. As Stott summarises:

> Actors that are lucky enough to work all of the time have an opportunity to see and watch an arc develop in their work and the way that they work reflects what has happened in their lives. I wouldn't do that for other characters but I could do it for these three detective characters that I've played.

Authenticity and entertainment

Reflecting the strong social realist traditions of police and medical dramas on British television, the relationship between authenticity and entertainment within the construction of narratives remains a central creative concern, and one which influences the character decisions of actors working within these genres. A sense of credibility in the presentation of the professional worlds of these dramas is significant not only because of their representational responsibilities but also – perhaps of more immediate production importance – because of the need to enable audiences to connect with characters and storylines through an overall acceptance of the plausibility of the dramatic environments in which these characters function. As Jacobs suggests in connecting developments in the 'medicalisation' of daily experience post-1990 to a further intensification of 'popular engagement with the fictional depiction of hospital life' (2008, 36), viewers have come to feel (often misguidedly) ever-more empowered by accessible knowledge of medical procedure and therefore increasingly sceptical of dramatic representations which appear to fall short of verisimilitude. However, this drive for credibility has to be compliant with the primary demands of effective storytelling, as Walsh acknowledges of *Holby City*:

[W]hen you're able to be really precise with the medical stuff then the whole thing lifts and is much better. We keep it as realistic as possible but we do all know that ultimately it's about the story not the medicine.

Here, medical authenticity is of value only in so far as it facilitates and heightens the drama, not when it begins to compromise dramatic power or appeal. Indeed, the primary draw of police and medical precincts in production terms is the dramatic weight of the mythic stakes that they offer in the construction of story: in many cases, literally life and death in the balance. Therefore, in this context, verisimilitude becomes the spoonful of sugar as opposed to the medicine itself.

As both Henshall and Walsh note of their work on *Holby City*, formalised production processes are in place to support actors in credibly inhabiting a medical environment, with actors offered opportunities to observe real medical procedures and to ask for clarification from a regular team of on-set medical advisors. However, both stress that such experience and information is of use only in further enabling the emotional truth of a character, their actions and their relationships, with Henshall remarking: 'If it's not going to help to push the character forward, then I don't need to know it.' In the same spirit, Walsh locates the worth of *Holby City's* medical advisors chiefly in their ability to offer information to guest actors playing patients which inflects their physical and emotional responses in the moment of a scene:

[T]he advisors will point out that your breathing would get heavier and you'd feel the pain there and this is what happens to your body as your adrenaline reacts. It can really help … I've seen whole performances really shift because one of our nurses has told someone that they have an elevated heart rate.

Equally, in reflecting upon her own work, Walsh articulates the value of medical authenticity in allowing her to truthfully inhabit the moment of the drama:

It's hard to stop 'pretending' to do something and actually do it. What's great about *Holby City* is you can't pretend to do anything, because you are genuinely and practically interacting with the stuff.

Moreover, in the case of actors working regularly on long-running medical dramas, the ability to 'actually do' rather than '"pretending" to do' increases the longer they continue to inhabit that world as that character. The cumulative experience of action within these environments renders it increasingly as automatically and instinctively 'doing' as opposed to consciously 'pretending'.

Emotional authenticity of action and response is deemed similarly paramount by both Hannah and Stott in the context of police drama, with Hannah highlighting the necessity of having established 'a framework of meaning and feeling … for when you're playing that character in the moment of a scene', and Stott commenting:

> I did research in terms of how you deal with murder, how you deal with what it's like for you as a police officer to go into that situation. The emotion and emotional survival in that environment was important to me.

Indeed, a significant challenge for television actors is quickly accessing the particular framework of authenticity for their characters within the pressured schedules of production. Walsh asserts the usefulness of costume choices as 'shorthands' or 'on-switches' for this, mentioning the particular trainers that her character wears for work and also her particular scent: 'I have a specific perfume for Cara which is really handy because … [i]t needs to be instant'. Comparably, Stott refers to his 'own little black box of secrets … Memories or associations that … trigger those emotions' in the production time available, which again has particular associations with Lee Strasberg's reformulation of Stanislavski's teaching.[2]

'Authenticity' thus takes on a nuanced meaning within these case studies. For Henshall and Walsh on medical drama, 'authenticity' can refer to the realistic depiction of medical procedures, skills and the physical effects of injury and illness for guest actors. For Hannah and Stott in a police drama context, 'authenticity' is much more intimately associated with emotional experience and how real-life detectives cope with the day-to-day scenes that they witness. Crucially, both of these formulations of 'authenticity' respond to the simple notion of being believable as their characters, and this believability comes from emotional, as well as professional, insights.

A further aspect of authenticity deemed important across each of this chapter's interviews relates to the mode of delivery in acting for television. Rather than being about 'scale' or 'size', it is repeatedly described as an appropriate modulation of 'focus', 'energy' or 'intensity' that effectively facilitates both compelling moments of drama and a sense of naturalistic plausibility within the world of the narrative and within the televisual form more broadly. Walsh communicates this as the 'sweet spot between doing something strong but in a way that is still authentic'. Collectively, the perspectives of the actor interviewees suggest that, for them, the form of authenticity that matters the most in the production of police and medical narratives for television is emotional in nature, and that all other concerns of verisimilitude work ultimately in the service of a truthful yet dramatic delivery of such emotion.

Conclusion

This chapter has examined police and medical genres as performative contexts for the work of British television actors, considering the associated opportunities and challenges that such contexts present.

Investigation of the forms of creative agency for actors within these genres revealed predictable limitations but also more surprising possibilities for creative influence, particularly in relation to deciding upon phrasal details that best present characters as 'truthful' and 'present'. This is stressed as crucial in the contexts of police and medical dramas specifically, in which professional terminology and moments of exposition regularly require phrasal adjustments to increase plausibility within the moment of the scene. Moreover, the actor interviews collectively evidence the various ways in which negotiations of 'authorship' play out between actors and other creative agents within the production process over prolonged periods. These negotiations may be more implicit and organic in nature, such as the process of 'leading' writers through making particular acting choices or the (most often unstated) mutual trust and respect that can develop between actor and director. Equally, actor agency may be more explicit in certain situations, as in the case of lead actors who also hold producer roles, or as the result of a unique personal perspective affording elevated creative value and therefore status to an actor within a particular production context (as with Henshall's experiences working in *Holby City*). Overall, the interviews suggest a greater degree of variety and complexity to actor experiences of creative agency in these dramatic forms than initially anticipated.

Furthermore, interviewee responses to the challenges and frustrations of character stasis and narrative repetition within police and medical dramas shed light upon the nuanced psychological and emotional dimensions with which television actors regularly imbue their work, often through generating correlations between character and self in order to impose a sense of logical development or 'journey' upon a role or across a series of roles through the larger span of a television career. Even if the results of these efforts are never realised in any discernible form within the finished performance texts themselves, they nevertheless assist the television actor in empathising with and understanding their characters, their motivations and their actions, and therefore instilling an enhanced sense of sincerity and purpose in their work. Indeed, as Hannah recognises: 'Much of that may never come out in the drama explicitly but it's there for you as an actor.' It is the fact that this remains private which is of crucial interest to this research. As explored in Chapter 1, textual analysis can only take us so far. These private processes, never made explicit in the final text, allow us to explore the process of creation with the scrutiny normally reserved for analysis of end product. These actors found strategies to confront the repetitive structural properties of the form both through the identification of emotional development in key scenes, and via the progression between roles and series, rather than episodes. These structural properties were experienced as a significant challenge, however, and often (particularly in the experience of Stott and Hannah) prompted them to seek out new roles, challenges and narrative developments elsewhere.

The actors' need to develop a framework of logic and sincerity around a character was inseparably combined with perceptions of 'authenticity' and its role within police and medical dramas. Unexpectedly, given that the workplaces depicted in these case studies are dominated by procedures, protocol and a highly specific lexicon, overwhelmingly 'authenticity' became less about the professional and procedural details of police or medical work, and more about establishing plausible character conditions which then enable a conviction of emotion and action from an actor, and therefore best ensure compelling storytelling.

References

Brown, M., 1996, 29 April. 'The Thick Blue Line'. *The Guardian*.

Brunsdon, C., 2000. 'Structures of Anxiety: Recent British Television Crime Fiction', in E. Buscombe (ed.), *British Television: A Reader*. Oxford: Oxford University Press, 195–217.

Buxton, D., 1990. *From The Avengers to Miami Vice: Form and Ideology in Television Series*. Manchester: Manchester University Press.

Cardwell, S., 2002. *Adaptation Revisited: Television and the Classic Novel*. Manchester: Manchester University Press.

Caughie, J., 2000. 'What Do Actors Do When They Act?', in J. Bignell, S. Lacey and M. MacMurraugh-Kavanagh (eds), *British Television Drama: Past, Present and Future* (First Edition). London: Palgrave Macmillan, 162–174.

Chapman, J., 2009. 'Not "Another Bloody Cop Show": *Life on Mars* and British Television Drama', *Film International*, 7:2, 6–19.

Creeber, G., 2004. *Serial Television: Big Drama on the Small Screen*. London: BFI.

Culler, J., 1975. *Structuralist Poetics: Structuralism, Linguistics and the Study of Literature*. London: Routledge.

Day-Lewis, S., 1998. *Talk of Drama: Views of the Television Drama Now and Then*. Luton: University of Luton Press.

Dingwall, J., 2012, 15 October. 'Rebus Creator Ian Rankin Reveals Why a TV Adaptation Won't Happen'. *Daily Record*.

Ellis, J., 2002. *Seeing Things: Television in the Age of Uncertainty*. London: I.B. Tauris.

—— 2007. *TV FAQ: Uncommon Answers to Common Questions about TV*. London: I.B. Tauris.

Fiske, J., 1988. *Television Culture: Popular Pleasures and Politics*. London: Methuen.

Gill, A.A., 1996, 27 October. 'They've Dunnit to Death', *Sunday Times*.

Holmwood, L., 2008, 22 February. 'ITV Ditches *Rebus* Amid Cull Threat'. *The Guardian*.

Jacobs, J., 2003. *Body Trauma TV: The New Hospital Dramas*. London: BFI.

—— 2008. 'Hospital Drama', in G. Creeber (ed.), *The Television Genre Book* (Second Edition). London: BFI, 34–36.

Jermyn, D., 2003. 'Women with a Mission: Lynda La Plante, DCI Jane Tennison and the Reconfiguration of TV Crime Drama', *International Journal of Cultural Studies*, 6:1, 46–63.

Jordan, M., 1981. 'A Study of the Relationship between the Novel and the Film (for Cinema or Television), with Special Reference to the Novels of Henry James' (unpublished Master's thesis, University of Warwick).

Mittell, J., 2015. *Complex TV: The Poetics of Contemporary Television Storytelling*. New York: New York University Press.

Moir, J., 1996, 11 February. 'Oh, What a Lovely Ward!'. *The Observer*.

Nelson, R., 1997. *TV Drama in Transition: Forms, Values and Cultural Change*. Houndmills: Palgrave Macmillan.

Newcomb, H., May/June 1985. '*Magnum:* The Champagne of TV'. *Channels of Communication*, 23–26.

News.bbc.co.uk, 2008, 17 July. 'TV Soaps "Stereotype Minorities"'. Accessed at: http://news.bbc.co.uk/1/hi/entertainment/7511439.stm (last viewed: 6 July 2016).

Redwood, F., 2003, 11 June. 'Script and Scalpel, Please'. *The Times*.

scotsman.com, 2011, 10 April. 'Rebus Set to Return to TV, but for Now its Star Remains a Mystery'. Accessed at: www.scotsman.com/news/rebus-set-to-return-to-tv-but-for-now-its-star-remains-a-mystery-1-1573818 (last viewed: 4 July 2016).

Strasberg, L. and E. Morphos. 1988. *A Dream of Passion: The Development of the Method*. London: Bloomsbury.

Strasberg, L. and L. Cohen. 2010. *The Lee Strasberg Notes*. London: Routledge.

Stubbs, D., 2015, 16 June. 'Watching the Detectives: Why the Police Procedural is More Popular than Ever', *The Guardian*.

Sutcliffe, T., 2009, 30 December. "Last Night's Television – Holby City, BBC1; The Many Faces of June Whitfield, BBC2', *The Independent*.

Sydney-Smith, S., 2009. 'Buddies, Bitches, Broads: The British Female Cop Show', *Film International*, 7:2, 46–58.

Tulloch, J., 1990. *Television Drama: Agency, Audience and Myth*. London: Routledge.

Wilsher, J.C., 1997. 'TV Series Drama: A Contradiction in Terms?', *The Author*, Spring, 11–12.

Yorke, J., 2014. *Into the Woods: How Stories Work and Why We Tell Them*. London: Penguin.

Notes

1   Whilst the present study will not focus on the complex existing debates regarding television 'authorship', Jason Mittell (2015, 86–117) offers an illuminating investigation of collaborative 'authorship' in twenty-first-century television drama production.

2   In his reformulation of Stanislavski's work, Lee Strasberg placed particular emphasis on accessing the actor's own psychological life and emotional experiences. The self became the primary site for character development in his teaching. See, for example, *A Dream of Passion: The Development of the Method* (1988) and *The Lee Strasberg Notes* (2010).

4

Comedy

Introduction

In comparison to the other chapters that comprise this book (most notably those relating to soap opera and police and medical drama), the work of actors in television comedy has been the subject of significant public and media attention, and actors have been lauded for their work. This is, in part, due to the visibility of the actors' skills in this particular form, which contrasts with the ways in which the broader performance styles and presentational structures of soap opera and police and medical drama can obscure the actors' work. As identified in the soap opera chapter, Baron and Carnicke note: 'When audiences encounter naturalistic performances ... [they] tend to overlook the crafted dimension of acting ... such performance elements are meant to disappear by calling attention neither to themselves nor to the skill of the actor.' (2008, 182) By contrast, implicit in critical praise for comic performance texts is an identification and appreciation of an actor's skill. Hight notes that 'sitcom ... tends to highlight and foreground performance in ways that other genres do not' (2010, 178), whilst Mills identifies that

> while most texts within the dominant naturalist mode of Western contemporary media try to hide the process behind their selection and use as much as possible, acting, and the meanings associated with the actors, often rests on a non-naturalistic display of their position within the text. (2005, 72)

He claims that this is 'at its most potent … when related to comedy' (2005, 72). It is therefore surprising that so little has been written about acting in television comedy. Back in 1981, Mick Eaton opened his chapter on sitcom in *Popular Television and Film* by asserting that 'in academic work on television the situation comedy has been all but ignored' (1981, 26). In his book, *Television Sitcom*, some 24 years later in 2005, Brett Mills still locates comedy as a neglected form of television. He offers a range of reasons for this, which include 'the belief that, as a comedic form, it has little to "say" about social concerns and the cultures it entertains; the belief that the examination of more "serious" forms is more pressing' (2005, 3). It is testament to Mills' pioneering work that this is no longer the case, and sitcom and television comedy more widely has, in recent years, gained the scholarly attention it deserves (*British TV Comedies* (2015) edited by Jürgen Kamm and Birgit Neumann is a recent significant addition to this field). The dominant modes of analysis within television comedy have been through the lens of humour theory (such as Neale and Krutnik 1990, Mills 2005, Marteinson 2014), genre definitions and studies (such as Gray and Jones 2009, Hight 2010, Baym and Jones 2012, Mundy and White 2012), case studies of particular programmes (such as *Little Britain*: Lockyer 2010, Lucas, Walliams and Hilton 2007, Lindner 2015; *The Office*: Mills 2004, Langford 2005, Walters 2005, Pankratz 2006, Dunleavy 2009, Hight 2010, Hanno Schwinda 2014, Jacobi 2015) and portrayals of gender (see the special edition of *Critical Studies in Television*: 'Acting Up: Gender and Television Comedy', edited by Leggott, Lockyer and White 2015, which built on the earlier work of Kirkham and Skeggs 1998, Koseluk 2000 and Feuer 2001). These analyses offer a thorough exploration of the debates surrounding television comedy. They rarely, however, examine performance or consider the actor's work.

In his 2005 book, Mills dedicates a chapter to sitcom performance, and his work provides a useful reference point for this study. However, what is missing from his chapter is any discussion of the ways in which these performances were generated, or use of actors' insights into the performances that he analyses. Mills himself acknowledges this, and indeed this chapter can be seen as a response to his belief that '[i]t is necessary to move away from an assumption that performances are nothing more than texts to be read, and instead move towards examining the rehearsal and production process which creates them' (2005, 73). In answering Mills' call, this chapter resituates comedic performance analysis not solely as a mode of textual analysis but rather as a mode of examination which focuses on the actors' contribution to the end performances we see on screen.

In preparing to interview actors about their work on comedy, we faced a particular anxiety about the task in hand: the sensitivity and complexity of articulating what makes something funny. We were mindful of Kamm and Neumann's warning that '[c]omedy and the comic … are notoriously difficult concepts to define' (2015, 2). We thus embarked upon this research with a certain amount of trepidation about analysing acting processes in comedy with the actors who generated such celebrated performances. What we found, however, was a willingness to discuss their work with us, and a high degree of precision when they did. In our interviews and in the analysis below we have ensured that the actors' work on comedy is at the heart of the analysis. Mills rightly recognises:

> When reading the scholarly literature on sitcom it is noticeable how the comic aspect of the genre is often sidelined, or taken as read, or incompletely examined … Yet the sitcom is only meaningful – and explicable as a genre – if its comic intent is understood; it is this which drives and defines it. (2005, 5)

This chapter will therefore focus on the particular demands of television comedy, and will foreground how the actors approached the 'comic intent' of the writing in their work. What emerges from these questions is a unique set of challenges for the actors, and a wide range of working methods on these projects.

The Case Studies

This chapter focuses on the work of four actors on two acclaimed comedies, *The Thick of It* (BBC 2005–2012) and *W1A* (BBC 2014–). We have chosen to focus on these two programmes as they have distinct similarities and yet, as shall become evident, had very different working processes for the actors. *The Thick of It*, created, written (as part of a writing team) and directed by Armando Iannucci, is one of the most popular and critically acclaimed comedies of recent years (winning the BAFTA, Royal Television Society Award, and Broadcasting Press Guild Award for Best Situation Comedy in 2006 and 2010). A biting political satire, over four series the comedy followed (and, as this chapter will explore, pre-empted) political decision making, chicanery and incompetence in a fictional governmental department, DoSAC (the 'Department of Social Affairs and Citizenship'). In parallel with the political reality it parodied, the first three series followed successive Labour ministers (Hugh Abbot MP played by Chris Langham and Nicola Murray MP played by Rebecca Front), before they were replaced in the 2011 General Election by a coalition government, after which time Conservative minister Peter Mannion MP (played by Roger Allam) led DoSAC.[1] The comedy revolves around the relationship between the minister and his/her group of researchers, assistants and civil servants (Oliver Reeder, played by Chris Addison, Glenn Cullen played by James Smith, and Terri Coverley played by Joanna Scanlan). The Prime Minister is never seen, but his presence is keenly felt through spin doctor and self-styled 'enforcer' Malcolm Tucker (played by Peter Capaldi), described by Laura Basu as an 'apoplectic foul mouthed bully' (2014, 91). The final series culminated in a Leveson-style inquiry into parliamentary standards, in which all of the protagonists gave evidence. This chapter includes interviews with Roger Allam and Rebecca Front.

W1A, written and directed by John Morton, has a similar satirical focus. Rather than politics, his object of derision is the BBC. The programme is a development of Morton's comedy, *Twenty Twelve* (BBC 2011–2012), which was based on the planning and delivery of the 2012 London Olympics. *W1A* follows the lead character in *Twenty Twelve*, Ian Fletcher (played by Hugh Bonneville), as he takes up a new post at the BBC. Like Iannucci's focus on a specific fictional (yet all too familiar) ministerial department within the apparatus of government, *W1A* focuses on one particular sector within the BBC, as Fletcher takes on his new role as 'Head of Values'. A satire on corporate governance, management of the arts and brand identity, Fletcher joins an ensemble of managers which include BBC Brand Consultant Siobhan Sharpe (played by Jessica Hynes), Director of Strategic Governance Simon Harwood (played by Jason Watkins), Head of Output Anna Rampton (played by Sarah Parish), and Producer and Head of Inclusivity Lucy Freeman (played by Nina Sosanya). *W1A* is presented as a mock fly-on-the-wall documentary, with a narratorial voice-over by David Tennant. The significance of this stylistic choice on the actors' work will be addressed below. The BBC has recently announced that *W1A* has been commissioned for a third series, which is likely to focus on the BBC's charter renewal. This chapter includes interviews with Nina Sosanya and Jason Watkins.

The similarities between these two programmes are striking with regard both to the content and the form. In terms of content, *W1A* and *The Thick of It* are biting satires of major British institutions. Unusually in British television comedy, they are projects by writer-directors, meaning that there is a direct line between the script and physical realisation of it in performance. Both comedies focus on the incompetence, shortcomings and idiosyncrasies of people in management positions, and much of the humour in both programmes is based on seeing high-profile, highly paid, ostensibly respected figures fumble, fail and embarrass themselves. Both programmes fall into Langford's category of 'painful comedy', in that, like Langford's example of *The Office*, they focus on 'very public failures' which make for 'deeply uncomfortable viewing' (2005, 29).[2]

These incisive and comic critiques of two 'establishment' institutions are symptomatic of a revival in satire as a form. Back in 2005, Mills stated that 'One of the reasons why comedy occupies such a maligned role in society may be because it no longer fulfils the subversive role it may once have done' (2005, 22). Over recent years, satire has seen a renaissance; Basu notes a 'great flourishing of political satire globally on television in recent years' (2014, 89). These are subversive, and though *W1A* might be gentler in its satire of the BBC than *The Thick of It* is about politicians (Jason Watkins calls *W1A* 'an affectionate satire; it sits in a strange world. It both satirises and celebrates the BBC'), both expose inadequacies in these institutions, and can be seen as part of a range of programmes which satirise institutions, the most recent of which, *The Windsors* (C4 2016), lampoons the British Royal Family.

The potency of this satire, and the unnervingly close similarities between comedies and the institutions they ridicule, can be found in two recent examples where art and life collide. Rebecca Front's concern about the security of *The Thick of It* scripts was not without foundation:

> These scripts are watermarked for security because … people were mindful of the fact that they didn't want stories leaking out. Not least because the government had a habit of copying the things we did throughout the show – it was quite a big risk, we didn't want to bring the country down!

At several points Iannucci pre-empted policies and initiatives, and in doing so offered what Fielding has called 'a running critique of New Labour and to a lesser extent of David Cameron's "modernised" Conservative alternative' (2014, 258). For example, a year into the coalition government (and three episodes into Series 4 of *The Thick of It*) Liberal Democrat Business Secretary, Vince Cable MP, announced a British business bank to support small- and medium-sized businesses. This was unveiled only two days after an almost identical initiative was ridiculed on *The Thick of It* when a hapless Liberal Democrat junior minister, without any authorisation, agreed to a £2bn 'micro-bank', declaring it 'is so fucking us it's brilliant' (Iannucci et al. 2012). Several papers covered the story, including *The Guardian*, whose headline asked 'Business bank: has Vince Cable been watching The Thick of It?' (Owen 2012). Similarly, Basu asks, 'What does it mean for the show to be adopted so enthusiastically by the system it so aggressively derides', when she analyses Ed Miliband's use of Iannucci's term 'omnishambles' (2014, 89). In a parallel example, in 2016 the BBC took the unusual step of pre-empting public embarrassment when their new BBC3 logo replaced the letters BBC with three lines, almost perfectly mimicking a scene in Series 1 Episode 4 in which Siobhan Sharpe unveils a near-identical BBC logo. Much to the hilarity of the press and social media, the Head of Marketing at BBC3 released a statement which read: 'Thanks to *W1A* we're cursed at the BBC when it comes to marketing.' (Carr 2016) *The Independent* led with the headline 'BBC3 admits its new logo looks like *W1A* spoof' (Hooton 2016). It is clear from both examples that these are comedies which are part of public consciousness, and which closely mirror the institutions that they depict.

Mockumentary and Comedy Vérité

It is, however, not just the content but also the form that is similar in these programmes, and the specific stylistic elements relating to the form had a fundamental bearing on the actors' work. The two programmes have strong stylistic associations with documentary forms of television. Both reject a three-camera set up, laughter track or live studio audience and were, instead, recorded on two handheld lightweight cameras on location. Characters are 'found' by the camera, frequently *in medias res* as the camera follows the action. Nina Sosanya calls *W1A* a 'mockumentary', and it is explicitly framed as such via Tennant's 'Voice of God' narration. Pankratz also identifies this quality in *The Thick of It*, which 'purports to be a fly-on-the-wall documentary using shaky, hand-held cameras, without a laugh track or incidental music' which she refers to as 'mockumentary aesthetics' (2015, 281). In this way, the aesthetic of both programmes foregrounds a sense that the viewer chances upon the action rather than what Mills and Hight have called 'conventional' sitcom, in which 'the laughter track, the theatrical shooting style and the displayed performance clearly demonstrate sitcom's artificial status' (Mills 2004, 69. See also Hight 2010, 177).

It is useful to consider *W1A* and *The Thick of It* in relation to what Mills describes as 'comedy vérité' (2004), which chimes with Roger Allam's use of the term 'cinéma vérité' to describe the style of *The Thick of It* in his interview. Mills' coining of the term 'comedy vérité' acknowledges the ancestral links between certain modern television comedies and the 'cinéma vérité' movement in documentary filmmaking. However, the precise definition of this term, in the context of the actor's work, requires some scrutiny here. In her analysis of *The Office*, Dunleavy explores the differences between the French 'cinéma vérité' tradition and the American 'direct cinema' as contrasting documentary traditions that have a bearing on contemporary television comedy. She cites Erik Barnouw's distinction that 'the direct cinema artist aspired to invisibility [and] … played the role of uninvolved bystander; the *cinéma vérité* artist espoused that of *provocateur*' (1983, 254–255, cited in Dunleavy 2009, 193).[3] As Mills notes, we can trace strong stylistic traditions from the 'cinéma vérité' to what we can now identify as the first wave of 'comedy vérité' programmes, such as

Marion and Geoff (BBC 2000–2003), *People Like Us* (BBC 1999–2001) and *The Office* (BBC 2001–2003), which were influenced by the docusoap boom in the 1990s (see Bruzzi 2000 and 2001). Jacobi states that '*The Office* was by no means the first to use a comedy vérité style, yet ultimately was the one to master it' (2015, 307). In all of these programmes the off-screen presence of the filmmaker was strongly referenced and, as many of these commentators have noted, much of the comedy derives from the ways in which characters self-consciously present themselves to the filmmaking team. At first glance, we might add *W1A* and *The Thick of It* to this list. They focus on the 'institutional milieu that has been particularly characteristic of British docusoaps' and which has been appropriated by comic forms (Dunleavy 2009, 194). However, as documentary forms have developed, so too have the ways in which comedies have remoulded them. This leads Mills to ask

> is *Twenty Twelve* a mock-doc? While it includes a voiceover and interviews to camera, the majority of the scenes ... would be impossible to achieve in a 'real' documentary, without the camera crew being visible. Similarly, mock-doc has often explored the differences between how people present themselves on- and off-camera, yet there seems no such tension in *Twenty Twelve* and we're shown events I would expect other mock-docs to present as ones the 'participants' would not want recorded ... I do wonder if *Twenty Twelve* represents the next stage in comedy's critique of documentary conventions. The fact that it seems audiences haven't been confused by it breaking the 'rules' of documentary shows how that genre's norms might have fallen apart. (2012)

Like Mills' question about *Twenty Twelve*, we argue that both *The Thick of It* and *W1A* represent the 'next stage in comedy's critique of documentary conventions', and depart from the 'comedy vérité' label. These labels have been of limited use for some time; as Hight notes in his discussion of comedy vérité and mockumentary, 'there is no consensus on the use of terminology' (2010, 182). In pursuing the question of definitions it is useful to turn to Nina Sosanya. She demonstrates a detailed understanding of the documentary style in which *W1A* is filmed in her interview. She positions *W1A* as the latest in a through-line in Morton's 'critique of documentary conventions' which stretches back to *People Like Us*. The documentary features of these programmes include, for example, the director's voice-over in *People Like Us*, the characters' direct address to camera in *Twenty Twelve*, and finally *W1A* which, Sosanya notes, was

> like *Educating Yorkshire* [C4, 2013] where people seem so used to being filmed, and the cameras are so small, and they're in their place of work 24 hours a day, and the people appear to forget about them. This was the style of *W1A*, particularly in the second series.

Neither *The Thick of It* nor *W1A* include any direct acknowledgement of the presence of cameras by the characters, and there is no explicit modification of behaviour due to the indirect effect of their presence, but both evidence a stylistic inheritance from the documentary traditions above. They sit between the 'comedy vérité' and the 'direct cinema' traditions, as there is no explicit relationship between the characters and the cameras and yet, as Allam identifies, the '[h]andheld cameras were used most of the time so that the viewer is more aware of the camera's presence. The camera isn't pretending not to be there'. As Allam notes, via the process of filming, and the style of these programmes and the satirical voice-over on *W1A*, they cannot be wholly described as creating the illusion of an 'uninvolved bystander' (Barnouw 1983, 255). In this light, 'docucom' is a more useful term to describe these programmes. This term adds to Taflinger's list of types of comedy which include 'domcom' (domestic comedy) and 'actcom' (action comedy) (Taflinger 1996, cited in Davies 2015, 105). With the prefix 'docu', docucom sits alongside 'docusoap' and 'docudrama' as a hybrid form which evidences a strong stylistic inheritance from documentary traditions and which develops symbiotically alongside it, rather than defining itself according to the now long-problematised binary of provocateur/bystander. This term, we contend, more accurately describes the work of the actor. As the following interviews will evidence, they aligned their work more closely with the combination of comedic and documentary inheritances than they did with a provocateur/bystander distinction.

It is for this reason that this chapter is entitled 'comedy' rather than 'sitcom'. Most of the actors in this chapter explored how their work on *W1A* and *The Thick of It* was distinct from sitcom, such as Nina Sosanya, who states: 'It's not a sitcom [...] It's a very different approach'. This may be because of the documentary style in which it was filmed. As stressed in Chapter 1, genre definitions are only of interest here to the extent that particular forms of television place specific demands on actors. To date, though debate surrounding these terms may be rich, there exist only passing references to how this style informs the work of actors. Hight contends that '[t]he adoption of a vérité style has implications for other aspects of a programme, such as an effort to include more muted forms of film acting rather than the more expressive television acting' (2010, 182). Similarly, Mills identifies the impact on acting of this move 'away from the theatrical visual style associated with sitcom and towards a more documentary-style one in which acting is relatively downplayed' (2005, 48), whilst Irwin suggests that 'performance [is] governed by the tropes of a documentary-style non-fiction naturalism' (2015, 69). Without more detail, such suggestions are of limited use. This chapter will therefore explore how the particular style of these programmes, as well as their content, affected the actors' work.

Interviews

Nina Sosanya

London, 27 November 2015

Nina Sosanya played BBC Producer and later Head of Inclusivity, Lucy Freeman, in John Morton's hit comedy, *W1A* (BBC 2014–). She previously worked with Morton on his comedies *Twenty Twelve* (BBC 2011–2012) and *People Like Us* (1999–2001). She also played Jenny Paige in the first two series of the popular comedy *Teachers* (C4 2001–2002). Sosanya has worked widely on television, also appearing as DCI Laura Porter on *Marcella* (ITV 2016), Kate in *Last Tango in Halifax* (BBC 2012–2016) and Kate Brockman in *Silk* (BBC 2011–2014). This interview focuses on her work on *W1A* and considers Morton's particular approach to television comedy.

How did you first get involved in W1A?

W1A is made by the director John Morton and the producer Paul Schlesinger. They also made *People Like Us* which was one of the first faux-documentary style comedies. I was in a couple of episodes, playing small parts. I'm assuming that's how my name was on the radar. The first I knew of it was when I was sent two scripts. I was sent the scenes for Lucy Freeman and I went in for a casting meeting. I knew that their style was very naturalistic, though I don't know if other people would use that word. The only way to do a good audition for them was to know absolutely every single word that John had written off-book, so I had a bit of an advantage in my first audition. I auditioned about four times for the part of Lucy and the last one was what they call a 'chemistry read' with Hugh Bonneville. In hindsight I'm not sure whether I got it because we did have chemistry or because we didn't!

So the text work you did in advance was very detailed?

John takes a long time to perfect his scripts. He's quite unique in my experience in that it's so specifically crafted. I assumed when I watched *Twenty Twelve* that a lot of it was improvised by the actors. I was quite wrong. It's absolutely word for word and stutter for stutter. That's where a lot of the comedy lies, in the rhythms of what he's written. So you have to get that right. There's one way to do his writing. That was the consensus that we all came to as a cast. It's so difficult, it's such a difficult job, but it is incredibly rewarding if you get it right. You know if you've got it right and John knows if you've got it right. There's a perfect way of doing his writing, and that's not usually the case. It's not that you can't bring your own sense of rhythm or your own sense of humour, but it's the case that if you don't see these rhythms on the page then I don't know how much of a chance you've got of being successful on this sort of work.

Having that sense of rhythm is not something every actor would have, is it?

I don't know whether it's a skill or whether it's just what chimes with what you find painful or funny. His writing is mostly about pain. It's about witnessing people in various stages of pain and social horror and watching them deal with it, and knowing what that feels like because we've all been there.

How much did you know about the character when you first became involved in the show?

It's a really interesting role to play actually, because I feel like Lucy is John's voice. She is the sanest person in *W1A*, and she's being driven insane, but a lot of the other characters are slightly more pushed; they're not stereotypes at all, but they are pushed and she's the suffering bit of sanity in the middle. That was one of the things they explained to me about the part; she doesn't have funny lines, she doesn't have funny character quirks. On the one hand that makes you go 'What's my thing? What does she do?' She doesn't have a catchphrase, she doesn't have any of those things so it's quite a hard line to walk surrounded by these insane people. But it does mean that the audience feel your pain. So in terms of her role within the company of characters that was the note they gave me. They also told me the facts about her: she's a producer, she works at the BBC. Then there's the whole challenge of being in a 'documentary' that isn't filmed as a documentary.

Can you describe how that feels?

In *People Like Us*, you had the voice of the director [played by Chris Langham] talking to subjects who were very much aware that they were sitting in front of a camera with it pointed at them. Then in *Twenty Twelve*, that voice was gone but you had characters talking straight to camera or straight to the director so it was still very much present even if it was not heard. As documentaries themselves have moved on, you have those shows like *Educating Yorkshire* [C4, 2013] where people seem so used to being filmed, and the cameras are so small, and they're in their place of work 24 hours a day, and the people appear to forget about them. This was the style of *W1A*, particularly in the second series. It morphed a little bit between the two series and now it's less about having that aware-ness of the cameras and of other people interpreting what you're saying. This allowed more intimate scenes to be included in the second series. The scenes with Lucy and Ian are more plausible as we can play with the fact that the audience believes that the cameras are less obtrusive. You're being very naturalistic and real, but you have this quarter of an eye, not half an eye anymore, on the fact that you're still in this false environment.

The camera work certainly adds to that quality …

The camera work is extraordinary. There's this unsung hero of a character who is the camera operator and he is such a big part of it. He might suddenly zoom in on somebody to get a reaction – he has to share exactly the same sense of humour and exactly the timing. What he picks up and what he leaves out of the frame is what makes it funny and that's down to John and Paul and John Sorapure, the DOP [Director of Photography].

Would he discuss his choice of shot with you?

Yes, sometimes you would discuss this with the director. Particularly if it's advantageous to what you're doing. Sometimes it is better not to know; I remember an example from a scene in *W1A* when 'B Camera' was focused on my fingers whilst I was talking. I was picking something apart at the same time as speaking. There was something wrong with the camera and John said 'You were doing something really interesting with your fingers, can you do that again?' Well, there was no way I could do that again, absolutely no way – because he told me! However, it is useful to know the size of the frame that you are in. You're a body in a wide shot but just a pair of eyes in an extreme close-up. That's the sort of thing that affects you physically; literally just knowing what the frame is will help you grow or shrink accordingly. When you don't know which size frame they are using, all you can do is tell the truth and hope that somebody else is going to take care of it. It's discussed when it's advantageous and when it is not, you learn to say 'Don't tell me.'

You talked about Lucy being one of the sanest characters. Did that impact on the way you handled scenes with other characters?

Yes it did. Rufus [Jones] is one of the very few people who is allowed to improvise because he has such a handle on his character, David Wilkes. My role with David is simply to be there for him to exist. For me those scenes are about what you choose to show and what you choose to hide. Lucy has this build-up of frustration and anger all squashed down by her infinite patience. The audience knows that one day she might bury him in her garden. In your head there's a whole film reel of you screaming and beating your head when you are really just sitting and listening politely.

She still exists within that world though doesn't she? She's part of that world.

Absolutely and that is where her frustration lies because she is part of it and wants to be part of it and is constantly drawn back into it. She wants to distance herself from the mad folk but she is definitely part of it. That is quite a tricky balance because you don't want to portray somebody where viewers scream at the TV 'Just get out!' She has to find ways of fitting and being within that world.

A big part of her pain seems linked to her appointment to Head of Inclusivity. Was that journey discussed for the character from the outset?

I certainly didn't know before I received the scripts. John writes whatever he is going to write and it takes him a long time to write because he is so specific and he knows precisely what he wants to say. You don't get prior warning as to what's going to happen. I've yet to come across an actor working for him who doesn't like that because you trust it. He's so good at what he's doing. I've been very lucky in that I have worked with two brilliant writer-directors. I did a theatre production of *House & Garden* by Alan Ayckbourn, with him directing his own work. Though they are very different, like Morton he's written every breath and every pause and he's written the comedy into the script. It's there and there is a way of doing it and it's his way and it actually is the correct way. You can try and do it some other way and you might be funny but it won't be as good. Sometimes performing John's work can feel painful because it's very real. For example, there's a scene where Lucy goes into Anna Rampton's office to say 'I'm leaving', she's made a decision, she's not a weak person, but it's just completely run roughshod. She doesn't manage to say it. She doesn't manage to leave.

That's a theme that runs through the series: very rarely do characters say what they mean, or make clear statements.

It's an interesting style. What do you call *W1A*? A comedy? A mockumentary? It's not a sitcom. The way that I approach a *W1A* script or a *People*

Like Us script is very different from the way that I would approach a sitcom. This has been in my mind recently as I've just auditioned for a sitcom. There are constantly two conversations happening in *W1A*. Therefore, it's actually about learning exactly what the words are cold and then when it comes to it, knowing that the character is thinking about something entirely different. It's a bit like rubbing your tummy and patting your head at the same time. It's a very different approach, on a sitcom I might ask, 'How am I going to make this line funny?' whereas with *W1A*, if I was thinking about how to make a line funny, then I'd be lost.

Did you feel like you were playing catch up with Hugh Bonneville and Jessica Hynes who had already worked extensively in that world on Twenty Twelve?

They are both geniuses, aren't they? They already know their characters inside out. Actually as you go along, one of the things that is really satisfying is that you realise it's just as hard for Hugh as it is for everyone else. Although it comes out like he's just speaking as he's thinking, it's so scripted and sometimes the things that he has to say are reams of double-talk and the comedy is in what they are really thinking about or the fact that they've said something slightly wrong or the fact that they are stuttering over this particular point because they don't really believe it. The actual content has to be so specific, and yet it has to sound almost effortless. We all drop lines. It is really hard; but it's great when you realise that it is hard for everyone!

Could you tell us a bit about the practicalities of working on the series? Was there a pattern to when you receive scripts?

For the first series we got the first two scripts quite well in advance. As it had been commissioned they had been written for a while and then a little later on we got the next two. The second series was similar; we had all the scripts before we rehearsed. Rehearsals are very rare on TV but they are an important part of working on John's projects. You have the read-through which is about timings and about characters, whether they are in it enough or whether they are in it too much. Then we'd have a week of rehearsals. There is a lot of material to cover in that week, so you might have an hour on your scenes across the week. John has the layout of everything very clearly in his mind, because it's a real place where we're shooting: in the first series it was in an abandoned part of White City, in some old offices that were then mocked up inside to look like the *W1A* building. Then the second series we did a lot more actually in the BBC itself. The amazing thing is that the designers only had to bring in things like the see-saws and the incredibly high stools. Almost everything else, the hedges and the names of the rooms are all real. There's a 'Tommy Cooper' room, an 'I'm Free' room, a 'Nice to See You' room. It's more bizarre than we are making it!

Is the rehearsal period the moment when you have time to develop the rhythms that you've talked about?

Yes, it was. There were also times when John would realise that something wasn't working and would re-write. It is also a technical process. He will use this time to sort the configuration of the blocking and check that he'll be able to capture what he needs.

Does the process feel valuable to you?

Yes. It's really rare to have this time. Sometimes I wonder if more rehearsal would be good or bad, I can't work it out really because there is definitely something to be said for that first take which is fresh and includes the unknown and so has fresh reactions. But then again familiarity also frees you up, so I don't know. It feels like the extremes are useful, but stuck in the middle would be no use whatsoever. You'd need either very little rehearsal so you're making it up and the cameras can catch the moment a thought comes for the first time, or you have a lot of rehearsal so that you'd know something so well, inside out and back to front, that you can then riff off that. With the week of rehearsal, we are able to get familiar with the choreography of the scenes so that's not something you have to contend with when you go out onto the floor. It is shot very quickly.

Does that speed make the relationship between the cast all the more important?

I think what really matters is an ensemble feel and it really feels, even though there are obviously the main characters, it does feel like an ensemble, it does feel like a company. Particularly during this second series when we had a green room that we would all sit in and you do build up a company feel and a shared sense of humour.

On W1A did you have any conversations with other actors about the style of performance?

I don't think so but I think that's only because of the nature of that material. Usually if you are able to have a company feel and can discuss things with each other, usually you'll discuss things that aren't explicitly explained in the script, so you'll discuss background or the life off-screen of the characters to build a world for yourselves. Often you'll discuss the structure of the scene and how you might push it in a direction that you feel it should go. I don't think I'm holding John up as some sort of God, but all of this is there, in the script. He's telling a very human story, he's portraying very human moments, he's not telling a grand plot, so actually those conversations would possibly be null and void. What we would do is just drill the lines and lament how bloody hard they are to learn and commiserate with each other when we can't get them right. They're all slightly different each time, so if Hugh Skinner [who plays Will Humphries] says 'Cool, yeah, no, yeah, cool' it's not 'Yeah, no, cool' it's 'No, yeah, cool' and he'd be picked up on it, it has to be absolutely right and precise. If you really look at it, it's not really how people speak at all; it's orchestrated like a piece of music. So it's somewhere between real and hugely artificial.

In terms of style it is true that there are levels of projection of performance within television. Something like *Doctor Who* is a half-step up just because of the nature of the stories that are being told and the nature of the audience. You know that because I'm somebody who will watch all sorts of things right across the board but I know that I'm a different viewer when I'm watching *Doctor Who* from when I'm watching something else. I'm expecting different things.

Is that ever discussed or do you just get a feel for it?

I think that's one of those things again that would be discussed with regulars but if you're going in and out; I guess if you're auditioning you would be told and if you were successful and got the role, then you would know. One of the odd things about being an actor and talking about acting is that it looks like you're part of a particular programme or series but really you only know your experience of it. I only have the experience of being me going into these things, I don't know what it's like for someone else. I remember I asked a director I was working with 'How do you feel you fit in with other directors?', and he had no idea, because he'd never seen other directors work. One director doesn't go and watch another director work. So everybody's operating on their own and it looks from the outside like a big cohesive thing but it's not really.

Do you think that there is such a thing as a good or a bad director from the actor's perspective?

It always depends on the work that you're doing. There are actors who refer to some directors as 'actors' directors' and others as 'technical directors', I don't know whether this is true or not, but 'technical directors' are, according to some actors, those who appear to be only interested in the shot or the lighting or in their editing. For them, the actors are what we call 'wetware': we're just moving props. If their take was technically quite perfect, it doesn't matter if you were any good or not. There are those other directors who, if it wasn't right for the actors, and if it wasn't right for the dramatic moment of the scene or the timing of the scene, despite the fact that they might not be totally happy technically, would overlook that in favour of getting the scene right. I think good directors are the ones that operate somewhere between the two extremes. They have a care, a concern, for both and being the person in between the two things. Sometimes you can feel as an actor on TV that you are the last bit: everyone has been there since seven o'clock in the morning, they've been lighting it and working out all sorts of stuff and then at the last minute you get called on and you've been in your trailer made up and ready for the last five hours and you just have to stand there and get it right because they've already been here forever getting it ready. You have to get your bit right and then they can move on. Sometimes you can feel a divide between the actors and the crew. A good director will bring the two together and remind everybody that they're all making the same thing, you're there for the same reason.

Can you be over-directed?

Sometimes a scene can be over-shot; you cover it and cover it and cover it from every angle and it feels like you've done the scene 50 times. It feels like a fish on a slab with no life in it. That's often when the director is worried that they haven't got enough coverage. A lot of this depends on how much time they've had. Some directors come to a scene with a storyboard for each shot, but if they've only just been employed, they're not going to have time to do that and they're going to have to think on their feet. Occasionally a director will want a close-up on every single character, a mid-shot on every single character, a wide from different angles; maybe through choice, or maybe because they simply haven't had the time to work out what they're going to end up with.

Whereas that's not the case with W1A?

That would be much tighter and much more planned. Also, there'll be a camera 'mopping up', as they call it, getting shots to cover anything we've missed. Directors also have less and less power. When I started my television work, the director seemed to be everything but now it's the producer and directors are given much less power it seems. More often than not they're shooting something the way the producer wants them to shoot it. This wasn't the case on *W1A*, but in general television today is more producer-led it seems. Also I find it quite odd in TV that the writer is not the king of everything. In theatre, the writer is the king of everything and their words are sacred and you do everything you can to make their lines work. Whereas in TV half the time people don't know who has written what it is they are saying. Who made the thing occur in the first place?

Did you feel prepared or trained for your work on television?

I didn't train, so on each type of job I've learnt. I trained as a dancer, and what I learnt from that was performance and discipline and how to listen. My job was to listen and to interpret what I was asked to do and to do it. So those skills are very useful. It's a kind of precision I suppose, which was particularly useful for something like *W1A*.

Have you ever been in a situation where you've thought that formal training in acting would have helped you?

You have nothing, no one tells you anything until you turn up and make massive mistakes and hopefully are re-employed in order to correct those mistakes. So the first TV thing I did, I benefited from my naivety in that I wasn't scared; now I'd be terrified. I was doing a scene on a television film called *Hercules and the Amazon Women* [Renaissance Pictures, 1994]. There was a massive tracking shot and a tracking dolly laid down and a huge crew with horses and extras, it was so expensive and I had no idea. I had a whole speech to do. I said to myself, 'All you have to do is tell the truth.' So I did that and then very nicely the director came over to me (rather than shouting it across 200 people, which was very kind) and said 'Great. When you do it next time, can you face the camera?' So I'd just done the whole thing facing the wrong way and it seemed really obvious with the track and there was this massive camera with loads of people behind it, but I chose to do it the other way because I was telling the truth. It doesn't work like that and that's the sort of painful lesson that you learn once and then you know what to do. That could have been the end of my career, over in that moment!

Jason Watkins

London, 28 April 2016

Jason Watkins has worked extensively on stage and screen since training at the Royal Academy of Dramatic Arts (RADA). In 2015 he won the BAFTA for Best Actor for his remarkable portrayal of the title character in *The Lost Honour of Christopher Jefferies* (ITV 2014). He has also worked on a range of television comedies, including playing Gavin in 49 episodes of the Sky sitcom *Trollied* (2011–2015) and Malcolm Tanner in *Love, Nina* (BBC 2016). This interview focuses on his work as Simon Harwood, Director of Strategic Governance at the BBC, in John Morton's comedy, *W1A*. Watkins previously worked with Morton on *Twenty Twelve*.

How did you get involved in W1A?

I was working on *The Lost Honour of Christopher Jefferies* whilst I was meeting for *W1A*. I had my hair dyed red to play Christopher Jefferies and cut short. I recorded myself reading for *W1A* whilst we were filming, and so when I got the job, Simon Harwood, my character, had short and red-ish hair. It therefore wasn't really my choice to have him look like that, but it certainly works to have short, neat hair and bright, fancy glasses. The other thing to say about the process was that when I met Paul Schlesinger [Producer of Hat Trick Productions] and John Morton, I had about three or four meetings that day, so I was dashing around on my Brompton. So I arrived on my Brompton and I think all that was useful [Simon Harwood also rides a Brompton bicycle in W1A]. They weren't sure about whether I was right straight away – they actually came down to Bristol to see me because I was right in the middle of filming *Christopher Jefferies*.

What strikes you about *W1A* is how it is pinpoint and exacting satire in a world where satire on television is less prevalent. I think comedy is perhaps more often character driven. Whilst *W1A* is, of course, still a slice of life, it is a slice of a rather extraordinary, strange world within the BBC and the language that that brings. It is a corporate language, a kind of boardroom speak. It is a satire in a way which is strange because it is an affectionate satire; it sits in a strange world. It both satirises and celebrates the BBC. It is bizarre and ridiculous and it both celebrates and exposes the weaknesses in the way that it is run. The BBC is a huge behemoth: it is still moving forward and I love it really even though it has its faults.

The character was, for me, very clear on the page. I didn't model Simon on anyone in particular although many people within the BBC came up to me and said, 'I know who that is, I know who you've modelled that one on', and I hadn't, I really hadn't. After I'd had the initial meetings with John and Paul, we had a clear idea of who he was. He is a fast-talking and bright person. He plays the game on the front foot, rather brilliantly;

he has a bright energy. This bright energy will cover a multitude of sins. It carries everything – faults and all. For me, Simon Harwood is one of those people who is playing the corporate ladder brilliantly and that is in the writing, it's not anything I do. By deflecting all responsibility, not making any decisions, delegating a poisoned chalice, he has played the game. He has survived by making his alliances with the right people, holding his position.

It's a fantastic position he's in – he's a buffer who has the ear of the person above.

Exactly, so he's actually not speaking for himself even in those circumstances. Even if he is, he is saying it is from somebody else. So my approach was to try and have a broad brush of bright energy and attack whilst observing the writing absolutely. John gave me a great note which was that Simon is having a really good day; every day is a really good day. He always has a really good day and nothing is bad. Everything is just great all the time. I thought that he was like me, Jason, on a really good day when I'm on form. I often don't like to cloud my characters with me too much, so my saying for him just became, 'Everything is just great, every day is really great and things are just great. This is a great day. We've done some good work.' For Simon, everything is possible and once you feel like that then you start to communicate that with others.

The inability of most characters to actually get to the end of their thought and articulate exactly what they want to say seems to dominate the way they speak. Simon can say 'no' to someone by saying 'yes' to them ten times.

Yes, that is a brilliant mechanism. They don't quite finish what they're going to say. He might say, 'Yes, yes, no fine, yes, no brilliant, yes, whatever you, yes, I mean.' He'll say this knowing full well that someone is digging their own grave in front of him. They're digging themselves into the ground which is extremely clever. People who work together develop a shorthand in which they never get to the end of what they're saying. They're always slightly ahead and they always pre-empt what somebody is going to say, or what they think someone is saying because there isn't time for them to finish their sentence. That was one key thing you learnt on *W1A*: the technical requirement of coming in bang on cue. I remember having dinner with my wife's family for the first time and, by God, you had to get in. You had to get in there because otherwise you wouldn't speak for two hours. I think there's something about that in this as well. You get your opinion in even when you're stitching somebody up. In Simon's case, even if he hasn't got that much to say, there are often scenes where he doesn't say very much and he's just waiting for it. He's letting it all happen around him. Then he'll come in at the right moment and only say a couple of words and then it's done.

An example of this is the new corporate structure which Simon develops. He basically sidelines Ian Fletcher and puts Alan Yentob in. Then of course the flip side of that is that Fletcher tells him he's devised his own structure which leaves Simon on the back foot. The thing is, John Morton knows that this is where Simon won't reveal that he's crushed or worried. Instead his response is, 'Yeah, great, go for it'. That is much more dangerous and scary, this ability to be strangely assertive. You hold your position. It's the same in the corporate world, you just protect your position. Simon will always do that. Even if he started as a junior script editor or something, he will have gone straight into the corporate structure as soon as he could because that was the bit he could operate in. You can imagine the conversations with Tony Hall [the Director General of the BBC who sits just outside the action on *W1A* but whose opinions and plans are frequently invoked by Simon Harwood]. Tony might ask, 'Have you got an opinion about that, Simon? What are you going to do?' I know that Simon would reply, 'That's a very interesting question, Tony, I think what I need to do is pull in a couple of – No that's really brilliant, I'll bring in a couple of – Let's do some curve ball on this. I take your point.' So he'd agree and agree, he'd bolster and affirm it. To use an actioning terminology, these are his actions but he does not actually deliver anything. Often, my character's lines or speeches start with, 'Listen, you're going to know more about this than I do … ', or, 'Listen, you know how you're going to play this, but … ', so he's handing it over and telling them that he'll never want to get in their way at all. A lot of his actions might be 'empowers' or 'inspires'. He's inspiring the other person and 'uplifting'. I would uplift Hugh's character [Ian Fletcher] but really I would be handing him his own dagger to kill himself.

You've talked about the language of the piece. It almost feels improvised – could you talk about the nature of the script?

Yes, I did an episode for *The Thick of It* actually; it was a special one-off and my character didn't make the cut, but at least I did the process. On that, we did a scripted version and then an improvised version of a scene. I did a scene with Roger Allam who was brilliant at doing both types of scene. By contrast, *W1A* is absolutely scripted. It's a challenge – a real challenge too. I remember in the first series whispering to Monica Dolan [who plays Tracey Pritchard], 'I think I'm at the limit of my abilities – I've just discovered where the limit of my abilities is, it's here, doing this.' It is very demanding and very technical. So the challenge, when you asked me the question about improvisation versus scripted, is that it is very, very strongly scripted and John is very particular about it. There are occasions when you think you're never going to get it. In the group meeting scenes we whizz around the table with those lines fizzing out like they're improvised but they are very precisely scripted. So you're really on your mettle.

You try to get up to speed as quickly as you can and try to find a route through it. Because the writing is so clear, if you just come in on cue, observe the structure of the speech as much as you can, and give it very fast and flat, the cumulative pace of delivery gives you the humour you need. You don't need to do too much inflection in your delivery of a particular line, it works fast and flat. It is about this pace between people, not your own individual spin.

So the comedy comes from the rhythms and build of the six people onscreen working together.

Yes, absolutely, it's very much like theatre and working in farces; there are structures to the comedy: there is a set-up, feed and a punchline. I've just done a re-make of *Are You Being Served?* I really enjoyed that because that was a brilliantly written episode which honours the original and it is an episode within itself. Why I mention *Are You Being Served?* is that it retains the live audience, and you begin to get a comic instinct about how to get a rapport with the audience. That rapport is familiar from theatre. In theatre you might have a joke that comes after the accumulation of lines or where you know that if you time a line in a certain way with the set-up, feed and punchline then you'll get a good laugh. That really comes out of having done it a few times with an audience, I find. But in *W1A*, you don't have an audience. So you rehearse it and block it, talk about it, practise it, then the crew come and watch and they may laugh or not. In my experience, often crews are exhausted and have seen it a few times before so you can't always use that as a guide and think that there might be a laugh there. With *W1A*, if you are leaving gaps then it's fatal. The joy and simmering giggling and slight satirical shock is lost as soon as you start messing with it, and breaking the cumulative momentum.

Does some of this come from the fact that the characters in W1A *take it so seriously – they won't ever stop and consider the weirdness of it?*

Well Hugh Bonneville can as Ian Fletcher. He can occasionally stop and see the madness around him, as can Nina Sosanya. They are windows for the audience into this mad world. Even more removed is the writer character, Dan Shepherd [played by Tom Basden] – that character is John Morton, literally the window going in and showing us what it is like.

When you had read-throughs, would you have conversations about structures or was it so evident from the text that you didn't need to?

You'd rehearse it. There's a week of rehearsals, or maybe two or three days actually, where you're just exploring. I'm trying to think of the differences between doing the first series rehearsals and doing the second series. I mean it's all a big discovery during the first one and you're still trying to work out who your character is, how he works best. There's a slight pressure of wanting to get it right and hoping that you can do what is required of you, recognise what it is and be able to deliver it but also have fun as well, try and have fun. By fun I mean you recognise where the comedy is. I don't know what Nina said about this …

She found that one of the key skills was to be able to find the humour off the page – to be able to identify the comic rhythms.

That's a good point. Her character is different from mine because she does see the horror of the absurdities. Occasionally, Simon experiences a slight beat of, 'Oh shit, I'm fucked; I didn't play that one right', but it's only ever a flicker and that's very real. That is something that Simon does very rarely. I agree that you have to see the comic possibility on the page, but for me, I find that if I try to avoid having a fixed idea of where the comedy is, then you can feel it come off the page. For me, it is often the case that it is only when it is off the page that you can recognise it. So that process for me, I would say, is that once it's off the page you can sniff that it's there. I find that once it is up in the room, I can feel what works, and what I need to do. I've always felt like that.

Could you say a bit more about the process of filming W1A?

I was familiar with the *W1A* process because I was in an episode of *Twenty Twelve* – I played a guy from the Church of England who was concerned about the shared worship area. There are two handheld cameras and it's quite unfussy, there are no big lights and there aren't big set-ups. But there are still continuity considerations to keep in mind when filming. I keep my physical movement quite minimal which fits Simon's character. He hits a pose, makes a comment, or asks a question and hands it over to somebody else and expects them to come up with the answer. You need to select for your character elements which work technically and which work psychologically as well. There is no point trying something that suits the character but not the medium or vice versa. It is a selection process based on the two demands – the character and the medium. Physical minimalism works for Simon and for the way that *W1A* is shot. It's something that I did for *Christopher Jefferies* as well, he was quite mesmeric in the way that he kept eye contact and I thought that I would keep that. The other thing here is not to interrupt the flow of the scene. This relates back to what I said about cumulative build. On most dramas, there is a general rule of one page per minute. So a half-hour script on the BBC would be about 26 or 27 pages, and

22 or 23 for commercial channels because of advertising. On *W1A* the scripts are 60 pages. So that tells you the pace at which it works. There's a saying in the theatre: 'If you can't be funny, be fast. If you can't be fast, fuck off.' It is true here!

Rebecca Front

London, 18 March 2016

Rebecca Front is one of Britain's most celebrated television actors, and is particularly known for her work on comedy. She has worked on a wide range of comedies since her television career began in the early 1990s, including *The Day Today* (BBC 1994), *Knowing Me, Knowing You* (BBC 1994–1995), *Big Train* (BBC 2002), *Nighty Night* (BBC 2004–2005) and *Up The Women* (BBC 2013–2015). She has also worked on a range of high-profile dramas, such as *War and Peace* (BBC 2016), *Doctor Thorne* (ITV 2016) and *Lewis* (ITV 2006–2014). Front played Nicola Murray MP in Series 3 and 4 of *The Thick of It* (BBC 2009–2012). She won a BAFTA and British Comedy Award for her work on the show. This interview focuses on her portrayal of the MP, who ran the Department for Social Affairs and Citizenship (DoSAC) and later became Leader of the Opposition.

How did you first become involved in The Thick of It*?*

I had worked with Armando Iannucci on quite a lot of his early work. We'd worked on radio together and then on television; on *Knowing Me, Knowing You* which was a multi-camera audience sitcom/sketch show. We'd also worked on *The Day Today* which was filmed more like *The Thick of It*. I was a great fan of *The Thick of It* and so was delighted when he rang me about it. I knew that Chris Langham had left the series and he rang up and talked about what they were going to do with the series. I was working with Armando as a writer at the time and so I assumed that he was asking me to join the writing team. Then he asked if I wanted to be in it, at which point I was quite shocked. According to him I just said 'Oh, that sounds fun' whereas I was thinking 'Yes! Fantastic! That sounds amazing!'

How much were you told about the character and how the series would play out?

That's one of the really interesting things about working on *The Thick of It*. When I first became involved, there were no scripts and actually there was no character. All they knew is that she had to be a government minister and the comedy would come from how Malcolm Tucker [played by Peter Capaldi] and the team react to that minister. There was going to be a cabinet reshuffle and she would be brought in. For comedic purposes she had to be an outsider and she had to be rubbish to some extent. I think they had quite a few ideas already about what they'd like to do because so much of it comes from Malcolm, from Joanna Scanlan's character [Terri Coverley] and from Chris Addison's character [Oliver Reeder]. But fundamentally they didn't know who she was; she didn't have a name or anything. We talked in an early discussion about how she could be a lawyer. I quite liked the idea of this because we know a lot of politicians go into it from law and it seems like the sort of career, given that Armando didn't want her particularly posh, that was a meritocracy where you could rise up whilst not being from a particularly privileged background. I've got a friend who is a lawyer called Nicola so I told them that Nicola was a good name, it's not too posh and it's not too working class, too old or too long. It really was that basic. So that's where we started from. Then, very early on, they got me into a room to improvise with Peter Capaldi, Chris Addison and Jo Scanlan. There were also a whole load of writers and that was my first experience. I'd done some improv but improvising in front of the writing team and then seeing how that process worked was a unique way of working.

Were you given rough scenarios?

I didn't know I was going to be improvising. We were chatting and it was lovely. Then I noticed a camera in the room and they asked if I minded doing a bit of improv, which I didn't. They said: 'Let's just say you're a back-bencher, you're the last person in the world that Malcolm would have picked to be his new minister and try that.' So we stood up, me and

Peter, and he immediately went into Malcolm which is terrifying. He's such a gentle and sweet man, so that is so scary. You have to think on your feet really fast when you're improvising. He'd immediately backed me against a wall and had started screaming at me, and I remember thinking that comedically I have to do something unexpected and there are two ways I could go. I could either crumble and cry but I feel that as I'm playing a woman I don't want to go down that route, or I could do the unexpected and start fighting back. So that's what I did, I squared up to him and started batting it back at him and he reacted brilliantly because he's a fantastic improviser. He reared back and said 'How dare you?' and thought that's it, that's what she's going to do. When she feels beaten down, she'll just come back fighting. The way the writers ran with that was brilliant: she is hopeless and that's what's so pathetic about her fighting back. I remember going home on the bus afterwards, my mind racing and just thinking that this was going to be amazing, it's going to be unlike anything I've ever done before.

What was the process from this early stage to recording it?

The next stage was my own research. I talked to a woman who had been a cabinet minister who was brilliant and gave me loads of insight; several of the things she told me ended up in the programme. For example, she gave me the detail of the character changing into trainers when she comes into the office. That came from this cabinet minister saying that one of the things she remembered most about being elevated from MP to cabinet minister was that she was constantly in and out of meetings and presentations in front of the press; so she was expected to dress smartly and wear heels and she said she was always in agony so she got into the habit of wearing trainers the minute she could. That gave us a lot of farcical moments to play with. I'm 5'4 and Peter is not far off six foot. So Peter squaring up to me when I'm in heels is one thing, squaring up to me when I'm in trainers is a whole different dynamic because he's right over my head and I'm looking up at him. I would feed this back to Armando: 'It might be funny if she wears trainers,' 'It might be funny if she's got lots of kids.'

Was the material that came from this research phase shared in meetings with the writers or was it more informal than that?

I would text and email Armando, and there would be lot of meetings and they introduced me to various other people who were advisors on the show. They would give me phone numbers that I could call if I wanted to know a bit of background detail about how I would have got to a meeting or those sort of things that would have mattered to an actor that don't necessarily appear in the show. For example, there was an early scene that didn't make it in the final cut, where Nicola is on a bus and she gets the phone call that she needs to go back to Number 10 because she has been given a place in the cabinet as part of a reshuffle. She's on the bus home, she's trying to juggle the nanny and the kids' birthdays and things and she gets this phone call and she tries to stop the bus. Understanding those kinds of things for an actor is very valuable as once she's in the cabinet, she's not going to be allowed on a bus anymore. Is she always going to be in the back of a limo? Will that be taken away from her the minute she gets sacked? All of those things are really useful to get a sense of what is at stake for her, and what she loses if she loses her job.

If we're talking about the process of how much comes from the actors and how much comes from the writers, a key point is that Armando and the team are incredibly responsive. During one of my early chats with Armando, he said: 'Of course, you've seen the show, you know we don't like to do too many office scenes where you're just sitting talking, we like to keep it dynamic, we shoot with a handheld camera. Quite often when we've got information to impart we do it in a corridor or you running into a lift for example.' I'm claustrophobic, so I said, 'Well, obviously not in a lift in my case.' So he then took that back to the writers and the plot of a whole episode is based on Nicola leaking information to the press because she's gone down the stairs with them rather than going with her colleagues in a lift. They are really clever about that sort of thing.

So you have this two-way process, was the next stage then rehearsals?

Yes, rehearsals again were very different from my other work. You didn't get the script in advance. At the read-through they would hand out scripts to everybody. These scripts are watermarked for security because by that time the show was quite a hit show and people were mindful of the fact that they didn't want stories leaking out. Not least because the government had a habit of copying the things we did throughout the show – it was quite a big risk, we didn't want to bring the country down! We read through cold, literally just turning the pages and reading which is so exciting because as you're turning the pages everyone is surprised at the same time. Then, having read it through once, we'd put the scripts down and all the writers would position themselves around the room and the actors improvised a loose version of what they had just read. Armando would say that he didn't need you to remember any of lines we've just read, for now those are totally unimportant, you'd only need the scenario – that in this scene Malcolm is about to be fired and you've just overheard the conversation. We'd improvise that for maybe an hour and then we'd move onto another scene and the writers would sit there and make notes. Certain things would come out of that, sometimes funny lines but more often it would be the way your character reacts and the dynamic between you and the status changes between characters. Then they go away and write the next draft of the script and it becomes more like a normal script process. You get sent the script that you're going to rehearse with which you then stick to (although it changes the whole time because the writers are in the room). Then you get sent the final script which you film.

It is interesting that you have an input at so many points in the process.

In a normal process, I'd be analysing the script by asking, 'How would I get from that point to that point?' and 'How do I play that?' There's a little bit of room in the way you choose to deliver lines, but with *The Thick of It* you have the chance of influencing the direction of the whole piece. You learn to not focus on making the writers laugh but just being true to your character and do what you think they would genuinely do. The writers are the ones who need to worry about whether it's funny. The improvisations at the script development stage also mean that you have less work to do to make the thought processes link together because you've already done that bit of work by the time you get to it. You'd receive the final draft very close to the wire, often the day before, but you've contributed to those thought processes and you know what they are going to be.

I remember a couple of improvised responses that stayed in the final cut. There's an episode where we're all holed up in a hotel for the party conference and I'm about to give a speech and suddenly all the content has to change. I was just genuinely getting really frustrated and I felt that, as Nicola, I couldn't do it. Everything was being taken out of my control and there was an armchair in the room and I remember picking up a cushion to punch it and then I think I dropped it and I just carried on jumping up and down on it. Similarly there was an improvised line of Peter's that I remember stayed in the final thing, which didn't actually come up until the shooting day. In the same episode, he comes into the hotel room and I can't bear to be near him so I just run off and lock myself in the bathroom. Peter suddenly ran over to the door, hammered on it and shouted 'Wilma!' like in *The Flintstones*. I remember being in the bathroom falling about thinking that was genius and I knew that was going to stay in. Generally, the script is 99 per cent written by the writers, but that's our input.

Would there be rehearsals before you started filming it?

Yes, that was another difference with *The Thick of It*. You'd have a few days of rehearsal which you very often don't get on something like *Lewis* [in which Rebecca played Lewis's boss, Chief Superintendent Jean Innocent]. It would be a fairly brief period with a few days here and there. We'd actually get to rehearse the scenes as they were written but the writers would still be finessing it. Nothing is set in stone, but you're not really improvising at that point.

So then you get on set and the way Armando likes to work is that you then film what's written as close to verbatim as you can get it, very much as you would with any normal filming. Usually you do two or three versions as written and then if there's time and you feel that there's something else you can bring out of it then you do a completely improvised version. At that point you can go completely off piste. You'd always be mindful of that fact that you know where they're going with the rest of the plot, but I was able to run into the bathroom in the scene I talked about earlier, for example.

The other thing which is very different is that with normal single and multi-camera filming, when you've blocked it, you have to stick with that blocking because all of the lighting and focusing is dependent on you hitting your mark. There's absolutely none of that in *The Thick of It*. I remember on my first day, James Smith [who plays Glenn Cullen] told me that I was going to have so much fun on this that I'd never want to film anything any other way. The first scene we did was me coming into the office and being briefed. Armando came in and asked if I could go in and take my trainers off in the outer office so that we could establish that as well. So I said, 'OK, which line do you want me to leave the room on?' and he said, 'Whatever you want.' That was so unusual. He said that the cameras would just follow me. To this day I have no idea how they edit it. The camera guys are running backwards the whole time and you're encouraged just to get up and go without any warning at all and they'll follow. Usually, filming for television is so static and quiet and you're focused on continuity and props and 'when did I put my hand on my face – I must make sure I do that the second time round'. 'When did I have my arms folded?' There was none of that in *The Thick of It*. I could just completely break all of those conventions.

Did you have discussions with Armando about things like reaction shots? There are so many moments where the cameras capture really small things which add to the comedy.

That's the benefit of working with two cameras. The two handheld cameras are on all the time on different people. By doing it again and again means they've got everything. I think that's why Armando can afford to be a bit more gung-ho about continuity. In single camera they will shoot you right the way through the scene whether you're doing anything interesting or not. So they have always got it but I think the difference here is that because they've got two cameras going, they are going to get different reactions each time. So if Peter is shouting at us and he is really loud on one take then they are going to get a different reaction than they would have got if he'd just been whispering right in my face.

Does that change the kind of performance you are giving? Do you have a sense of this being a mockumentary or something else?

I never thought of it as a mockumentary. There was never any reference to the cameras whereas with *The Office* you have someone looking into the camera and they know it's going to be broadcast as a documentary about David Brent. This isn't, this is just something else. As with a real film, you would forget the camera was there. So for me, I was that cabinet minister being bullied by someone; I wasn't remotely conscious of whether the camera was catching that. How much you heighten moments for a laugh is an interesting point with comedy, and I suppose instinctively you do with everything. There's always a little bit of your brain that's thinking, 'It would be funnier if I did this actually' while at the same time trying to be completely truthful to that character in that situation which is all that you can do as an actor. Try and be that person in that situation but with maybe ten per cent of your brain thinking, 'On the other hand it will really make Armando laugh if I do this.' So there's always that little bit of you thinking, 'I know what will be quite funny' and occasionally you will scupper yourself doing these things because you make yourself laugh.

I imagine that happens quite a lot. It sounds more unpredictable in comparison to other projects.

Absolutely, particularly when you're working with people who are so quick. I remember the episode at *The Guardian* offices in which I'm trying to think of things to announce and Chris Addison mentions that we can always pitch the idea of encouraging people to buy wooden toys for their children. I say something along the lines of: 'We're not going to pitch the wooden toys. Nothing would entice me to mention the wooden toys, it's a rubbish idea,' which is a classic sitcom set up. Of course Armando cuts to me announcing wooden toys. This was one of the hardest things for me to shoot, I barely got through it. If you watch it you can see that I was really struggling with it, I was constantly corpsing. In the same scene, Jo and Chris had to remind me to smile, and at one point Jo draws a little smiley face and pushes it across the table and she's got it the wrong way round and I think she's telling me to look serious. Chris then leans forward and turns it round and that got me every time. That was something that had just come up at the last minute but I wasn't quite prepared for it, so a lot of things do get added, and yes, it is unpredictable and I kept corpsing. It's incredibly exciting, it's the sort of feeling that you get on stage and you don't usually get it with normal filming. What you hope for in normal filming are moments when the scene transcends the restrictions of the blocking and the lighting. The scene just lifts and then you get that amazing feeling of, 'Oh that went really well and I felt like I have forgotten that those cameras were there' and that's brilliant. The great thing with *The Thick of It* and that guerrilla filming style is that you're feeling like that almost all the time.

I suppose that adrenaline suits the story you're telling, doesn't it?

Yes, it plays beautifully to it. We had a screening in Westminster and we had all these cabinet ministers and MPs watching it which was fascinating because they were all telling us their stories afterwards. A woman who had been a junior minister told me about a speech she had to deliver about a new initiative. She was sitting on the stage with a room full of journalists; somebody else from her party was up there and introducing her saying: 'We are delighted to have so and so here tonight, she's about to announce this new initiative' and as she sat there, one of her aides came up and whispered to her, 'I'm afraid you've been fired.' The aide took the speech off her and somebody else gave it and that was it, she had just lost her job. So this sort of guerrilla filming style is the style you need. They're on the precipice the whole time, an inch away from falling off the cliff.

So you said you got the script not long before you started filming, did you get an overview of the series as well?

Yes, I think with that series we did. We knew certain events but not how it would play out. We knew in the series that there was going to be a running storyline of a guy who was going to be camping out because he had lost his house. He was a male nurse; the storyline was going to reflect badly on both parties. I think I knew that I was going to be sacked at the end and that Malcolm was going to be sacked. We had these certain pointers but we didn't know all of the details until we were in this process of first draft scripts and rehearsals. But by the time you turn up on set you know roughly what is going to happen in the next few episodes.

Is that useful to know that?

To some extent. In Method Acting terms it probably would be quite nice to not know anything, but no I think it is useful. As long as you and Armando are confident that you can put all that away and not play it. That's the important thing: it's remembering not to play 'you're doomed', you've got to keep playing it as if you're hopeful and that you're not aware of that information. I think it is quite helpful to know that.

Were there any moments where information was kept from you, like the real life MP who was suddenly told she was sacked?

Yes. Armando likes doing that occasionally. Every now and then he'll scuttle in and whisper to somebody, which again I really like. In my first episode when I had just arrived, apparently there was a scene where Chris Addison is outside talking to James [Smith] and Jo [Scanlan] and he does an impression of Nicola. In a later scene in which I'm talking to Chris, Armando came in and whispered to me, 'He does an impression of you. Let's say you've heard that he does this impression.' So we do the next take and mid-way through it I just stopped as if I'd forgotten my next line and said, 'I hear you do an impression of me' and he just froze. I had to keep pushing until I got him to do it. Things like that are great.

There are other things that you know or decide upon but choose to withhold as an actor. For example, I was really struggling with why Nicola puts up with the treatment that she receives. Of course, she's holding onto that bit of power, I get that. But why does she so often put herself into situations where she knows she's going to be confronted by Malcolm? The only thing that I can think of is that she likes it. He's rather nice looking and alright he's shouting at her and being unpleasant, but at least he's paying her some attention. So he walks into that big open-plan office and he's coming to see her and she might like that in a weird way. That, to me, started to make sense of what was there in the scripts. So when, in the last series, Malcolm is sacked, it meant that it gave me something quite interesting to play because what they had originally planned was that Nicola, like everybody else, was originally relieved that Malcolm has gone. She comes back into the office and they are all saying 'ding-dong the witch is dead', but actually the way I played it was that she's really disturbed by it. For me, the reason that she is disturbed is that she feels that she has lost this one connection that she had. She was actually a little bit in love with him. My instinct in the next rehearsal was to say, 'You know what I think, I think she's in love with Malcolm' and then I thought that actually in real life there's no way that Malcolm would know that and he's too involved with himself and what he's doing to be aware of it. It's actually slightly unhelpful for Peter to know that. Actually, I'm not sure I told Armando. Sometimes you make those decisions that are just for you and it will impact on what you're doing. In that case no one had asked me why I was looking like that or why I got a bit shaky when he got in the room; it seemed to be working. So they're useful things to play but not useful things to share.

The series ends with a Leveson-style inquiry which feels very different from the rest of the series.

That was really extraordinary because Armando really cranked it up to the next level. We all knew that there was going to be this Leveson-style tribunal, but the last two scripts were withheld from all of us and we were only given the information that we could conceivably have seen if that tribunal was being televised. So I could see the transcript of what Jo had said because that had happened the day before in the story order, but I wasn't allowed to know what Peter was going to say. When we went in, we didn't know who was on the bench. Armando wanted to make it a terrifying ordeal so that our experience as actors was similar to our characters'. We knew our scripts, and we did two normal versions and then a loosened-up version, but we hadn't seen the room until we walked into it, intentionally again because he wanted us to look out of our comfort zones. As you know from acting there's a difference between walking into a room that you're familiar with and walking into a room that you don't know. It just gave us that feeling walking in and wondering, 'Where should I put my coat?' I remember getting there was very cloak and dagger. They took me up to my dressing room and I sat there for a bit and got into costume and I remember Peter was in the next dressing room and we had a little chat. Someone told us, 'I'm sorry, but you're not allowed to talk. Well, you are but you're not allowed to know what Peter's been saying.' I got taken down to the room and somebody briefed me outside saying that in a minute we'll open the curtain and you'll go in and from that moment on you're on camera. We're not going to show you the room until then. It was brilliant, again it was really thrilling, and quite hilarious. I remember I was really shaking doing it which is quite hard to recreate. When you're about to do an interview or something that really matters to you, it's quite hard to recreate that feeling of absolutely being on edge and your palms sweating and I remember actually genuinely feeling that.

Roger Allam

London, 28 April 2016

Roger Allam has worked extensively in television drama and comedy, including portrayals of Charlie Baxter in *The Creatives* (BBC 1998–2000), Detective Superintendent Mackintosh in *Ashes to Ashes* (BBC 2009), John Mallory QC in *The Jury* (ITV 2011), and as General Campion in Tom Stoppard's screenplay of *Parades End* for the BBC (2012). At the time of this interview, he was recording Season 2 of *The Missing* (BBC 2016), in which he plays Adrian Stone. Since 2012, Allam has played Detective Inspector Fred Thursday in four series of ITV's hit drama, *Endeavour*, a prequel to the *Inspector Morse* series. This interview focuses on Allam's portrayal of Peter Mannion MP in *The Thick of It*, who he played in Series 3 and 4 of Iannucci's comedy. Mannion replaced Rebecca Front's character, Nicola Murray, as the Social Affairs and Citizenship Secretary running DoSAC as part of a Coalition government.

You've worked extensively on television, as well as in theatre and film. Could you talk about your work on The Thick of It *in the context of your wider experiences of television acting?*

The Thick of It was different from anything else that I've ever done on television. This is true of both the process and the way it was filmed. We all used to meet and read through a draft of an episode script. This would be early in the process. The draft was always very funny; they were very talented writers. Following the read-through, Armando would ask us to improvise – to expand something already in the script, or to improvise something new. You had to dive into that really and be willing to make an idiot out of yourself. Then the writers would go away and on the strength of that and their own ideas, would write a new draft. Then we would meet to read the final draft later in the process. Again, this would be in front of the writers. It was a way of exploring various possibilities for them. When you received the script ahead of filming, you'd be able to see the results of some of those improvisations in it.

But really, it was the actual filming that was different. Everybody always says, 'Oh you improvised it didn't you?' And of course, no we didn't. It was always a very good script. But in the filming of it there were always two cameras on the move, rather than a single-camera set-up where you do a master-shot, mid-shot, and then close-ups from various points of view; so it is a looser, freer way of filming from an acting point of view. Consequently you didn't feel so trapped by continuity, by someone saying, 'You scratched your cheek when you said that in the mid-shot.' There was less attention paid to that side of things in the interests of pursuing a kind of cinéma vérité, documentary feel. Sometimes, after a few takes, Armando might ask you to extend something, take a situation a bit further, and we would play with particular moments perhaps taking them a lot further.

I guess what Armando did was rather in the style of the Hollywood film director Robert Altman. I remember Armando telling me that every episode they did, whether it be an hour-long special or a half-hour episode, when they did the first assembly of it, it would always be about twice as long as they needed it. He said that in the process of editing and cutting it down they would always cut five minutes too much so that they could put back their favourite bits. So that was the approach. From an actor's point of view, my attitude to it was much more freewheeling as I was providing material, a lot of which I knew wouldn't make it into the final film. Whenever you are filming you are providing the director with options for the edit and often the director will come up and ask you to try something in a particular way to give him or her another option. You are providing the director with a lot of cloth from which s/he can make something tight and well-fitting. But here it wasn't just different options, it was new material, and sometimes that material made it into the final programme, and sometimes not.

Did you have conversations about your character which allowed you to improvise in this way?

When I first met Armando and auditioned for *The Thick of It*, he wanted to see whether I could make material up in the way that politicians do. He'd give me a scenario – like a big directive that has just been agreed, something like 'Green Conservatism'. I just had to make things up about it. I would be flailing, trying to justify the directive. Moments like that are very useful for the character. Peter Mannion was constantly flailing for the right response and only just keeping afloat; trying to just survive. Politicians have this utter need to talk. They have all these fillers to stop the other person talking. The need to make announcements. Often Peter Mannion's lines would start with 'What I am saying to you is … '. He says this before he has thought what he will say. These useless phrases which are just a noise designed to occupy the space whilst they think. It's like an everyday version of filibustering.

Armando told me that the whole project came about because he wondered what politicians actually do, day by day, behind closed doors. What do you do if you are a minister or secretary of state? What is your day like? There is this desperate need to announce initiatives and get headlines and publicity so that you can seem to be doing something. Mostly, you look at these things and the reality is a bit shit. The offices are a bit shit. So what do these people do and how do they function? It's all set around those questions really. So you base your character on responding to questions like that. Once the writers are on board, they start to define more detail about your character, but I viewed him in this context: he's someone who is always at a loss within his particular world.

Could you tell me about how you worked on the particular language of The Thick of It?

I love looking again at my favourite classic Hollywood movies for inspiration, looking at actors like Humphrey Bogart and Cary Grant. For example, there is a scene in *His Girl Friday* (dir. Howard Hawks 1940) in which Cary Grant is on the phone to someone while having an argument in the room with Rosalind Russell, who is trying to type an article at the same time as shutting Ralph Bellamy up who is keeps trying to interject; a four-way row. They all speak at about double speed; it's technically absolutely brilliant, very funny and a very long scene. There is only one cut in the middle of it. They must have rehearsed it a great deal, like a play. It was shot just in mid-shot which meant that they could overlap their dialogue and keep their own comic rhythm; something that the wide-shot, mid-shot, close-up process makes more difficult as the sound department will want you to keep the close-up takes clean of overlapping. I noticed a similar use of mid-shot in some re-runs of *Rising Damp* (ITV 1974–8). I was working with Frances de la Tour at the time and asked her about it. She said that it was down to Leonard Rossiter, who directed some of the episodes, but even when he didn't, always insisted that the camera didn't come in too close, precisely so that the actors were in charge of the comedy. In *The Thick of It* the two cameras on the move gave us the liberty to overlap like that. So the storytelling and comedy, and your work as an actor, is really informed by the way that the piece is shot.

Does the question of continuity mean that you have to get the first shot right and that you are limited by these decisions?

No, that's not necessarily true. The first master-shot is like a plan and you can ask about which moments they are on you and which you can still develop or change. Sometimes you can use the question of continuity to help you. You might find particular reasons for each of the moves you have established in the wide-shot so that there is something emotional behind the simple gesture of say picking up a coffee cup. It can become like a piece of choreography that helps give shape to the emotional story of the scene as the scene is gradually assembled as the shots move in closer.

In the context of this precision, Armando's work seems particularly unusual. Could you say a bit more about the process of filming it? Did you discuss reaction shots and making sure that particular moments are captured?

Armando would certainly ask for reaction shots to make sure of catching particular moments. There weren't two cameras on the move the whole time, sometimes he would come in close with one camera, so he could have the best of both worlds.

Could you say a bit more about the phrase 'cinéma vérité'? Was this a question of style?

Cinéma vérité was a useful shorthand term for the style. Handheld cameras were used most of the time so that the viewer is more aware of the camera's presence. The camera isn't pretending not to be there. This gives a feel of the messiness of real life. Though of course as an actor, technically, you are always aware of where the camera is whatever the style. Also, when you are in a comedy, you are aware that you are in a comedy. Going back to the language, the writers would write lines that were very funny. Peter Capaldi had some particularly brilliant lines. In fact they had a special swearing writer. They would give him the script and he would give it the odd tweak and polish. You know full well as an actor that if you have a line like 'I'm bored of this, I'm going for a Twix', or 'I'll stuff that meter so far up your arse you'll know the price of your next shit', you know that they are funny lines, but you have to find a way of saying them that honours that fact but is also believable and 'real' for your character and the situation. In *The Thick of It* saying lines like that was part of the world we were in, and John Gielgud's famous line 'Style is just knowing what play you're in' is relevant here. My character was often at a complete loss for the right thing to say and was also often trying to adhere to policy directives from above that he didn't believe in. So he would often fail in his attempts to find the right language and only in his frustration would he become truly articulate. This led to lots of rich comic situations like losing it over wearing his shirt outside his trousers, or when they were on that retreat to team build and ended up on a children's slide trying to get a mobile phone signal.

How does this compare to your work on dramas such as Endeavour?

The Thick of It was like a little island of freedom within BBC comedy in that there didn't seem to be any interference from BBC executives that

I was aware of. This meant that the conversations and interactions you had as an actor were all with the creative people involved directly in making it. That's rare, and is a very different experience from working on *Endeavour* and *The Missing* Season 2 (BBC 2016). *Endeavour* is for ITV and is broadcast on a Sunday at 8pm, so it is pre the 9pm watershed. So no imaginative swearing for a start. There are two sets of executives; the ones who work for Mammoth Screen who make it, and the ones who work for ITV Drama who commission and broadcast it. There is only one writer, Russell Lewis (as opposed to a group on *The Thick of It*), and there is a different director for each film. There are 23 days filming per episode of just under 90 minutes. It is shot using classical film grammar, though occasionally using handheld. The way a scene is built up is as described above, with master-shots, mid-shots and close-ups from various points of view. We will finish filming on a Tuesday, have a read-through of the next one on Wednesday and start filming it the following Monday. There is probably only one day with the director to talk through the script, investigate it and iron out any inconsistencies and difficulties. After the read-through the ITV execs will have notes for the writer, and after that there will be discussions between the Mammoth execs, the writer, director, and myself and Shaun Evans [who plays DC Endeavour Morse] about the script. Then Russell will start rewriting. All this means that the script will keep changing once you start shooting it, expanding and contracting right up to the last week of filming. All TV is constrained by the discipline of the slots. *Endeavour* has to be 88½ minutes long in a two-hour slot. *The Thick of It* will always have to be a 30-minute episode or an hour-long special. *The Missing* was more complicated in that there were about five different TV companies involved including the BBC and an American company. There were eight hour-long episodes, each having only 12½ days to film it, so it was a very tight schedule filming mainly in Belgium. It was a very complex story set over three different time frames and not told sequentially. This meant that each episode would be swapping back and forth between the different times. I have very little contact with the executives and producers, so when the script kept changing I just had to accept it.

This must make charting your character's path through the narrative very complicated.

I tried putting all my character's scenes into their story day order, so I would know what I was doing at what particular time. It was a useful exercise for me but not ultimately playable as sometimes something I had done on Story Day 1 might not be revealed until Episode 7. So in the end I tried thinking of each of my scenes as a kind of separate snapshot.

All these things; producers, execs, constant script changes, no rehearsal, can be very frustrating in TV work and make you feel powerless and lacking any control. You have to try and deal with them and turn them to your advantage as best you can. When you are part of a team that is working well, like myself, Shaun Evans [DC Endeavour Morse] and Anton Lesser [Chief Superintendent Reginald Bright] do in *Endeavour*, you can find the space to sort out problems, work out what is going on in a scene, what is not being said (which is sometimes more important than what is), or what is behind what you are saying, what a simple exchange might be freighted with. This can be very rewarding and satisfying.

Acting in Television Comedy

The actor's relationship with the script

It is clear from these actors' experiences that the script functioned in very different ways for them, and that their relationship with it depended on the working methods of the writer-director. This is particularly pronounced in the examples of *W1A* and *The Thick of It* because both are based on linguistic dexterity and parody the way in which people communicate in government and the BBC. Much of the humour is associated with 'media-speak', political chicanery, and what Roger Allam describes as an 'everyday version of filibustering'[4]. Both Allam and Front talk about the particular lexicon of politicians, and their techniques for simultaneously avoiding a clear answer whilst appearing to make decisive statements. In addition to this focus, Jason Watkins notes that the script for *W1A* was almost three times the length that he would expect for a half-hour BBC slot, meaning that the sheer pace of the comedy was highly unusual.

One would be forgiven for thinking that both projects included improvised passages (indeed, Nina Sosanya admits that she assumed *Twenty Twelve* was improvised). Both are rich in verbal tics, overlaps and idiosyncrasies. The frequent circumlocutions, hesitations and half-completed phrases align both programmes with documentary traditions in that the writers attempted to capture the way that real people speak, albeit in a complex and stylised way; as Sosanya notes: '[I]t's somewhere between real and hugely artificial.' The result is that speech patterns are notably messier than is often the case in traditional sitcom. However, as is clear from the interviews above, though *The Thick of It* and *W1A* have a similar vocal precision and linguistic style, the process of arriving at this end result could not have been more different.

W1A: Linguistic precision and cumulative build

Nina Sosanya and Jason Watkins both identify the detail of John Morton's script. As Sosanya observes, 'It's absolutely word for word and stutter for stutter' whilst Watkins states that 'it is very, very strongly scripted and John is very particular about it'. Foremost in their recollections was the need to observe the rhythms of the writing in their performance. Sosanya stresses: 'That's where a lot of the comedy lies, in the rhythms of what he's written. So you have to get that right.' Ostensibly, this could be considered true of any script, but the actors here went over and above the way in which actors have viewed their work on script elsewhere in this book. Rather, as Sosanya states: 'There's one way to do his writing. That was the consensus that we all came to as a cast,' and that deviation from this resulted in the scene losing some of its potency. This may, in part, be a result of the writer also directing the piece, but from the actors' testimony, it appeared to be more a feature of this particular style of writing than a condition of their work with Morton as writer-director.

Image 6   Nina Sosanya as Lucy Freeman in *W1A*

One of the key strategies that Sosanya and Watkins employed was to view the script not as a series of comedic opportunities to inflect and embellish particular lines, but rather to view their work as one element in a comic structure built collaboratively by the ensemble. The comedy of the piece is thus frequently a product of several different constituent parts which had to work in harmony to provide the set-up for the later pay-off. This was a specific feature of Morton's writing which Sosanya distances from her work on traditional sitcom: 'On a sitcom I might ask, "How am I going to make this line funny?" whereas with *W1A*, if I was thinking about how to make a line funny, then I'd be lost.' This represents a nuanced understanding of comic structure. It is not unusual in sitcom for a comic build to be reliant upon an ensemble, but what distinguishes *W1A* is the size, complexity and pace of the group scenes. Frequently, such as in the regular 'Way Ahead Task Force' meetings (for example, see Series 1 Episode 1 and Series 2 Episode 4), the comedy relied on about eight actors working at great speed to negotiate the set-up and pay-off, as Jason Watkins identifies:

> In the group meeting scenes we whizz around the table with those lines fizzing out like they're improvised but they are very precisely scripted … the cumulative pace of delivery gives you the humour you need. You don't

need to do too much inflection in your delivery of a particular line, it works fast and flat. It is about this pace between people, not your own individual spin.

This appears to contradict this chapter's opening comment about the visibility of acting skill in comedy. It is true that individual acting work is downplayed and subsumed in favour of the ensemble here. However, such is the speed and precision of the dialogue, the effect is an almost dizzyingly impressive performance by the ensemble, meaning that though it takes a different form, the actors' skill is still immediately identifiable and visible.

It is therefore of little surprise that one of the focuses of Sosanya's and Watkins' interview was on how they developed this precision. Jason Watkins was particularly detailed in this regard. He states: '[M]y approach was to try and have a broad brush of bright energy and attack whilst observing the writing absolutely.' Much of Watkins' interview is concerned with gaining absolute specificity with regard to the angle of this attack. He analyses his character's lines in terms of actions – transitive verbs with a clear sense of what he is doing to the other person: '[H]e'd agree and agree, he'd bolster and affirm it. To use an actioning terminology, these are his actions but he does not actually deliver anything.' This 'actioning terminology' is a post-Stanislavskian reformulation of 'objectives', one of Stanislavski's approaches to script analysis which allows the actor to identify his or her aim moment by moment in a scene. The development of 'objectives' into 'actions' was first proposed by Stanislavski's Moscow Art Theatre actor and later renowned acting tutor, Richard Boleslavsky, who suggested that 'you could take a pencil and write "music of action" under every word or speech … you would have to memorize your actions. You would have to know distinctly the difference between "I complained" and "I scorned"' (2003, 60). Though this particular lineage has been overlooked in research, this process has become a common approach of actors via the work of theatre director Max Stafford-Clark (see Stafford-Clark and Roberts 2007). The technique was well-chosen here, as it allowed Watkins to gain precision without interrupting the flow of the scene. However, what is distinctive is that Watkins reformulates this technique in the service of his work on comedy. Rather than simply using a verb to identify what he is doing to the person he addresses, he uses this process to identify the duplicity of the character. He juxtaposes the action of 'uplifts' and 'empowers' with the fact that 'I would uplift Hugh's character but really I would be handing him his own dagger to kill himself'. Watkins' comments relate back to the obsession with language in *W1A* and the media-speak of the characters who rarely say what they mean. Sosanya also notes this duplicity: 'There are constantly two conversations happening in *W1A*. Therefore, it's actually about learning exactly what the words are cold and then when it comes to it, knowing that the character is thinking about something entirely different.' For Watkins and Sosanya, the script was thus a detailed and precise document which they had no part in the creation of, and which arrived to them in its final state. Their challenge was to execute this precisely, to observe its structure and specific syntactical properties, and to view the comedy within it as a product of the rhythms and cumulative build across the work of several actors.

The Thick of It: Improvisation and agency

The script for *The Thick of It* was a rather different entity for the actors. As is clear from the interviews, the actors had a significant input into the content of the script during its creation (via the initial character improvisations at the very beginning of the process that Rebecca Front recalls so vividly), its development (through the extensive post read-through improvisations on particular scripted scenarios) and its performance (by means of the 'loosened'-up version of the script which the actors frequently improvised). It is not to underestimate the skill of Iannucci and his writing team to acknowledge that the actors had a very active role in the creation of their characters and in their paths through particular scenes. Despite being leading figures on television, Rebecca Front and Roger Allam were both keen to point out that this was a highly unusual and privileged position to be in. Allam states that '*The Thick of It* was different from anything else that I've ever done on television' whilst Front notes that it was 'unlike anything I've ever done before'. But what difference did this make, and how did improvisation function to change their processes on *The Thick of It*?

Firstly, the improvisations at the beginning of the process functioned in a similar way to the hot-seating session that Rachel Bright took part in ahead of her introduction as a regular character on *EastEnders* and also the early conversations the actors in soap operas had with the executive producers. These processes and the improvisations on *The Thick of It* informed the script that the actors received. As Allam remarks: 'It was a way of exploring various possibilities for them [the writers]. When you received the script ahead of filming, you'd be able to see the results of some of those improvisations in it.' Similarly, Front was impressed by the way in which the writers incorporated some of her character choices from her early improvisations:

> [Malcolm Tucker] immediately backed me against a wall and had started screaming at me, and I remember thinking that comedically I have to do something unexpected and there are two ways I could go. I could either crumble and cry but I feel that as I'm playing a woman I don't want to go down that route, or I could do the unexpected and start fighting back … The way the writers ran with that was brilliant: she is hopeless and that's what's so pathetic about her fighting back.

As the actors in soap found, seeing the imprint of this early work on the development of the character was clearly a satisfying element of the process. As Front notes, '[W]ith *The Thick of It* you have the chance of influencing the direction of the whole piece.' However, the extensive use of improvisation went much further than merely allowing the actors to make early suggestions to the writers. For example, the improvisations at the script development stage, immediately following the episode read-through, constituted an unusual form of rehearsal for the actors, as Rebecca Front acknowledges:

> We'd improvise that for maybe an hour and then we'd move onto another scene and the writers would sit there and make notes. Certain things would come out of that, sometimes funny lines but more often it would be the way your character reacts and the dynamic between you and the status changes between characters.

In these improvisations, it is clear that the generation of material was not the sole aim of Front's work, but rather she also focused on the turning points of her character within the scene; the decisions she took and the shifts in dynamics and status which resulted from these decisions. This process, Front found, was useful in navigating the psychology of the character through the episode:

> The improvisations at the script development stage also mean that you have less work to do to make the thought processes link together because you've already done that bit of work by the time you get to [record] it. You'd receive the final draft very close to the wire, often the day before, but you've contributed to those thought processes and you know what they are going to be.

In the quick turnaround of television production, to have had a hand in crafting these turning points was clearly very useful for Front. Spending an hour improvising a scene meant that she had significant time to explore and map them. Through this process, the complex work of determining the logic behind these 'thought processes' had already been done to an extent. In television acting (as opposed to theatre) this work is frequently a private process of script analysis by the actor. As we have explored earlier in this book and elsewhere (Cantrell and Hogg 2016), without shared rehearsal time, television acting tends to necessitate the actor working privately and with only the script as a resource to determine character motivation and thought process. Here, by contrast, the improvisations allowed this to be explored in action as the character. It was thus an element of *The Thick of It* which called upon the actors' creative response in the context of performance rather than on their skills of script analysis in private study. In this light, the improvisations can be seen as a valuable and unusual form of rehearsal for the actors.

The final stage of improvisation, in the recording itself, again positions the actor as a creator of material, and as such, one of the authors of the script.[5] Allam recalls: 'Whenever you are filming you are providing the director with options for the edit … But here it wasn't just different options, it was new material, and sometimes that material made it into the final programme.' Within the hierarchy of the apparatus of production, this affords the actors significant status, which Allam credits to Iannucci's 'little island of freedom within BBC comedy' and which he contrasts with his other work. This process gave the actors creative space in television acting, a form which has historically been associated with the actors having far less agency than is the case in their other work (be that in theatre or on film). For Rebecca Front, this creative space manifested itself in two interesting ways, both based on her access to character information in the script.

The improvisations in the 'loosened-up version' allowed Front significant space to experiment and provide alternatives to the scripted responses. Front explores this in detail in her interview and the positive impact this had on her experience is clear. What is particularly interesting for analysis here, though, is the fact that the improvisations took a variety of forms and did not all conform to the simple notion of the actors improvising around a given scenario that they had previously performed 'verbatim' from the script. Front explains:

> In my first episode when I had just arrived, apparently there was a scene where Chris Addison is outside talking to James [Smith] and Jo [Scanlan] and he does an impression of Nicola. In a later scene in which I'm talking to Chris, Armando came in and whispered to me, 'He does an impression of you. Let's say you've heard that he does this impression.' So we do the next take and mid-way through it I just stopped as if I'd forgotten my next line and said, 'I hear you do an impression of me' and he just froze. I had to keep pushing until I got him to do it. Things like that are great.

In her interview, Front also provides examples in which she was on the receiving end of Iannucci's deliberate manipulation of information in the takes. It is testament to the ensemble atmosphere and the sense of creative engagement by the actors and director that these unusual processes could be so profitably embraced. This process not only relies on the actor's ability to improvise, but it also positions them as the experts on their character – and as such able to respond instinctively in role rather than rely on the script to navigate their character's attitude and response to events (as did her improvisations earlier in the script development process). Thus, the actor's work was not limited to what was written, but rather the script was a component of their process, and a key reference point for their improvisations away from it.

Image 7   Rebecca Front and Roger Allam as Nicola Murray MP and Peter Mannion MP in *The Thick of It*

This is, however, only half of the story, and it should not be assumed that the power relationship on *The Thick of It* is characterised only by the director choosing to withhold information from the actor. Front had evidently found it hard to explain Nicola Murray's attitude towards Malcolm Tucker in the script. Rather than discuss this with the director or the other actors involved in the scenes, she decided on a rationale in her own mind, but kept this private. The revelation that Front decided that Nicola Murray was 'actually a little bit in love with him' will no doubt come as something of a revelation to fans of the show, but the key factor from the actor's point of view is that this was not something that Front considered useful to share. Rather, it informed her portrayal and made sense of elements of the script that had appeared contradictory or unjustified. Front states: 'Sometimes you make those decisions that are just for you and it will impact on what you're doing ... they're useful things to play but not useful things to share.' This example again demonstrates that actors' working processes on television are much more complex and nuanced than the industrial contexts in which they work would suggest. In both these comedies, some of the actors' work is shared in preparation and in recording, but there are also many hidden elements which the actors work on in their own private time, and which can only be accessed through direct interviews with them.

The approach to the script was thus very different on these two projects. The script for *W1A* was arranged like a piece of music, and the actors (and Watkins in particular) found that a lot of their work was based on ensuring that none of their character choices interrupted the flow of the scenes. The actors' approaches on Morton's script were more about capturing the rhythms (both within their characters' lines but more often across conversations and repartee between many characters) than it was about their ability to mould and adapt stresses and emphases for comic effect. By contrast, the actor's own imprint on the script of *The Thick of It* was evident at all stages. The work on Iannucci's script relied less on observing the original rhythms (though this was still a preoccupation) and more about their skills as improvisers. Thus, rather than focusing on the complex cumulative build in *W1A* and paying attention to the minutiae of the script, in *The Thick of It* the actors were encouraged to become creators of new material too.

All of the actors interviewed, but Watkins and Front in particular, found this process to be an exhilarating and all-consuming experience during filming (as Watkins says, he was 'at the limit of his abilities'). Here, we will refer to this quality as 'creative danger'. It is based on adrenaline, absolute creative involvement and the sense of a lack of control in the overall shape of the scene. In this context, the 'danger' is the distinct possibility of missing a cue, 'corpsing', or the take being abandoned because of an actor's mistake. Anyone who has experience of improvisation or performing live comedy will be familiar with this feeling. However, there were different reasons for this 'creative danger' on *W1A* and *The Thick of It*. For Front, it was the feeling of danger and adrenaline which comes from a sense of creative freedom. This meant that she was acutely creatively and imaginatively involved in the process:

> It's incredibly exciting, it's the sort of feeling that you get on stage and you don't usually get it with normal filming. What you hope for in normal filming are moments when the scene transcends the restrictions of the blocking and the lighting. The scene just lifts and then you get that amazing feeling … The great thing with *The Thick of It* and that guerrilla filming style is that you're feeling like that almost all the time.

For Watkins, it was a similar release of adrenaline which comes from the quick-paced, minutely observed grammatical structure and ensemble build that characterised his experience of many scenes on *W1A*. For all of these actors, a component of the 'comic intent' in the scene was their limited grasp on how it played out. As creators and interpreters of the comedy through improvisation, and in the pace of exchanges between multiple characters, the 'creative danger' was present because the comedy always threatened to become out of the control of individual actors, and thus placed a strong emphasis on the collective labour of the ensemble.

'Docucom' and the relationship between actor and camera

Front's comment about the 'guerrilla' filming style is a useful reference point here as the actors' processes, including the ways in which they worked on the script above, are inextricably linked to the way in which *W1A* and *The Thick of It* were shot. As Allam notes, 'the storytelling and comedy, and your work as an actor, is really informed by the way that the piece is shot', whilst Watkins comments:

> You need to select for your character elements which work technically and which work psychologically as well. There is no point trying something that suits the character but not the medium or vice versa. It is a selection process based on the two demands – the character and the medium … the way that *W1A* is shot.

However, rather than allowing the analysis of camera work and editing process to subsume the actor's contribution, this section will examine the nature of the relationship between actor and camera with specific reference to the 'comic intent' of the programmes.

On *W1A*, one of Sosanya's storylines revolves around a potential attraction between her character and Ian Fletcher. The second series includes some scenes which are more intimate than the large group scenes explored above, and include only the two of them (for example, see Series 2 Episode 4). The particular documentary aesthetic Sosanya notes, in which 'people seem so used to being filmed, and the cameras are so small … people appear to forget about them', allows such scenes to exist within *W1A*. As Sosanya explores, 'The scenes with Lucy and Ian are more plausible as we can play with the fact that the audience believes that the cameras are less obtrusive.' The shot selection and editing style in *W1A* by turns suggests both privileged access (such as quick cuts from several angles in a group meeting) and restricted access (such as muted conversations inside the meeting room when the camera is outside and shots that are blocked by a bystander or which begin out of focus). The filming style of *W1A* shares many similarities with *The Thick of It* in that the location work tends to be recorded on two cameras and, as they are handheld, they can follow the action rather than the action being blocked specifically for a three-camera set-up. This put a significant onus on the camera operators to work with the actors to tell the story. Sosanya notes:

> There's this unsung hero of a character who is the camera operator and he is such a big part of it. He might suddenly zoom in on somebody to get a reaction – he has to share exactly the same sense of humour and exactly the timing. What he picks up and what he leaves out of the frame is what makes it funny.

One of the challenges of this form is that as it is shot so quickly and because the contrivance is that cameras are capturing real behaviour, retaking is complex, as Sosanya experienced:

> I remember an example from a scene in *W1A* when 'B Camera' was focused on my fingers whilst I was talking. I was picking something apart at the same time as speaking. There was something wrong with the camera and John said 'You were doing something really interesting with your fingers, can you do that again?' Well, there was no way I could do that again, absolutely no way – because he told me!

Though Sosanya frames this as a challenge that she had to overcome, it provides an insight into the way in which the shooting style allows the actors a certain amount of freedom: presumably B Camera focusing on Sosanya's hands was not storyboarded but rather the recording style allowed the camera operator to respond to what the actor did in performance. It was certainly an element that was not shared with Sosanya, and as soon as this instinctive action was remarked upon by the director, repeating it became complex. Though not as pronounced as the use of improvisation in *The Thick of It*, this documentary filming style appears to have allowed the actors a certain freedom in performance and with this freedom came spontaneity in their work.

It is of little surprise, however, that this freedom was not evident in all scenes. Sosanya is perhaps unusual in that frequently her scenes involve only one or two other people. This arguably allows for a freer approach to recording it. For example, her scene with David Wilkes (Rufus Jones) in Series 2 Episode 2 has an average shot length of 2.7 seconds and, with the exception of a single two-shot, is in medium close-up throughout. By contrast, Simon Harwood is a true committee man. The vast majority of Watkins' scenes are, as above, multi-character meetings, and have a very short shot length (for example, an average of 1.7 seconds in the first meeting scene in Episode 1 Series 2). As his quotation below indicates, Watkins was very aware of the dual demands of the script and the medium when developing his characterisation:

> I keep my physical movement quite minimal which fits Simon's character. He hits a pose, makes a comment, or asks a question and hands it over to somebody else and expects them to come up with the answer ... Physical minimalism works for Simon and for the way that *W1A* is shot.

In these tightly scripted and exceptionally quickly performed group scenes (which Watkins says 'fizz[ed]' in recording), he decided to employ a minimalist physicality for Simon Harwood. By doing so, he succeeded in uniting the demands of the character with the demands of the form. Harwood is a smooth operator in this forum, and Watkins' precise and spare gestural range allowed him to achieve a neatness in filming which, given that the average utterance (and shot) was less than two seconds long, suited this speed and ensured that he did not obstruct the pace or cumulative build of the scene.

The docucom style of *The Thick of It*, by contrast, resulted in a 'messier' performance for the actors. As mentioned earlier, Roger Allam states that '*The Thick of It* was different from anything else that I've ever done on television' and it is was the process of recording which he identifies as being particularly noteworthy: '[R]eally, it was the actual filming that was different.' He notes that the 'cinéma vérité' shooting style deployed by the two handheld cameras resulted in 'a looser, freer way of filming from an acting point of view'. This section will explore what 'freer' means in this context, and how this relates to the 'comic intent' of *The Thick of It*.

Allam states that this shooting style 'gives a feel of the messiness of real life'. In contrast to Watkins' experience, both Allam and Front recalled the physical and verbal freedom which came from this shooting style. This manifested itself in three particular ways. Firstly, it almost completely avoided issues of continuity, which have been dominant concerns of actors in other case studies in this book. Front notes:

> [W]ith normal single and multi-camera filming, when you've blocked it, you have to stick with that blocking because all of the lighting and focusing is dependent on you hitting your mark. There's absolutely none of that in *The Thick of It* … The first scene we did was me coming into the office and being briefed. Armando came in and asked if I could go in and take my trainers off in the outer office so that we could establish that as well. So I said, 'OK, which line do you want me to leave the room on?' and he said, 'Whatever you want.' That was so unusual. He said that the cameras would just follow me.

This allowed a much greater degree of spontaneity in the actors' work. Allam also comments upon the way in which the actors' creative freedom can be compromised by a conventional single-camera set-up:

> [I]n the filming of it there were always two cameras on the move, rather than a single-camera set-up where you do a master-shot, mid-shot, and then close-ups from various points of view … Consequently you didn't feel so trapped by continuity, by someone saying, 'You scratched your cheek when you said that in the mid-shot.'

Enabling the actors' sense of instinct and spontaneity is particularly important in *The Thick of It* as it ensures that the form matches the content: the messiness and unpredictability in the actors' work (both in the scripted and improvised takes) parallels the subject matter as the characters manically try to disguise their own incompetence and avoid public disaster.

The second effect of this shooting style on the actors was the way in which it enabled them to achieve pace in their scenes. Allam draws parallels with the shooting style of *His Girl Friday* (1940) and *Rising Damp* (1974–8) when he explores the ways in which the two camera set-up allows for overlapping dialogue. Comparing a particular scene in *His Girl Friday* to his own experience, he notes:

> It was shot just in mid-shot which meant that they could overlap their dialogue and keep their own comic rhythm; something that the wide-shot, mid-shot, close-up process makes more difficult as the sound department will want you to keep the close-up takes clean of overlapping … In *The Thick of It* the two cameras on the move gave us the liberty to overlap like that.

The approach to recording *The Thick of It* thus allowed the overlaps that Allam mentions. Again, the 'messiness' of the dialogue (particularly overlaps and interjections) helps to create this pace and the sense of lack of control within DoSAC. Here, as before, the form and content work together. In Allam's experience this strongly links to the 'comic intent' of the programme and allowed him to be much more spontaneous in his timing and delivery.

The third benefit of this shooting style is associated with repeat takes. Rebecca Front's experiences stand in contrast to Nina Sosanya's experiences on *W1A*. Where Sosanya found repeating instinctive behaviour to be complex, in *The Thick of It* the shooting style meant that repeat takes were opportunities to try something new and to experiment, rather than to minutely recreate what had already been captured. Front explains:

> In single camera they will shoot you right the way through the scene whether you're doing anything interesting or not. So they have always got it but I think the difference here is that because they've got two cameras going, they are going to get different reactions each time. So if Peter [Capaldi] is shouting at us and he is really loud on one take then they are going to get a different reaction than they would have got if he'd just been whispering right in my face.

Therefore, a product of this 'freer' approach with two cameras was that Iannucci could consciously 'over-shoot' and use repeat takes to try out different options in performance. The difference here is that the material recorded was not the usual range of wide-shots, mid-shots and close-ups, capturing a similar take from multiple angles, but rather a dynamic and contrasting range of performance decisions by the actors. This was evidently creatively satisfying for them and distanced their work on *The Thick of It* from other television projects. As Front remarks: 'I remember on my first day, James Smith told me that I was going to have so much fun on this that I'd never want to film anything any other way.'

This section has demonstrated that the actors' processes and the performance style of the piece are inextricably linked. Whilst modes of shooting have been given significant scholarly attention, the effect that this has on the actor (and, indeed, the effect the actor has on the shooting style) has been overlooked. The actors in these case-study programmes were acutely aware of, and responsive to, the industrial contexts of their work, and so too were the directors with regard to the ways in which the actors' work could inform their processes. The result is innovative and carefully tailored approaches in which the actors worked effectively and creatively on these comedies.

Conclusion

This chapter has analysed the work of four actors in two highly successful and innovative television comedies. These case studies were chosen because they demonstrate the amount that can be learnt about television comedy by talking to the actors who work on it. If performance is only analysed via the well-trodden path of textual analysis, this chapter would conclude that the programmes are similar. The centrality of the writer-director, the handheld location shooting, and their docucom form which uses documentary traditions to lampoon national institutions all suggest that the actors worked in similar ways. Yet this was not the case. From an actor's point of view, the two projects could scarcely have been more different.

Throughout this chapter, Mills' warning that '[i]t is all too easy to simply end up describing a performance' (2005, 68) has informed the analysis. Rather, this chapter answers Mills' call for a 'move towards examining the rehearsal and production process which creates [it]' (2005, 73). The result is that this chapter has uncovered a varied and distinctive set of approaches. The specificity of the rhythms in Morton's script and the pace at which it was delivered was one of the defining features of *W1A*, and both Watkins and Sosanya developed informed strategies to ensure that their work foregrounded the comic intent of the writing: namely that they privileged the ensemble over self and cumulative build over individual contribution. By contrast, the actors were involved in the generation of material in addition to their interpretation of it on *The Thick of It*. This not only positioned them as experts of the character, it also provided them with an unusual form of rehearsal. The emphasis on the actors' creativity in the moment of execution contrasts neatly with the actors' focus on script analysis in *W1A*. Therefore, despite the two programmes' shared fascination with language and verbal expression as the dominant site of comedy, and the similar style in which they are filmed, behind these similarities were two very different working processes.

A notable feature of this chapter has been the strong alignment between the actors' work on script and the ways in which the two programmes were shot. The docucom shooting styles called upon the actors to deploy their work on script in different ways from the approach to traditional sitcom. The 'messiness' of *The Thick of It*, much like the improvisations throughout the process, released the actors to be physically and verbally experimental in the different takes, and to seek out alternative possibilities at almost every stage of the process. This freedom resulted in both actors experiencing what we have called 'creative danger' in the process. 'Creative danger' was also evident for the actors in *W1A*, but the reasons for this are quite different. In *W1A* it was the speed and specificity of their utterances, rather than their freedom, which led to them experiencing this quality. Mills raises a concern that 'the comic aspect of the genre is often sidelined' and that 'sitcom is only meaningful – and explicable as a genre – if its comic intent is understood' (2005, 5). This chapter has analysed a variety of hitherto unexplored ways in which actors foreground 'comic intent' in their work.

References

Barnouw, E., 1983. *Documentary: A History of the Non-Fiction Film*. Oxford: Oxford University Press.

Baron, C. and S.M. Carnicke, 2008. *Reframing Screen Performance*. Ann Arbor: University of Michigan Press.

Basu, L., 2014. 'British Satire in *The Thick of It*', *Popular Communication*, 12, 89–103.

Baym, G. and J. Jones, 2012. 'News Parody in Global Perspective: Politics, Power, and Resistance', *Popular Communication*, 10:1, 2–13.

Boleslavsky, R., 2003. *Acting: The First Six Lessons*. New York; London: Routledge.

Bruzzi, S., 2000. *New Documentary: A Critical Introduction*. London: Routledge.

————2001. 'Docusoaps', in G. Creeber (ed.), *The Television Genre Book*. London: BFI Publishing, 163.

Cantrell, T. and C. Hogg, 2016. 'Returning to an Old Question: What Do Television Actors Do When They Act?', *Critical Studies in Television*, 11:3, 283–298.

Carr, N., 2016. 'New Year. New Look. New Beginnings.' *BBC Blog Post*. Accessed at: www.bbc.co.uk/blogs/aboutthebbc/entries/0f9df107-a2d2-4687-a691-887ed6fd4aa9 (last viewed: 21 June 2016).

Davies, P., 2015. 'Class and Other Hotel Matters in *Fawlty Towers*', in J. Kamm and B. Neumann (eds), *British TV Comedies: Cultural Concepts, Contexts and Controversies*. Houndmills: Palgrave, 99–113.

Dunleavy, T., 2009. *Television Drama: Form, Agency, Innovation*. Houndmills: Palgrave.

Eaton, M., 1981. 'TV Situation Comedy', in T. Bennett, S. Boyd-Bowmann, C. Mercer, and J. Woollacott (eds), *Popular Television and Film: A Reader*. London: BFI.

Feuer, J., 2001. 'Situation Comedies, Part 2', in G. Creeber (ed.), *The Television Genre Book*. London: British Film Institute, 67–70.

Fielding, S., 2014. *A State of Play: British Politics on Screen, Stage and Page, from Anthony Trollope to The Thick of It*. London: Bloomsbury Academic.

Gray, J. and J. Jones, 2009. *Satire TV: Politics and Comedy in the Post-Network Era*. New York: NYU Press.

Hight, C., 2010. *Television Mockumentary: Reflexivity, Satire and a Call to Play*. Manchester: Manchester University Press.

Hooton, C., 2016. 'BBC Three Admits that its New Logo Looks like W1A Spoof', *The Independent*. Accessed at: www.independent.co.uk/arts-entertainment/tv/news/bbc-three-admits-that-its-new-logo-looks-like-w1a-spoof-a6795871.html (last viewed: 21 June 2016).

Iannucci, A., J. Armstrong, S. Blackwell, I. Martin, T. Roche, 2012. *The Thick of It*. London: BBC.

Irwin, M., 2015. '*The Rag Trade:* "Everybody Out!" Gender, Politics and Class on the Factory Floor', in J. Kamm and B. Neumann (eds), *British TV Comedies: Cultural Concepts, Contexts and Controversies*. Houndmills: Palgrave, 66–82.

Jacobi, P., 2015. 'Life is Stationary: Mockumentary and Embarrassment in *The Office*', in J. Kamm and B. Neumann (eds), *British TV Comedies: Cultural Concepts, Contexts and Controversies*, Houndmills: Palgrave, 295–310.

Kamm. J., 2015. 'Ignorant Master, Capable Servants: The Politics of Yes Minister and Yes Prime Minister', in J. Kamm and B. Neumann (eds), *British TV Comedies: Cultural Concepts, Contexts and Controversies*, Houndmills: Palgrave, 114–135.

Kamm, J. and B. Neumann (eds), 2015. *British TV Comedies: Cultural Concepts, Contexts and Controversies*. Houndmills: Palgrave.

Kirkham, P. and B. Skeggs, 1998. 'Absolutely Fabulous: Absolutely Feminist?', in C. Geraghty and D. Lusted (eds), *The Television Studies Book*. London: Arnold, 287–298.

Koseluk, G., 2000. *Great Brit-coms: British Television Situation Comedy*. Jefferson, N.C. and London: McFarland.

Langford, B., 2005. 'Our Usual Impasse: The Episodic Television Situation Comedy Revisited' in J. Bignell and S. Lacey, *Popular Television Drama: Critical Perspectives*. Manchester: Manchester University Press, 15–33.

Leggott, J., S. Lockyer and R. White (eds), 2015. 'Acting Up: Gender and Television Comedy', Special edition of *Critical Studies in Television*, 10:2.

Lindner, O., 2015. 'The Comic Nation: *Little Britain* and the Politics of Representation', in J. Kamm and B. Neumann (eds), *British TV Comedies: Cultural Concepts, Contexts and Controversies*. Houndmills: Palgrave, 326–340.

Lockyer, S., 2010. *Reading Little Britain: Comedy Matters on Contemporary Television*. London: I.B. Tauris.

Lucas, M., D. Walliams and B. Hilton, 2007. *Inside Little Britain*. London: Ebury.

Marteinson, P., 2014. 'Thoughts on the current state of humour theory', *Comedy Studies*, 2: 173–180.

Mills, B., 2004. 'Comedy Verite: Contemporary Sitcom Form' in *Screen*, 45:1, 63–78.

————2005. *Television Sitcom*. London: BFI/Palgrave.

————2009. *The Sitcom*. Edinburgh: Edinburgh University Press.

————2012. 'Make Me Laugh: Creativity in the British Television Comedy Industry', Blog. Accessed at: www.makemelaugh.org.uk/blog-archive (last viewed: 29 June 2016).

Mundy, G. and J. White, 2012. *Laughing Matters: Understanding Film, Television and Radio Comedy*. Manchester: Manchester University Press.

Neale, S. and F. Krutnik, 1990. *Popular Film and Television Comedy*. London: Routledge.

Owen, P., 2012. 'Business bank: has Vince Cable been watching The Thick of It?', *The Guardian*. Accessed at: www.theguardian.com/politics/blog/2012/sep/24/business-bank-vince-cable-thick-of-it (last viewed: 21 June 2016).

Pankratz, A., 2006. '*The Office* and the Hyperreality of New Britain', in J. Kamm (ed.), *Mediatised Britain*. Passau: Verlag Karl Stutz, 201–217.

————2015. 'Spin, Swearing and Slapstick: *The Thick of It*', in J. Kamm and B. Neumann (eds), *British TV Comedies: Cultural Concepts, Contexts and Controversies*. Houndmills: Palgrave, 281–294.

Schwinda, K.H., 2014. 'Chilled-out Entertainers' – Multi-layered Sitcom Performances in the British and American version of The Office', *Comedy Studies*, 5:1, 20–32.

Stafford-Clark, M. and P. Roberts, 2007. *Taking Stock: The Theatre of Max Stafford-Clark*. London: Nick Hern.

Taflinger, R.F., 1996. 'Sitcom: What it is, How it works'. Accessed at: http://public.wsu.edu/~taflinge/sitcom.html (last viewed: 29 June 2016).

Walters, B., 2005. *The Office*. London: BFI Publishing.

Notes

1 Though clearly identifiable, the political parties are never named.

2 Jacobi has called this 'cringe comedy' (2015, 300).

3 For more on cinéma vérité and the relationship between this mode of documentary and television comedy, see Hight 2010 and Jacobi 2015.

4 We might compare this to Kamm's analysis of 'civil-service speak' in *Yes, Minister* and *Yes, Prime Minister* (2015, 121–125).

5 This contribution is acknowledged as 'Additional material by the cast' in the credits for *The Thick of It*.

5

Period Drama

Introduction

As the 'period' modifier suggests, television dramas of this kind can be defined very simplistically as productions that are set partly or wholly in past eras. Referred to variously and interchangeably as 'period dramas', 'costume dramas', 'historical dramas' and 'heritage dramas',[1] television's dramatic representations of a British past continue to capture viewer imaginations both domestically and internationally.

Offering a useful point of distinction in terms of form and content, Nelson stresses that, whilst 'period adaptations of historical novels have long been a tradition of British television, "costume drama" might be seen as a more recent phenomenon' (2008, 49). Nelson goes on to outline 'costume drama's' prioritisation of melodrama, star casting, spectacular sets, lavish costumes and fast-paced action, with big-budget, popular entertainment appeal superseding the concerns of period veracity and fidelity to source which are now associated more with the traditional literary adaptation for television (2008, 49–52). Longer-form, popular-appeal traditions do exist in the creation of historical drama on British television, with notable examples such as *Upstairs, Downstairs* (ITV 1971–1975) and *Poldark* (BBC 1975–1977) spanning multiple series. Period dramas of this time also regularly cohered more closely with the 'televisual everyday' performative modes expected of popular long-form drama, as this chapter's interview insights from Siân Phillips regarding her work on *I, Claudius* (BBC 1976) suggest, employing studio-based techniques of character presentation which Phillips parallels with the soap opera strategies of the day. Prevalent production patterns through the 1980s and early 1990s, however, saw British period dramas further align themselves with the more expensive yet shorter-form strategies of their cinematic counterparts. Internationally successful mini-series such as *Brideshead Revisited* (ITV 1981) and *The Jewel in the Crown* (ITV 1984) worked to encourage the 'quality' connotations of the 'filmic event' as opposed to the 'televisual everyday', acting as forerunners for increasing numbers of shorter-form or stand-alone period television productions aiming to emulate these 'event' connotations but on a smaller budget. Production patterns were once again reinvigorated by the BBC's landmark 1995 adaptation of *Pride and Prejudice*, effectively meshing an 'event' aesthetic with the more pronounced melodramatic approaches and ambitious narrative spans of popular television fiction. *Pride and Prejudice* also consciously downgraded the importance of 'faithfulness' to Jane Austen's literary work in favour of foregrounding sexuality, visual spectacle and episodic 'cliffhanger' endings more commonly associated with the television soap opera. Such hybridity of form has since reached further extremes with the recent cycle of open-ended period serials such as *The Paradise* (BBC 2012–2013), *Mr Selfridge* (ITV 2013–2016) and, most notably, *Downton Abbey* (ITV 2010–2015), eschewing literary sources in preference of more particularly televisual storytelling strategies. Additionally, even more recent developments in open-ended period formats extend across established televisual genres, with dramas such as *Ripper Street* (BBC 2012–) and *Call the Midwife* (BBC 2012–) combining historical settings with police and medical narrative components. As evidenced by these ongoing processes of adaptation, British period drama remains a lively and inventive form that continues to attract international co-production interest along with international audiences.

British screen representations of the past have also drawn sustained academic attention, with significant contributions from, for instance: Sue Harper (1994), Sarah Cardwell (2002), Andrew Higson (2003), James Chapman (2005) and Jerome de Groot (2008, 2015). Reflecting broader research predilections towards the cinematic, with the exception of one example (Cardwell 2002) within the range of noteworthy scholarship indicated above, there has been limited primary focus upon the televisual context. On occasions when such a televisual emphasis has been seen as warranted, it has most often been in relation to the detailed reading of particular texts deemed for some reason 'exceptional', often adaptations of canonical literary sources, such as Christine Geraghty's 2012 study of *Bleak House* (BBC 2005). Presciently, one of the defining features of the BBC's *Bleak House* was its unusual use of a twice-weekly, soap-like format, anticipating a subsequent renaissance in long-form presentational modes for British period television drama more broadly. Indeed, more recently, due in no small part to the remarkable international success of *Downton Abbey* in triggering a contemporary production boom in more long-running, populist British dramas located in the past, scholarly activity around period television as a distinct and dynamic form in its own right has increased substantially. Monographs such as Katherine Byrne's *Edwardians on Screen: from Downton Abbey to Parade's End* (2015) and edited collections like James Leggott and Julie Anne Taddeo's *Upstairs and Downstairs: British Costume Drama Television from The Forsyte Saga to Downton Abbey* (2015) investigate both rich histories and new developments within the period genre on television. Predominantly, however, these investigations have been undertaken chiefly through text-based scrutiny, as opposed to examining production backgrounds and industry perspectives.

This is not to suggest that some valuable work has not already been generated in considering these dramas as sites of performance. Cardwell, most notably, provides useful discussion of period dramas as performative texts, considering the ways in which audiences' 'imaginative engagement with the "past" that is being presented to them' is complicated by the work of actors who 'serve to highlight the contemporaneity and televisuality of the programmes in which they exist' (2002, 88, 89). However, Cardwell stresses that such performative complications most often add to rather than subtract from textual meanings and viewing pleasures. For example, like Nelson (2008, 50), Cardwell observes the 'star system' of British period drama, in which high-profile, well-respected actors are repeatedly cast in familiar roles, facilitating a 'complex layering process' of awareness – and, indeed, enjoyment – for audiences: '[T]hey often appeal to the viewers to use their knowledge of the actors in order to supplement their perceptions of the actor's performance-in-role.' (2002, 91) In reflecting upon the various meanings and pleasures created by such a nuanced alternation between present performances and imagined pasts, Cardwell summarises:

> The performative nature of television texts also reasserts their contemporaneity, through their use of actors and props that exist in the present. In addition, actors' appearances outside programmes assert their existence as contemporary, real people, whose job it is to 'act' as if they were other people ... The active mental negotiation of our perceptions of the contemporaneity of the performance, and our imaginings of the 'past' that are inextricably tied to the text's representations of it, augments our viewing experience. (2002, 91–92)

Whilst Cardwell's insights into this 'past/present dichotomy' (2002, 92) within the period drama as performative text are clearly illuminating, it is equally clear that text-and-reception-based analytical approaches of the kind used here can only take us so far in truly understanding the ways in which actors 'whose job it is to "act" as if they were other people' (2002, 91) function in the specific context of period drama. This chapter's combination of actor testimony and analysis of such testimony aims to contribute to developing further the valuable ideas that Cardwell introduced.

To this end, without delving unnecessarily deeply into the associated complexities of historical representation, social commentary, commercial determinants, audience escapism and 'quality' aesthetic appeal (all vibrant debates that are ongoing within the rich body of research cited above), there are a number of factors in period television production which demand further investigation in terms of the actor's work specifically. As Higson notes in relation to historical film: '[M]uch of the debate ... tends to be about how accurate they are in terms of historical detail.' (2011, 230) Indeed, there is an equally forceful critical predilection within the televisual context, from academics, journalists and audiences alike, to read period inaccuracy in negative terms, as creative mistake, artistic immoderation or, at the very worst, commercially driven popularisation. Such critical interpretations are exemplified by Caughie's assessment of those period television dramas in which '[h]istory becomes the present in costume, showing us only … lingering generalities of tone and style … without the formal distance and historical particularity which might enable us to experience difference and change' (2000, 211). Responding to this, elsewhere we have identified the ways in which

> Caughie suggests a creative and conceptual reductionism that can result from stylising or contemporising the past … bringing the past more conveniently 'up to date' for consumers: framing it within the more 'user-friendly' codes and conventions of history as present-day entertainment commodity. (Hogg 2013, 87)

As this chapter's interviews evidence, these concerns around historical representation and contemporisation find form also in the television actor's work on period roles, often undertaking historical research of various forms (both personal and formalised within the production process) with the aim of embodying period characters as plausibly and truthfully as possible. Furthermore, as this chapter will go on to consider, costumes, props and sets constitute a particularly potent conditioning factor for the actor within a period production context: when utilised well, they offer significant value in terms of an actor's ability to immerse themselves simultaneously in both the imagined past being represented and the action of the present performative context.

However, such drive towards historical accuracy from actors is balanced by their awareness of these dramas as big-budget, contemporary entertainment products which must also follow a variety of recognised standards within the popular period form. As Higson asserts, credibility 'depends in part on [the] deployment of history effects, and in part on adhering to established conventions for representing a particular period' (2011, 231). Moreover, period dramas for television can be seen to constitute part of a larger British 'heritage industry', offering up stylised experiences of British history for present-day consumption. According to Higson and John Hill, the reason for the domestic and international appeal of such heritage experiences in media form is essentially twofold: they depict glamorous and idealised stereotypical visions of Britain's geography, architecture, past and people (Higson 2001, 250), whilst simultaneously employing aesthetic strategies and cultural signposts which distinguish them from the Hollywood mainstream (Hill 1999, 79). In the case of heritage media commodities that are also literary adaptations of canonical British novels, there is an added cultural cachet, enabling mass access to esteemed literary texts by converting such texts into more 'user-friendly' (Hogg 2013, 87) contemporary media vehicles. The ways in which actors function as key agents in generating plausible 'history effects' (Higson 2011, 231) through their period work, at the same time as tackling their involvement in the often elaborate technical and aesthetic construction of these dramas as high-cost, culturally prestigious, internationally distributed heritage entertainment products, are revealed further through this chapter's interviews and subsequent analysis.

Period Drama Case Study: *Downton Abbey* (ITV 2010–2015)

Created by veteran period actor and screenwriter Julian Fellowes and first aired in September 2010, *Downton Abbey* quickly became one of the critical and commercial landmarks of British television drama in the twenty-first century. Launched as an international co-production between the UK-originated Carnival Films and the US company Masterpiece, to be shown initially by ITV in Britain and PBS in America, the drama went on to find global popularity, with broadcast rights acquired in over 220 countries and territories (*ITV Press Centre* 2013). Spanning six series and 52 episodes over five years of production, including a number of Christmas specials, *Downton Abbey* charts the lives of the aristocratic Crawley family and their servants from 1912 through to 1926, representing personal dramas alongside global historical moments and developments such as the sinking of the Titanic, the onset, events and aftermath of the First World War, and the creation of the Irish Free State. The show effectively combined the visual splendour of 'event' period drama with a long-form narrative emphasis upon personal relationships – romantic, familial or professional – more attuned with the storytelling sensibilities of popular television. Notably, such hybridity of form was reflected in *Downton Abbey*'s casting strategies, bringing together high-profile figures from the established period 'star system' with actors more familiar to British audiences from earlier soap opera or other popular-drama roles. Indeed, a number of the cast members have made effective use the show's global profile as a professional springboard to subsequent Hollywood work for television and film. The international appeal of *Downton Abbey*'s production strategies heralded a renewed industry interest in long-form 'upstairs and downstairs' British period formats depicting both the privileged and their servants, aiming to emulate the winning televisual formula that achieved success 'on a scale almost never reached by British or European series' (Amandine Cassi, cited in Egner 2013).

Although *Downton Abbey* has garnered considerable critical and industry acclaim, with numerous Emmy and BAFTA award wins, amongst others, the drama has also been the target of critical hostility, particularly in relation to its perceived excessive creative licence in representing the past. Whilst *The Guardian*'s Vicky Frost reads soothing positivity in *Downton Abbey*'s 'warm bath' idealisation of British history (2013, 17), other commentators took a more negative stance. US critic James Parker deems *Downton Abbey* '[p]reposterous as history, preposterous as drama, the show succeeds magnificently as bad television', but with the interesting caveat that '[t]he acting is superb – it has to be', suggesting that the work of the cast somehow mitigated against the perceived historical and narrative failings of this 'aristo-soap' (2013). In the UK, A. A. Gill offers a less forgiving appraisal: '[E]verything I despise and despair of on British television: National Trust sentimentality, costumed comfort drama that flogs an embarrassing, demeaning, and bogus vision of the place I live in.' (Cited in Kamp 2012) The substantive elements of such criticisms echo the aforementioned significance of historical accuracy in the appraisal of period dramas, along with resentment towards the commercial 'packaging' of an idealised history for present-day consumption and the well-established critical disdain for soap-like populist narrative strategies. As this chapter's interviews attest, the production process on *Downton Abbey* strives for historical authenticity as far as it can but, ultimately, as with police and medical representations, the drama must come first. Responding to such criticisms, *Downton Abbey*'s executive producer Gareth Neame clarifies: 'Downton is a fictional drama … It is not a history programme.' (Cited in *BBC News* 2012) This chapter contains interviews with both Penelope Wilton and Lesley Nicol regarding their work on all six series of *Downton Abbey*, offering actor perspectives on both the 'upstairs' and 'downstairs' production components of the drama.

Period Drama Case Study: *Poldark* (BBC 2015–)

Adapted from Winston Graham's historical novels by screenwriter Debbie Horsfield and directors Edward Bazalgette and Will McGregor, the BBC's latest version of *Poldark* launched with an opening series of eight hour-long episodes in March 2015. Pre-established audience interest regarding this adaptation came not only from those familiar with Graham's literary work but also from those who remembered the BBC's earlier highly successful adaptation of the same name which ran for two series from 1975 to 1977. Set in late eighteenth-century Cornwall, *Poldark* is well-suited to the current melodramatic narrative expectations of the period form, following the dramas of disgraced nobleman Ross Poldark (Aidan Turner) in restoring his ruined family estate and his reputation, whilst also finding love. The BBC's latest iteration of *Poldark* enjoyed considerable public and critical praise, with a commission for a second series secured in April 2015 (*BBC Media Centre* 2015) and a third series announced in July 2016 (*BBC Media Centre* 2016), before the second series even aired. Such success was further echoed in the drama's receipt of the *Radio Times* Audience Award at the BAFTA TV Awards in 2016. *The Telegraph*'s Allison Pearson (2015) describes the Series 1 finale as 'devastatingly good', arguing that *Poldark*, in the broader context of current period drama trends, offers an unusual combination of stylised 'comfort' alongside powerful dramatic sincerity: 'There are rare occasions when a popular drama series breaks free of its clichés and delivers something that properly belongs to art.' This chapter includes an interview with Jack Farthing who portrays George Warleggan, Poldark's chief antagonist, in the BBC's current adaptation.

Period Drama Case Study: *I, Claudius*

The chapter's final interview offers a further interpretive dimension to 'period acting' for television, sharing thoughts from Siân Phillips regarding her extensive television work, from the earliest days of live performance conditions to the present, but chiefly through the lens of her role in the much-celebrated television production of *I, Claudius* (BBC 1976), along with her other experiences of high-profile period dramas. Having worked in British television drama for over 60 years, Phillips offers a unique perspective on the various periods of technical and artistic development within the form, discussing recollections from early single plays and iconic BBC period productions such as *Shoulder to Shoulder* (BBC 1974).

Interviews

Penelope Wilton

London, 11 September 2015

Trained at Drama Centre London in the late 1960s, Penelope Wilton has become one of the most familiar faces on British television. Wilton has worked prolifically on both stage and screen for almost 50 years, awarded an OBE in 2004 and a DBE in 2016 for her services to drama, and winning an Olivier Award for Best Actress in 2015. Her numerous roles for television memorably include long-suffering wife Ann Bryce in the situation comedy *Ever Decreasing Circles* (BBC 1984–1989) and courageous politician Harriet Jones in *Doctor Who* (BBC 1963–1989, 2005–). This interview centres upon one of Wilton's most famous recurring roles as Isobel Crawley in *Downton Abbey*. Wilton appeared in all 52 episodes of *Downton Abbey*.

How did you get involved with Downton Abbey?

The producers got in contact with my agent and sent through scripts for the first three episodes. Julian Fellowes had written some very good scripts. The thing that immediately appealed to me was the fact that he had introduced a whole ensemble – a wide range of characters, and in the first three episodes I could see that there was a lot of potential for these characters to develop. Of course at that stage I had no idea that there would be six series, but I could tell that this was a story that could develop over the course of the nine-episode first series that was planned.

Though I wasn't aware of this at the time, Julian had written a synopsis of the other episodes. However, I didn't know where the story was going to go. I received the three that were complete, and I got the sense that this was something with which I wanted to get involved.

Did you meet Julian Fellowes to discuss the project?

Not at that stage. All I had was the scripts to go on, and I decided to be involved on the strength of what he had written. That, after all, is all you have to go on. As an actor, it is those words that I am speaking, and so the script is the most important element.

How did your involvement begin?

We had a read-through of the scripts as a company, but there wasn't much time for preparation. The filming schedule is very tight, as Highclere Castle, where we filmed, is open to the public for a lot of the year.

One of the interesting features of acting on *Downton Abbey* is the focus on the ensemble. You'll see that close-ups are very rare. Instead, a lot of it is shot in mid- or long-shot. This is different from a lot of television. It is a reason that the programme looks so opulent and beautiful – like a painting you can see the room and the position of the people in it. It meant that, as an actor, your awareness is slightly different. There would be lots of scenes that I was involved in which were set in the drawing room, and would include about eight or ten people. I might only have a couple of lines, but as they were working with a long shot, I would be on camera most of the time. In these group scenes, there would often be three or four plot lines that come together, and therefore several relationships that would be affected. I found that I had to closely consider the script, and be absolutely sure about the context of the scene so that I could be clear about the significance of what was being said. You had to be clear about this because often we would film out of sequence; you'd shoot the end of the scene before you had shot the beginning. Often scenes would begin at another point, so you had to be very clear about the sequence.

These group scenes were a main feature of my experience on *Downton Abbey*. The dinner party scenes might take two days to film. This was all on location at Highclere Castle. There were some technical skills associated with this. For example, you had to be aware that the sound of a fork or piece of cutlery hitting the table was too loud for the microphones and would interrupt the dialogue, so you had to place your knife and fork down very gently. However, you couldn't look like you were placing them down carefully, so we all had to be aware that it had be silent but appear as natural behaviour. Then there was the complicated technical challenge of filming the scenes and the choreography of the blocking. The actors playing the waiting staff, those eating, and the sound and camera crew all had to be tightly choreographed so that you didn't find that you reverse a shot and suddenly Carson [the butler, played by Jim Carter] is on the opposite side of the room, or that a waiter's arm cuts across a shot. It is a complex dance involving many people and the rhythms have to be just right. I remember working on Woody Allen's *Match Point* [2005] and there was a very complicated shot which went downstairs, tracked through rooms and followed a conversation. He loves shots like that and the timing of them has to be very precise; all of the components have to be synchronised.

On *Downton Abbey*, you also had to observe completely the etiquette of the day. In the dinner party scenes there were a whole host of rules of behaviour that you had to follow. These rules were different according to the period, which progressed from 1912 to 1926, and things got more relaxed. This is something that we would read up about and do our homework on. For example, you would never put your hands on the table; you would completely avoid touching it. You had to have very good deportment – which was something that was dictated by the corsets that we wore in the early series. This was also true of the men. The starched front panel of their dinner shirts was a nod towards armoured breastplates and again meant that they sat up with a very straight back. You can imagine that this becomes quite a challenge when you are filming all day. But it also allows you to really embody the period.

Did these period elements affect your characterisation?

Yes, the style of the era and the etiquette was central to the way that we spoke to each other and the sorts of relationships that you would have with people. We had an expert, Alastair Bruce [the Historical Advisor on the show], who would teach the actors about particular aspects of the time. These details included how you greet people. For example, when you shook hands with someone it was a brief hold, you wouldn't pump their hand. You would always be introduced to a room by the butler. In fact, something interesting about this period is that the house staff were completely free within the house. They would be able to go from room to room and would rarely be asked to leave. Therefore, regularly, people would have intimate conversations with someone else with members of the staff in the room. This is one reason why the programme worked so well. The staff would know a lot, if not everything, about the family who owned the house. Alastair also taught us about the etiquette for cloth-ing, particularly for glove and hat wearing. We all wondered why our gloves had a run of small buttons up the side. He explained that, when eating, you should unbutton the glove and roll it up and then button it back up again, so it sits, rolled up, on the wrist. Then, following dinner, you would roll it down again, and by doing so avoid getting any stains on the white cotton. Similarly, though it seems odd to us now, women would wear small hats which they wouldn't take off indoors as it would have made their hair an odd shape. They would have to retire upstairs to remove their hats. From an acting point of view, these help you to see the character as being distinct from you. It makes you stand in a different way, behave in a different way. There was also a difference in inflection of speech then too. An upward inflection at the end of a sentence has crept into the English accent over recent years, and this wasn't the case in the period in which *Downton Abbey* is set. This was particularly true of the young actors on the show, who had to ensure that they didn't speak with this upwards inflection. However, there were never points at which there was a tension between those period elements and the storytelling; they worked seamlessly together.

The stylistic features of the period also affected, or rather were reflected in, the ways in which the characters communicated. Isobel Crawley is a moderniser. However, even then, there are emotions that she feels which she can't express. To modern sensibilities, there is a reserved-ness to her manner, which is shared by other members of society at that time.

Unlike the inhabitants of Downton, Isobel is not landed gentry, but rather a member of what we might call the upper middle classes. She had trained as a nurse. She has been left comfortably provided for, and has used this to develop particular social reforms. Over the course of the programme she has campaigned for women's suffrage, and helped women forced into prostitution, and she successfully argued that Downton should be used as a convalescent home for injured soldiers in the First World War. Her attitude and also her behaviour is more modern than the Granthams, but still has to conform to particular codes of the time. She is part of that time but also apart from the world of Downton, which made her very intriguing to me. I'm sometimes asked what she would be doing if she were around today. Perhaps the editor of *The Guardian's* women's page, or the editor of a woman's magazine. She would write about subjects affecting women.

Long-running television narratives mean that characters can evolve, and yours certainly did. Were there elements of the character that were there from the outset which you kept at the forefront of your mind as the character developed?

Yes, one of the delights of working on *Downton Abbey* was the fact that the series ran across a long time frame. The first series was aired in 2010, and the final series in 2015, but the time frame within the series started against the backdrop of the sinking of the Titanic in 1912 all the way through to the mid-1920s. This allowed my character to develop and for her to be able to see the development of so many causes that she cared about. Each historical period allowed her views to be developed. It made her a very interesting and rewarding character to play. I did certainly hold on to the idea that she is a reformer, a moderniser, someone moving forward, which was often at odds with the attitudes of Downton. So whatever happened to her, I had that in mind, and it was always there in her conversations and relationships with others.

When you work on a series for a long time, you can build the character gradually – it doesn't have to be instant like it is in a film. For instance, at the end of Series 3, my son Matthew Crawley [played by Dan Stevens] dies in a car crash. In the writing, this history was not forgotten by the characters. Often in series in which storylines weave in and out, major events are forgotten quickly by characters, I suppose in an effort to move the plot along. However, Julian did the opposite on *Downton Abbey*. My character did not forget the past, but rather was in mourning for the next year. Society had clear rules for the length and nature of mourning, and Julian stuck to these. That was very satisfying and meant that the character became richer – she was shaped by her experiences and I had time to play this, rather than another plot twist immediately taking over. This made the project different from other series that I have done.

Because so much of your character and her reasons for being at Downton centred upon her relationship with her son, did you find that his death destabilised your sense of character?

No, not at all. Quite the opposite. In fact, it opened up so many other aspects of her as a character. Of course, the relationship with her son was a lovely one and very satisfying to play, but his death meant that, after her mourning, she had to move on as best she could and develop other interesting relationships far more.

How important were those relationships, between characters but also between actors, during your time on the series?

When acting on television, and on a programme like *Downton Abbey* in particular, you have to get used to a lot going on, so you have to concentrate hard. On stage you have silence, but on set you have cameras, technicians, boom operators, so you have to be very concentrated in order not to be distracted by what is happening around you. It is a different discipline from acting on stage. For example, we might be filming a scene and then they need to do a reverse shot and so they need to raise my eye line a bit. So they move the sofa I was sitting on and give me a modern stool to sit on. So the environment around you changes regularly. On stage, you get used to the set, the lighting and the sound all contributing, live, to the story. On screen all of this is changeable or added after you've done the scene. Therefore, you need to rely on the other actor. You feel the intensity of this reliance and it is one of the most satisfying things about television work.

Once you have this trust with the other actor, the next element is the camera. In a sense, it is a three-way relationship. It becomes like a dance, and when it works well, you can feel it. Like a dance, the three of you are perfectly in time with the rhythm of the scene and you can all judge the tempo of the moves and dialogue. You really can feel how all of this is working in harmony. When this harmony breaks, it is equally evident. One of the huge benefits of working on *Downton Abbey* was that the camera and sound operators worked on the show for many years and so they were skilled at working quickly and precisely with the actors. We were all very used to working together on this dance and when it all comes together it is a very satisfying feeling.

One particular challenge of *Downton Abbey* was the fact that, with the exception of dinner party conversations, the scenes are often very short. It was rare to find a scene that lasted for more than about two pages in the script – a couple of minutes of recording. Whilst this meant that learning the script was straightforward, it also meant that you had to get straight to the heart of the scene. There was no time for warming into it. You had to know exactly what you wanted to do with it. This is where the trust you have in the other actors is again crucial.

Could you tell us a bit about the timetable for filming and receiving the scripts etc.?

As I said, the filming was over a set period because of the availability of Highclere Castle. It was complicated to film because often you would be on location and doing outdoor shoots. The scullery and the kitchens were not suitable at Highclere, so they built the sets at Ealing Studios. I would receive the scripts in advance of filming and Julian would sketch out the shape of the series that we were working on. We weren't told much about how our characters might develop in future series, but I didn't want to know. It is more true to life – we don't know what is going to happen to us, so it focuses you on the present.

We would have a read-through but there wouldn't be much rehearsal apart from a line run, a blocking and camera rehearsal, and then we would film it. This is one of the big differences from theatre. In the theatre, you re-rehearse and try it out in different ways. On television, on

Downton Abbey, you felt that you should try these different ways out in performance, with the cameras running. You wouldn't want to do a run through which felt fresh and interesting but which you hadn't recorded. That needs to be captured. Also, if you were to run it too many times, the energy would be lost.

Beyond Downton Abbey, *working on different television productions and across different genres, are there ever discussions around different 'house styles' or modes of performance?*

Not in my experience, no, but different genres do ask different things of you, and that is a judgement that you make as an actor when going through the script. Working on a show like *Doctor Who*, for instance, requires something different from *Downton Abbey*. It is broader and more heightened, because you are dealing with a world of the imagination rather than the real world. But I have never had explicit discussions about these things. It is something that you feel and act upon for yourself. I certainly wouldn't see it as my role to give guidance to actors on *Downton Abbey* – that is the director's role.

You've worked in television for the last 40 years. Has the job of the television actor changed in that time?

The technical context has changed hugely. The cameras used to be so heavy and unwieldy that you would have to film in a studio and there were scenes that we film now that would have been impossible – the camera operators can easily carry the steady-cams now and walk through the action, or spin during a dance, for example. But the fundamental job of the actor on television hasn't changed. It varies hugely from project to project, but the reliance on the other actors and the relationship with the camera have remained constant.

The other change is that young actors seem much more at home on set or in a studio than I was when I started. I trained at Drama Centre and at that time there was no training for television at all. The young actors on *Downton Abbey* seem to take it all in their stride.

How did it feel to put the full stop on Downton Abbey *for the final series?*

Well, sad, of course, but it also felt like the right time. It's wise to end whilst you're still wanted, and it is important that the cast – particularly the younger actors – move on to other opportunities.

Lesley Nicol

Interview via Skype, 12 May 2016

Since studying at Guildhall School of Music and Drama in the 1970s, Lesley Nicol has worked in television for over 30 years, appearing as a visiting actor in shows spanning a number of popular genres, from situation comedies such as *Blackadder II* (BBC 1986) and *Dinnerladies* (BBC 1998–2000), to police dramas like *The Bill* (ITV 1984–2010), *A Touch of Frost* (ITV 1992–2010) and *The Last Detective* (ITV 2003–2007), to medical dramas including *Casualty*, *Holby City* and *Doctors* (BBC 2000–). This interview focuses upon Nicol's best-known recurring role as Beryl Patmore, the house cook in *Downton Abbey*. Nicol appeared in all 52 episodes of *Downton Abbey*.

How did you get involved in Downton Abbey*?*

I knew one of the producers of the show, Liz Trubridge, and I met her one day in the gardens of Chiswick House whilst we were both walking our dogs. This was the year before *Downton Abbey* happened and we had this conversation about her getting this lovely new job. Liz had worked with Julian Fellowes the year before on a film and then he had come up with this television concept and brought her on board, and I was delighted for her. At the end of the conversation she said that there might be a part that I would be right for and that they would be in touch, as they would begin casting early in the following year. As an actor, if you had a pound for every time someone said that they thought they had a part for you, you would be rich. I'm not denigrating what Liz said but productions so often evolve in ways that mean initial casting ideas eventually change and so I did not hold my breath. However, the call did come. I subsequently discovered that there had already been an important casting meeting at ITV and they had brought on board big names like Maggie Smith and Hugh Bonneville, and they also wanted to include existing ITV faces so they had cast Rob James-Collier from *Coronation Street* and Siobhan Finneran from *Benidorm* [ITV 2007–], for example. That mix of home-grown talent and international stars was important to them. There happened also to be this part still vacant of Mrs Patmore, the house cook, and Julian stood up at a casting meeting and said that they had this idea for the character and should they just bring in the actor they had in mind – me – and put her on tape and see? ITV said yes because they were rather more relaxed about things at that stage, having already secured these other actors. I went in to read some scenes for the tape and I met with the casting director and Liz, and thankfully they offered me the part and did not see anyone else. That never happens unless you are a big star, so I was very lucky.

Did you immediately feel that the part was a good fit for you?

When I read a script, I do get a clear feel for whether I can do something or not with a character. With this, I was fascinated by the whole concept and the writing was fantastic. I already knew that there were some incredible actors on board and so I was very excited about being involved in the production as a whole, but I could also see things that I could do with the character and how I could fit into that, so it felt right.

Once you were cast, did you then start to do some character research before filming began?

I found a book about a period country house and its cook and so I did some reading around but what was really most useful was the historical advisor who was employed by the production and who showed us round the location when we first arrived and offered us a wealth of historical detail on the workings of a period house. That was far more valuable than reading a book because it personalised it and brought the history alive in that environment in which we would be working. When I initially read for Mrs Patmore, she was just a cross, red-faced cook who shouted a lot. As an actor, you have to think that nobody is just that, and so you have to burrow underneath that and start thinking about why she is like that. The historical advisor helped with this enormously. He explained that the kitchen is the engine of the house, things happen fast, pressures are running high and, if someone makes a mistake, it will be Mrs Patmore's fault, and so she cannot tolerate mistakes. She has to run things very strictly. The character started to make more sense and become more nuanced in my head when placed in that historical context. The importance of Mrs Patmore's role also as a mentor for her assistant Daisy [played by Sophie McShera], and the necessity to be hard with Daisy sometimes, in order to ensure that she was being trained for the future, also started to make sense when placed within that period. The advisor lined us all up, as the downstairs staff, in order of importance, because downstairs was as hierarchical as upstairs, if not more so. Once you had a clear sense of that hierarchy, the relationships on the pages of the script started to become even richer. For example, the 'Mrs' title for my character was absolutely a sign of respect within that hierarchy, as it was clear to me that Mrs Patmore had never been married.

In addition, as the production went on, Julian observed what actors brought to the roles and adapted them accordingly. Julian mentioned to me recently that Mrs Patmore was never intended to be funny, in his head, but because of my approach to the role and the connection I developed with Sophie who played Daisy, that gave him a whole different set of creative opportunities and directions for those characters. He then began writing for us.

Did you meet with Sophie McShera before filming began, to test that relationship for the screen?

No. In America they are big on 'chemistry reads' as part of the casting process for television, something I have never experienced as an actor. However, I do often get asked if I had a 'chemistry read' with Sophie. Instead, I remember clearly being in a rehearsal room at Ealing Studios before we started filming – we had about an hour to chat with the director before things started – and someone telling me that the girl playing Daisy was just down the hallway if I wanted to say hello, and we were fortunate enough to hit it off immediately. It was good luck rather than production planning, though. The dynamic between us is genuine, on and off the screen, as we have become very close, and I admire her tremendously.

Did you have access to all the scripts for the first series from the outset, to start getting to grips with your character?

Again, no. I think we had three or four of the scripts. Of course, Julian was the only writer, so it was a lot of work for him. No writers' room for *Downton Abbey*! We had an initial read-through of those scripts in a massive room with all the cast, and then behind us was everyone else – the crew and all the departments. So we were all together before filming started to try to get a handle on the world of this story. I wasn't told all that much about Mrs Patmore initially. I was largely working in my own head with the information in the scripts I had at that point. Because, in television, there is not much time on the day to investigate things in terms of rehearsal or discussion. Really your job becomes about what you are filming on that day and how best to serve those scenes. That is your primary task. In terms of our scenes in the kitchen, it became very clear very early on that, because of the nature of those scenes and the need for authenticity, time of day within the story was very significant. The time completely governs the pace of the action and the jeopardy. If it was just before an important dinner upstairs, things would be more intense and tempers would be heightened. If a scene was after an important dinner, the pace would change completely. So timing and the rhythms of the house governed, and that was about authenticity but it also affected characters and their relationships at particular moments. Mrs Patmore would have a different persona in the midst of cooking than she would relaxing over a pot of tea afterwards, for example. We had to tip off new actors working in the kitchen scenes about that pace. We even had a chef in the props department who would advise on where we would be in the process of making something at that point in a scene, and what we should be doing to make it look authentic. That logic in terms of the workings of the kitchen was very important because it would be crucial to our characters. Sophie and I had a crash course in choreographing a kitchen scene, with little or no rehearsal, furnishing it with credible kitchen activity, and then knowing how to replicate that activity multiple times. It has to be consistent across various takes for the edit. So those technical skills were very important because there was never time, so you had to nail it very quickly and then repeat it.

Also, the costumes, sets and props were so amazing in creating that world to inhabit, and there was so much detail that an audience would never see on screen. There was an interconnecting set of kitchen and servants' hall which meant that you were immersed in that world. In terms of costume, all the female characters started out in corsets, which does make you move and hold yourself in a certain way. I somehow managed to lose mine after about three years! Initially, though, it did help to get into the world of your character.

As things went on, it was never a problem for me to get into the mindset of Mrs Patmore after breaks in filming. The main reason, aside from the quality of the writing, was some advice I got from Anne Reid, a wonderful actress and a dear friend. When I got the part, Anne advised me to figure out who she is but never to overcomplicate what I did with Mrs Patmore and, where appropriate, to embed some of my own characteristics in the character. What happens then is that you can return to those things without any significant effort, because it is in your DNA, and it will also bring different colours to the character without ever having to over-think it. That was fantastic advice because it feels effortlessly real. For example, some of the humour of Mrs Patmore was very close to my own humour, and then Julian started responding to those things in the writing. So it became second nature for me to return to that role.

Of course, a big part of that was the mastery of the writing. What Julian would do is slowly unravel a character and show different sides as time went on. For example, he eventually revealed a softness and vulnerability to Mrs Patmore that was not clear from the outset. As those different dimensions surfaced, you would take them and play them as an actor, without ever having to think about what would come next, because you trust in the writing and want to prioritise serving your character in those scenes in that moment.

Did you have a notation system of any kind for your scripts, to keep a handle on the journey of your character?

Every actor is different. Phyllis Logan [who played Mrs Hughes] had an impressively complex notation system of colours and stickers which I always admired. I would just write on the front the page numbers of my scenes so I could find them easily. I also had a notebook in which I would write a summary of the journey of Mrs Patmore through an episode. I would note down all my scenes and what happened in them so I would always have an understanding of order, so you could then play a scene out of continuity. Nothing is ever shot in order in television so knowing what happened before and what comes after is important. Where am I on this journey? What has already happened? What do I know at this point? Those were the big questions for me. There is never any chronological logic to filming for television, at least in my experience. It is all based on other factors about set and actor availability and so on. Sometimes you might be filming two episodes at once, which is even more of a sequential challenge, because a lot can happen in an episode, so you need to know where you are. I remember Julian saying at the start to the core cast: 'I am going to have to ask you to be responsible for your character's journey. Even if you are not speaking, know where you are in the story because we will notice if you do not.' I made sure that I did that.

What did rehearsal mean for an actor on Downton Abbey?

For us in the kitchen, those technical aspects that I mentioned about time of day and what we were doing were very important. We would come on set and have a line run. The director would then block it and tell you where you needed to be at each point and where the cameras would be. All this would be quick. If you had a character question, that could be voiced then, but you were aware that there was never much time to have an in-depth conversation about character. A lot of the time, the discussions were around the choreography of the scene. You then do a run for the crew so they can figure out sound and lighting, for example. You then go away whilst the set is lit for half an hour or so. If the scene is a tricky one, you might run it again more informally with the other actors in that time. The cast on *Downton* was incredibly supportive as a collective so if you had a challenging scene people would sit with you and run it for as long as you needed. If something needed discussion, that would happen then, and we all felt very comfortable making suggestions with one another but often it was clear from the script alone. Then you would go back and shoot it. So the space for an acting rehearsal was sparse.

It was more about technical rehearsal where you could voice any character concerns quickly if you had them. I have been asked in the past if we
ever improvised – absolutely not. The job was to deliver the lines accurately and if you didn't then you would be told.

One thing that was a challenge, and the historical advisor helped here
too, was that, as Mrs Patmore and Daisy became closer, you had to be
increasingly aware of physical and emotional contact that was appropriate for the period. If there was an emotional exchange, for instance, you
had to fight the urge to hug each other. Physical contact in general was
pretty much off-limits so you had to be mindful of the period and how
people expressed themselves at that time. As you became more familiar
with one another, as characters and actors, you had to fight against those
modern expressions of intimacy and affection in front of the cameras,
because that was not how it was in that period.

Are there demands on an actor that are specific to period television work?

I think those specific demands are largely about period accuracy. However,
if the writing is good – and Julian was impeccable on his period knowledge – and you have support there in terms of the historical advice, then
a lot of the work is already done for you as an actor. None of us actors
went into *Downton* as experts on the period but you are guided in the
right direction by the workings of the production – the scripts, the historical advisor, the costumes, the sets and so on. Also, as you live it and
get immersed in it, it becomes easier.

Beyond Downton, *what were the key things you learnt from your previous
and extensive television work in supporting or guest roles?*

I learnt that it is far more difficult to enter a long-running production
as a visiting actor and so, on *Downton*, we made sure that visitors felt
as welcomed and comfortable as possible. It is a daunting thing to be a
visitor because if things are going well it is like walking into a family that
you are not part of and that is challenging. It is hard to turn up and nail
a scene with very little time, surrounded by strangers who all know each
other already and have their pre-established working patterns. For me,

having experienced that visitor perspective, being on *Downton* for the whole run and knowing the entire crew was a real luxury. If you were not sure about something technical, you could ask, because you got to know people. As a visitor or early on in a production, you do not always have the confidence to ask technical questions about how close the camera is on you, for example. Working with people for prolonged periods makes that communication easier. If you are only there for a day, however, your job is more simply not to screw up. There is never time to mess up. I have seen that happen – when someone has not got a handle on their lines and it is mortifying to watch. If you are a visiting actor, that is your worst nightmare. If you are working with people all the time, they know you and respect you, and you would be supported if you made a mistake, but as a visitor it is very different. As an actor you are being judged every single day you work. In my line of work, people will accept practically anything about you as a person, whatever your age, sexuality, religion, politics and so on, nobody cares, as long as you come prepared and you can act. That is the bottom line. If people know you are good, they will take care of you, no question.

Is there anything you wish you had been told about working in television before you started?

Anyone of my generation, trained or not, was not trained for television. I was trained at Guildhall and it just was not happening in the 1970s. It probably took me years to figure out what I was actually doing with my television work. I was awful! I had done a lot of theatre and that is what drama school trained you for but television is such a different ball game, and I had no idea. That is one of the reasons that *Downton* has been such a joy because I have had the confidence to ask people technical things that I have never really been clear about for television because I was never taught those things and I did not previously have the courage to ask, as a visiting actor. I am still learning and that is the way it should be I suppose. On a long-running show, you have that space to watch things back and learn from your mistakes. I know some actors will never watch themselves. I cannot understand that. I know anyone watching them-selves is bound to be critical and you will be watching yourself, which you should not really be doing, because the scene is not just about you, but that is human nature. However, watching still makes sense to me because that is your work and you can learn from it. I loved watching *Downton* and sometimes the cast and crew all watched it together which was lovely.

It is hard to remember what I did learn at drama school. I was 17, leaving the North-West and going to London. It was about growing up, first and foremost. I am sure I learnt some useful techniques and skills there but you also learn a great deal afterwards, on the job. The bottom line in any acting work is to convince people that you are not acting.

One thing that I know they do now at ArtsEd [Arts Educational Schools] in London is to get the actors to work as a crew, doing camera, continuity or sound, for example. I think that is wonderful. Not only do you get an insight as an actor into what the different departments do but also you learn to respect their work, just through that little glimpse. It reinforces that idea that you are all a team working together on something. For everyone, the hours are brutal, and in the US it is even more extreme, and people are stretched to their limits. The crew are in there every single day. That is rare for actors, even if you are the lead, so you have got to respect that and help each other out where you can. For instance, do not throw your costume on the floor; hang it up, because not to is disrespectful and creates extra work for others.

Are there differences between theatre, film and television in terms of challenges for an actor?

I suppose the core things in investigating a character and their arc and presenting that as accurately as you can are the same but the energy levels required are different. I was in *Mamma Mia* in the West End for two years and doing eight shows a week, four of which are over two days, is a big deal for your stamina. You might be working long hours in television but there is a different energy required. For example, working in theatre you need to wake up every morning and check you have a voice. If you do not then you need to tell somebody. Television does not require the same things from your vocal equipment. So there are different demands on your tools as an actor, day-to-day.

What is the difference between a 'good' director and a 'bad' director in television, from an actor's perspective?

Some television directors are really skilled and focused on the technical side, and so are more interested in the shots than what the actor is doing. That can be frustrating for an actor if you need some direction, and I am sure it can be frustrating for them too because they do not really know how acting works so they cannot really advise in that sense, or they are not interested in doing so. Sometimes in television the director's focus is on making things look beautiful and hoping the actors can figure out the rest for themselves. The perfect combination is a director who has the technical ability but also has an interest in the acting, and can suggest possibilities for you to explore. That is bliss. We have not got very long to do anything in television so suggestions and discussions are always welcome, if it helps to make things better. Also, as an actor, your confidence is a delicate thing, and so a mutual sensitivity and trust with a director is always valuable. However, on a long-running show, directors come and go but you are there all the time. So, in that sense, sometimes it is your job to make them feel comfortable. We are all human and feel the need to be accepted.

Jack Farthing

Telephone interview, 3 May 2016

Trained at the London Academy of Music and Dramatic Art (LAMDA), Jack Farthing left his studies early when he was spotted and cast as Benvolio in Shakespeare's Globe's 2009 production of *Romeo and Juliet*. Since then, Farthing has become an established name across stage and screen, playing George in the 2014 film adaptation of Laura Wade's play *The Riot Club* (dir. Lone Scherfig) and appearing in a range of British television dramas and comedies such as *Dancing on the Edge* (BBC 2013), *Silk* (BBC 2011–2014), *Cilla* (ITV 2014), *Blandings* (BBC 2013–2014) and *Pramface* (BBC 2012–2014). In this interview, Farthing reflects upon his latest television role as George Warleggan, the central antagonist in the BBC's BAFTA-award-winning period drama *Poldark*.

How did you initially become involved in Poldark?

Mammoth Screen, the company who make *Poldark*, also made *Blandings*, in which I played Freddie Threepwood. They're a company with a wide range of production interests, and they have made a number of period pieces for television. So they were aware of me because of my earlier work on *Blandings*, and it was the same, wonderful executive producer, Damien Timmer, heading up *Poldark*. I went through the audition process, initially auditioning for the character of Francis [eventually played by Kyle Soller] and then I was asked to audition for the character of George as well. Ultimately, they wanted me for George. I read as George with Aidan Turner [who plays Ross Poldark] and Heida Reed [who plays Elizabeth Chenoweth], as they had already been cast, and I suppose they wanted to see how we worked as a combination, and then I was offered the part of George. It was a funny one though because I really wasn't expecting to be right for George. I thought Francis was far more likely for me in casting terms, I think because I hadn't played an out-and-out villain before, although I'm now hesitant to refer to George in those terms anyway, as he's far more complex than that, as I soon learnt. There's also the description of George in the source novels that isn't at all like me, whereas I thought I could fit more with the description of Francis in the books. That was my gut feeling. However, I have done this a couple of times now where I've thought I wasn't right for something and then it's been the thing that's worked out. It sometimes makes me think that others must see somebody very different to the person I see in myself! Often, you're not able to judge fully how you come across to others, and you have to rely upon the perspective and the judgement of those people making these shows to see something in you. I was so lucky, because Mammoth had seen me do this one particular thing with the character of Freddie in *Blandings*, something comedic and odd and a world away from my *Poldark* character, and I was fortunate that they had the open-mindedness to see me in a very different light and as capable of doing something really different, something which I wasn't even convinced of myself at that moment. Often with television, actors are put in boxes and it's easier just to keep them there, so it was a real gift for Mammoth to say 'try this' and for me to have realised that it worked for me.

Have you since discussed with the production team what they initially wanted in George as a character?

I think Mammoth wanted something quite double-sided for George, to be more than just a villain, in that he's got this poor lineage that he's managed to paint over with money and the artifice of aristocracy. He is still somebody making a real effort to appear to be somebody else. So I think the production company wanted a smoothness and iciness to him, rather than a physicality like Ross. The meticulousness of George's clothes and his hair are an expression of who he wants to be rather than who he is in his DNA. There's a conflict within him but, in trying to leave his heritage behind, he's a shrewd and devious money-maker who often has to make ruthless decisions to achieve his goals. He has his own vulnerabilities and insecurities like any of us, and so seeing him as just a villain is to ignore all of that, and I probably didn't see all of that when I initially looked at the character in the books. Also, it's always fun to play someone who's pretending to be something they're not or who's hiding something. So much of being an actor is about pretending or about look or presentation, and so it's interesting when the character also chimes with those things that you're facing as an actor on set and in the hours before you're filming and you're getting yourself ready. George also goes through those things in his world. His life is a gruelling performance of sorts. He's desperate to sound right and appear right to his audience.

Is it important to find points of empathy and understanding, even with the most dubious of characters, in order to find a route into playing them?

Definitely. I think it's very hard to play someone who you've judged and categorised as something in advance. I think the point of us all is that we're not just one thing. We behave surprisingly and we are different things to different people. To assume that characters would be any different would be a simplification, and a reduction of possibilities for an actor. Also, when you have novels by Winston Graham and scripts by Debbie Horsfield, that complexity is already there on the page. George's villainy is clearly part of him but it's not something that feels alien to me. It is the end product of thoughts that we might all have. He's resentful, he's insecure, he's vulnerable, and he's proud – feelings with which we're all very familiar. So it's unhelpful for me to think of George as a villain because that means that I have to 'play bad', which I think is useless for an actor, and impossible to do well. It's much more interesting to play real motivation. For all George's moments of moustache twirling he also has moments of surprising depth – these windows into him that you don't expect, such as the way that he behaves when he's with Elizabeth. I like embracing those surprises and contradictions.

Interestingly, in the books George has a living father as well as an uncle. For various reasons, in our adaptation it's just an uncle. In the books, the father, Nicholas, is very moral, whereas George's uncle [played by Pip Torrens in the BBC adaptation] is far more crooked. So, in the source books, George is in between and taking from both. In the absence of his father in our version, the way I've played it is that George's father's voice is still very much in his head, even though we never see his father on screen. I'm not sure if I've ever discussed these things with Debbie but I very much think that George would much rather win over Ross Poldark fairly. That sophistication of character is definitely there in the script. He doesn't necessarily want to cheat to win. And playing that complexity in George is far more satisfying than playing him as just an underhand villain.

After casting, what were the next stages you went through in preparing for the role?

I had a couple of months from being cast to filming starting, and I think I was able to see six scripts out of the eight episodes from Series 1, although these would inevitably change somewhat during the filming. The way we're working things currently is that one series roughly corresponds to two of the books but before we started I had read the first four books, just because they sweep you along so quickly and, although our story is all there in the scripts, these books are an absolute treasure trove of detail. Graham was so meticulous in the way he wrote about the time and the locations. It's useful to find little details that you can hang on to and it's also of value in getting a grasp on the historical context. So I had the books and the scripts that I pored over until we got to filming.

Is character research important to you, particularly for period work?

Yes. Alongside reading the books and the scripts, I started doing some preliminary research before filming began – reading contextual things and finding pictures. I like finding paintings of the period, which are all about poise and pose, which is especially useful for George and his performance of gentility, in thinking about how people felt they were best presented at that time. I read a very useful book called *Lord Chesterfield's Letters to His Son*, which is a series of letters written in the mid-eighteenth century by a nobleman to his illegitimate son, instructing him on how to be a gentleman, which was gold for me in thinking about how someone, like my character, might learn to be a gentleman as opposed to being born into it. A lot of it is about observing people and never revealing too much emotion, which certainly fed into my work on George. We also have a great historical advisor on *Poldark*, who we met after the read-through and she pointed us in the right directions. I've also watched so many films depicting that period.

Do you have any rituals of preparation in getting ready for any role?

I think I just like to immerse myself in the world of the character and learn as much as I can. I like to feel as though I have a broad grasp on the context and the look of the time. The research for me is always an exercise in making myself feel as little a fraud as possible. I like the idea that, if suddenly something was changed in the script, I'd have a handle on it. Obviously there's very little improvisation in period drama but I like to think that my mind is present enough to deal with anything that might come my way, and for that I need to feel comfortable in the world of the story. That's why it's nice to have research time in advance so you can do all that stuff before and then have it all in there, not necessarily consciously, and not that you always refer to it, but it's there. Clearly you have to be in the scene and play the moment and be present, rather than think about that painting you saw, but it's there in the background. One thing I always do is I have a notebook that I fill with stuff, like passages from *Lord Chesterfield's Letters* or little pictures or instructions I've found on how to take snuff. That way, I have all these little details to refer to without trawling back through all that preliminary research. Often I won't even look at it but I always take it with me!

Did you have any preliminary discussions with the writer or other members of the production team in advance of filming starting?

I don't think we had any substantial discussions until after the read-through. The audition process was relatively lengthy and they'd put a lot of thought and preparation into that. So, by the time I was in the room with the other cast members, we were having conversations about character and character relationships that would stand. We had the initial read-through of all the scripts which was useful in some ways and useless in others, as things inevitably change when you're actually filming. Then we had a few days to talk with our first-block director, Ed Bazalgette, and Debbie Horsfield. That was useful, to confirm things that we'd already discussed at earlier stages and to make sure that relationships were clear and that nobody had any remaining questions unanswered. There were never any big question marks to resolve or issues to wrestle with – it was just lovely to have that time to realise how full and complicated a writer's vision of your character is. Sometimes you don't get that time as an actor and you're left to your own devices. Debbie is a phenomenal writer and distils a huge amount into quite tight television scripts. It's valuable to learn her thought processes, in terms of what she's included and what she'd had to leave out, and I hound her probably more than most of the actors! She's amazingly available on email and I'm always asking her things. I think that level of communication is quite unusual. Debbie is also an executive producer on *Poldark*, which is helpful, in the sense that she's present, not always physically but emotionally and in her level of investment in the production in a creative sense. There are constant revisions to the scripts during filming. For example, the weather fails us so we have to move a scene indoors or scenes have to be amalgamated for whatever reason. So these things come up that you don't expect – suddenly you've moved geographically or an important line has been moved from one scene to another, and that means there are questions and clarifications that I feel I want from the horse's mouth. Debbie is amazing at that – I will send her a little email and she will send me back an A4 side of type, full of ideas and reasons and complications and new ideas. That's such a valuable resource for an actor.

Is working out of continuity in filming for television a challenge, in keeping a handle on your character and their journey through the story?

It certainly can be a challenge. We film in blocks. The second series of *Poldark* which we've just finished filming is ten episodes in three blocks, which is ten hours in just under seven months. The first block was Episode 1 to Episode 4, the second block was Episodes 5 to 8, and the third block was Episodes 9 and 10. We had a different director for each. The way it works is that the exteriors and interiors we then film in any order but staying within the block. There is some sequential stuff but then a lot of jumbling. That does make it challenging to try to get a handle on the path the character is taking. One of the things I do with any filming job is I write lots of notes to try to get a handle on the chronology. What you want is to not have to think about it, and you can do that if you've already answered the big questions about the journey, so that you know when you get to key points you're not going to be surprised by anything. You have to make sure that you've addressed all those questions in advance and have a really good grasp on the journey so that you can access those different stages out of sequence. At the same time, it is easy to get frustrated in that lack of continuity in filming and forget the work that the editing and the audience does. If you see a character in a scene following the scene at his mother's deathbed, the work is done. However the character is behaving, you know that his mother's just died. It's very rare when you're watching something that you question those things. So I think it's important not to get too fixated on it as an actor. I think the most important thing is being present in that moment in the scene and talking to the people you're performing with and listening to them.

Throughout this discontinuity in filming terms, are there constants about George as a character that you hold on to, to keep you centred and help you through?

There must be but possibly things I'm less aware of – I just rely on them instinctively. The clothes that he wears are hugely important because he's so defined by his performance of status. His clothes and his pose are markers of what drives him internally. There are ongoing discussions with the designer and all the wonderful people who work in wardrobe about costume details. I love talking to them about the details as part of the process. For example, the props team whilst filming recently said that they had this Malacca cane and so we talked about when might be appropriate to use it, in terms of the social contexts of certain scenes. I feel that those sorts of details are so defining for a character like George because everything about his appearance is so carefully selected. Nothing is without thought. So props and costume are really important constants for me, because they chime so much with George as a character, and I'm fortunate that these aspects of characterisation are a major concern in period drama. Locations are also very significant to me. We filmed the first scenes in a location called Chavenage House in the Cotswolds, which was the location for Chenoweth – Francis and Elizabeth's house – and, forever after, going there feels very *Poldark*! It's an environment that has become so closely linked for me to that world and the world of my character. To be presented with those period sets and locations as a living world, transformed with such precision, is a massive credit to the art departments involved, and is so useful for an actor. To get everything accurate for the period and to choreograph lavish banquets, for example. An astonishing level of detail goes into furnishing this world for the story, only a small fraction of which you see on screen in the end. Those aspects of the performance in these dramas deserve far more recognition. As an actor, nothing beats walking onto a period set and feeling that it's real and that you've been transported somewhere. Nothing else can give you that same sense of context for your performance, so I think it's a huge advantage for an actor. On the other hand, creating these detailed, multifaceted environments takes longer to film than a contemporary piece. That can be a challenge because you're tied to a world for long periods that isn't entirely familiar. It can change how spontaneous and open you feel you can be because, to an extent, you have to remain within the parameters of historical accuracy. Also, on a TV period drama, there's probably less time for everyone to do what they need to do, actors included, because the art department needs longer, wardrobe needs longer, hair and make-up need longer between takes and so on, because of the need to maintain that sense of period. So it's more work for everyone involved. Ultimately, the most important thing has to be the story but period accuracy plays a huge part in making that story credible. Whilst I would say that, if your priority is historical accuracy, you should go to a museum rather than watch a drama, it is still very important and has to be taken seriously.

Are you self-critical in watching the final product on screen and recognising scenes that were filmed earlier as opposed to later in the production process?

I am certainly guilty of that. I can always pick out the first scene I've shot. It is pure actor's neurosis – nobody watching would pick up on that! It probably does get easier but I do still find it very difficult watching things back and not focusing on what I perceive as the negatives of my performance, and imposing my own hang-ups on what I see. Although, I suppose if I ever sit back and say, 'That was brilliant' then I'm probably done for!

What does rehearsal mean for an actor on a production like Poldark? *How long do you have and what would be prioritised?*

The initial read-through process on the second series was eight episodes in two days. We read 1 to 4 on day one and then 5 to 8 on day two. We didn't read through Episodes 9 and 10 because they were still being polished up until the point we started filming, so we decided just to roll with it. We have little time for rehearsal in a traditional sense. You have the initial read-through, subsequent chats, and then – say we're starting filming first thing – we'll have hair and make-up done in the morning, then to wardrobe to get completely ready. You go to set, by which time the director will be there and will have refreshed themselves on what they think this scene should be. We'll read the lines and then we'll go over where the action will take place, under an archway, for example, with brief discussion about whether or not we think this will work from a performance point of view. You then have one run through, just to make sure it works. If it's all good, the crew is then called in for a crew rehearsal, in which we run through again with all the crew present, for them to see if they can capture things on camera from all the angles that they require. We then go away for a short period, they light it, and then we return and shoot it. However, if it is a very complicated scene, we'll be given more time. I don't just mean technically complicated: fight scenes will be given more time but also, for example, in the series we've just filmed, there were storylines that required a great deal of sensitivity because of their subject matter, and so they were afforded more time. The standard scene, though, is very much, 'Run through the lines, run through the blocking, and get a camera on it.'

Would more rehearsal time be a blessing or a curse?

You could see it both ways. For me, the more time you have helps to try different things and to get things wrong and experiment. There are definitely, however, circumstances when you know how the scene needs to go and you want to retain its spontaneity. In those situations, it's useful to keep that initial fiery, sparky thing, which can be bled out through lengthy rehearsal. With a play you're rehearsing and then you go home in the evening and have time to reflect and digest, to then go back the next day, and that's lovely. When you rehearse for camera, however, you're rehearsing to then do it, which can tire the muscles through repeating. If you over-rehearse comedy, for instance, it can be catastrophic because you can completely lose what's required, that freshness, through repetition.

Would you have more informal conversations with other cast members in advance of filming scenes?

When appropriate, for sure. Sometimes there isn't time to do that on set so it might occur later, over dinner, for example. The great thing about *Poldark* is that we've developed a wonderful company of people who are all mates, so it's very easy to ask someone if we can have a quick run through some lines before the next day, to get their opinion on something I'm not quite sure about. There's a lot of that. Also, the more you work with people, the more you can predict how they will approach something, actors and directors included, and so everything becomes quicker. You do develop a shorthand.

Did the very famous, earlier BBC adaptation of Poldark *play any part in your performance decisions? Did you go back and watch any of that?*

No, not at all. I think most of us actors actively avoided thinking about that too much because, of course, you want to offer your own take on the characters and the story. If anything, you want to look at the source novels rather than an earlier adaptation. We had the books and Debbie's scripts and her fresh ideas about them, and that's what excited us all. It'd be interesting though, I'm sure. I probably should watch it but it's a product of very different era of television and so, for my work, it's not particularly relevant or helpful really.

Are there things you wish you'd been told about working in television before you started working in television?

When I started auditioning for television, I think I had a notion of what I thought I should be doing which actually turned out to be wrong. I only started figuring out what worked when I started thinking about characters for television in exactly the same way as I thought about characters for the theatre. There's the same level of preparation. A lot is made of the differences between theatre and screen acting – and of course there are differences – but it's nothing more than differences of focus. I really don't think that there's a grand dramatic shift in what it is to be an actor for television. But I think I thought there was, initially. So maybe I wish I'd been told just to go into auditions and do what I felt was natural and right for the character, as opposed to some sort of televisual equivalent. To see a disconnect between the largely theatrical training that goes on in British drama schools and what actors do on screen is wrong, in my view. The main difference for me, in acting for screen, is that you have to do most of the work yourself, independently, in advance of the performance itself. You don't have a rehearsal room and a director and other actors to shape things with, and that's the major difference from theatre. Certainly, that independent work is hard, and being able to work on those things collectively is one of the major luxuries of doing a play – the time and the space and having everyone there to exchange ideas. In terms of the way that you approach a character, break down a character, look at a script, break down a script and ultimately present a performance – those elements are all essentially the same. Both on stage and on screen, you're ultimately trying to present something as natural, as convincing, or as least fraudulent, as possible.

How useful was it to work with very talented television actors so early on in your career, as part of a learning process?

Very. Even just to observe them, not necessarily discuss things with them about what was right and wrong, but just to watch them do their thing and to see that their points of focus were was massively helpful. The most valuable learning process is simply to be there and to watch and to do it. On every show I've done I've been lucky to work with people who have a wealth of experience about what it is to be an actor, in whatever medium. It's really important to remain open and alert to what those people are doing and to take from that what you can.

Is there such a thing as a 'good director' or 'bad director' for television, from an actor's perspective?

I think every actor requires something different, in terms of attention, feedback or compliments. Every actor is aligned with slightly different degrees of interference or assistance. I think my requirements change from show to show. Sometimes I feel under-served by a director and other times I can feel smothered but I don't think I have a consistent set of requirements. Generally, I think probably I prefer to talk more rather than less because I never fully trust what I'm doing so I like dialogue. If you can develop that dialogue and really feel in safe hands with that director then you can really go for it. You know that they have the show, the story and your interests at heart.

Are you conscious as an actor of different 'modes' of performance for different television genres?

I think, as a viewer, it's apparent that there are. You can tell that there are clear differences in tone between different types of television drama. However, I think that probably comes from the script rather than from any discussion with or amongst the actors involved. Everything you read you have a gut response to and feel that you have a handle on what it should be. Following that, the first week of filming is then a process of watching people and getting a read on their take of it all, and perhaps subconsciously attuning to one another to make sure you're all broadly the same track. Largely, though, I think it's the job of the writer and the director to establish the tone. It seems to me that the actors are required to try to serve the truth of what's on the page, and it's then up to the people operating outside of those performances to calibrate the tone and to offer the actors guidance accordingly. The writer and director are the outside eyes and so best positioned to do that. It's hard for an actor to be aware of broader tone in that way, because you're focused instead on your character and on motivations, wants, wishes and thoughts. I think all I can do is make it as real as possible and then the job of the director is to tinker with that and bring the levels up or down as befits the tone.

Siân Phillips

York, 6 June 2016

Awarded a CBE in 2000 and a DBE in 2016 for her services to drama, Siân Phillips has worked in television since she was 17, with an acting career on stage and screen spanning over 60 years. Phillips studied at the Royal Academy of Dramatic Arts (RADA) in the 1950s, professionally experiencing the evolution of British television drama from its live origins to present-day digital developments. In this interview, Phillips offers insights into the acting challenges of early live-transmission television, whilst also considering her work on two celebrated BBC period dramas: *Shoulder to Shoulder*, a serial exploring the history of the women's suffrage movement, in which Phillips plays Emmeline Pankhurst; and *I, Claudius*, for which Phillips won the 1977 BAFTA Television Award for Best Actress and Royal Television Society Award for Best Performance in the role of Roman Empress Livia Drusilla.

Could you offer some insights into what working in early, live-transmission television drama was like?

I was 16 when I first started acting professionally. At that age one is pretty fearless – nothing gets to you. In that period very few people had a television set, so you felt that nobody was watching and judging you when you worked on television. Even my mother and father did not have a television set, so you did not feel a sense of mass observation and scrutiny. It was a far more small-scale affair in those early years. It seems to me that this phase of live television went on for a long time, but then of course everybody had a television set after the Queen's coronation; they all bought one to watch the coronation. So then, suddenly, you would walk down the street the morning after you had been on television and people recognised you. By that point, it was quite a thing to be on television. However, I still didn't find it scary because there was so much hysteria in the studio. Rather than nerves, you would get quite euphoric, quite high on it, and I think that is what I really loved about it. The energy and spontaneity of live performance. It was so different from film; as it was live it was so exciting.

One of the major challenges at the start of my career was that these early live plays on television were not actually written for television. They were West End successes from a decade before and they were just brought in, chopped up, and you just played the acts of the play for the cameras. I was in a television version of play called *Granite* [BBC 1958] by Clemence Dane, which even then seemed dated. I was in a scene with Donald Pleasence and my character had to get a candlestick and smash the window with it at one point. The floor managers told me not to worry as it was sugar glass. They told me that everything would be fine. As we were performing live, I smashed it and of course they had not put sugar glass in the window, and I pulled my hand back and there was blood everywhere. It just went on pouring out for the rest of the play. Blood on the set, blood on my clothes, blood everywhere. When you are faced with dramas like that, you don't care what people are thinking, you simply try get through it. *Granite* is a play that goes through the seasons – spring, summer, autumn and winter – four seasons across four acts. You have to do all your costume changes on the studio floor as you had no time to go and change. You would finish your scene, run off, and the dresser would start to rip your costume off you. My dresser started to put my winter clothes on as we were about to go into the act set in the summer. I was silently trying to tell her that she had got it wrong whilst she was jamming me into the winter costume. But I lost the battle and I walked back towards the set where everybody was dressed in their summer costumes. I had to stay like that, in my overcoat, galoshes and hat for the rest of the act. You are beyond worry as there is nothing you can do in that moment.

Live broadcast in this period, before what we now call the 'Golden Age', was very challenging. For example, I appeared in *Strangers in the Room*, an Armchair Theatre production in 1961, with Wilfrid Lawson, Donald Houston and Richard Pasco. We had a scene standing around at a cocktail party. We were on the air and we realised that they needed to start striking the set to prepare for the next scene during the one we were currently performing. We had never rehearsed it. I was talking to Donald Houston, I think, and we were chatting away in this party scene and I saw two stagehands crawling towards us. They took the table away and so every time I put the glass down a stagehand would hold it out of shot. Then, you see, there was a point when we had to sit down. We just had to half squat! These were the kinds of challenges that you were dealing with day-to-day as an actor in early live television.

However, things had not wholly improved in what we now call the 'Golden Age'. I remember that I was rehearsing a show called *Women Can Be Monsters* [ITV 1968] written by Ernest Gébler. We were in the middle of rehearsals when a strike was called and we were told that we were not going to do the play. However, out of the blue I was called about a week later and told that we would perform the play – and that it would be recorded that night. I had no costume, so I dressed myself from my own wardrobe. As a cast, we had no idea what we were doing as we had never had a camera rehearsal. The cameraman said to me: 'Siân, if you know where the next set-up is, you go and I'll follow you, and if I know, then you follow me.' That is an indication of the adaptability required of a television actor during this period.

Would there generally be a rehearsal period for early television work?

Yes. It was a very different industry from television today. We rehearsed for television like we did for a stage play. It would not be in as much depth, but it was the same kind of process in terms of an acting rehearsal.

For example, even as late as *Heartbreak House* [BBC 1977], we had about a month to rehearse. For *Platonov* [BBC 1971] with Rex Harrison, we had around seven weeks, because Rex had never done television before and did not understand the process, so he needed a bit more time. He was such a catch for the BBC to have, they gave him as long as he needed. These rehearsals were largely based around character and story discussion as opposed to technical rehearsals, unlike today's television rehearsals.

How is television work different from film or theatre for an actor?

Television is very fast. By contrast, shooting for film seems terribly slow – every shot is composed, the lighting is arranged, your mark is arranged. Even the loosest kind of movie is so carefully considered and constructed that you may do 30 takes before it is accepted as what the director wants. On television, you need to behave as though it is film but it is not. This is why you have to concentrate so hard – it has the integrity of film but the speed of television. You are not supported in the way that you are when you are doing a movie. There are so many distractions on television so it becomes about your own work and your own concentration. In many ways it is a process of dissatisfaction, and you have to get used to this. You have to accept that you might feel dissatisfied, but because there is so little time, you have to move on. Theatre is an actors' medium. When the curtain goes up, the actors are the ones who are responsible. You feel the differences particularly keenly when you are working on theatre adaptations for television. When you combine theatre and television you are really at the sharp end as an actor. You are combining the industry structures of television with the integrity and responsibility for telling the story that you associate with theatre. In television it is not only your responsibility, however. The mechanics of the production are also working with you.

You were working in television before you trained at RADA. Was it more challenging because of a lack of formal training at that time?

RADA did not train you in television at all. I think that most actors will automatically adapt, though. It is interesting; I had this discussion with some actors on the job that I am working on currently. We were discussing the fact that there are some actors who are wonderfully eccentric on stage and give virtuoso performances (whether or not their performance sinks the play) but when these actors work on television, it looks too big. You can see that they are acting. That is the one thing that you cannot be seen to be doing on television: acting. So this set us thinking, what is it that you have to do? We all agreed that the one thing that the camera always picks up is whether or not you are thinking. If the camera is on you then something has to be going on – it can be seen if it is not. You have to know what you are thinking otherwise it is dead. It is a very difficult thing. It can look like you are doing nothing but you need to have a very intense relationship with the camera. It is about circles of concentration. In a theatre your circle can be vast, it can reach to the edge of the lights, to the edge of the stage, or into the back of the auditorium. In television it is much, much smaller, but it is very intense. Radio is a hot medium – you need to add warmth and colour to everything. Television is a cool medium. It has to be brought right down but you still need to feel that intensity.

Performing a theatre play on television is completely different from live recordings of plays within the theatre and we should not confuse those two things. In the theatre, you are projecting to the back of thousand seats. I do not like it when people film stage performances. Frantic Assembly do it all the time. It is one of the only things that I do not like, because the type of performance is so different. If I was working with a camera I would not be projecting my performance to the back of a thousand-seater theatre. I dislike that but everybody does it now. I get very anxious when I know there is a camera somewhere and I am delivering my lines to the back of the theatre.

What is your personal approach to working with a television script?

Well I do learn it. I understand that some actors prefer just to have the gist of it so that it leaves you just on the edge of a precipice. I do not think that I can do that, so I really do have to learn it properly. However, I do try and stay as open as I can, because if you completely plan your performance before you arrive at the studio, you invariably find that the director has had a contradictory plan and you can get rather upset when your idea is dismissed. So I try not to plan too much out. I know the script inside out and I know what my character is doing but within that I try to leave myself open to making decisions on the floor. The important thing to remember is that only the director has the overall context and so some of his or her decisions are based on this and, as an actor who has not seen the whole process, I have to go with the wider view that they can take on a production. So, preparation but also openness.

To move more specifically to period television drama, how much period research did you do for something like Shoulder to Shoulder *as an actor?*

Oh well that was a wonderful experience. The BBC at that time committed a lot of time to development and research. You went into the rehearsal room and there was a long trestle table with a host of books, swatches of fabric and so on. It was a big rehearsal room and the trestle table ran the whole length of it. The project was about the suffragettes and none of us knew anything about them at the outset. We were offered so much information – details about eating and drinking, political pamphlets, and all the reference books you might need there on the table. We must have become such bores! The script was excellent but we did so much research that we all became experts on our characters and we all wanted additional stories from their lives included in the script as a result.

Is that sort of historical research usual in television, as part of the production process for actors?

It depends on the project. The BBC always does that when they are producing anything historical. Sometimes actors don't want to delve too much into research though, and leave it more to the other departments. The costume department at the BBC is very good, so you always know you are going to look right with them (down to the buttons – it will be right, the jewellery – it will be right). That is a great help, and it gives one a lot of confidence. For example, Livia in *I, Claudius* – very little is known about Livia. I did no research. I let the costume department do their job – their own research, I let the make-up people do their research, and the wig department do theirs. I was playing a character in a play by one person, Jack Pulman, freely adapted from a novel written by another, Robert Graves, freely adapted from history! So I figured that all I could do was play Jack Pulman's story, which is a bit of a Jewish comedy. But the costume department had been working on it for about a year. Everything had been researched endlessly and was ready to go. At other times, as with the suffragettes in *Shoulder to Shoulder*, as actors we got fascinated by the politics of the period and I think on the whole that interest paid off in the performances and in the final version of the story.

For something like I, Claudius, *how far in advance did you have access to the scripts for each episode, and how did you approach that style of performance?*

Oh we had the scripts way in advance, and they did not change. Jack Pulman had written a wonderful series of scripts. Although, when we first worked on it, on the first episode, we just could not get it right. All of us wanted to do too little acting, we wanted to do our television technique. And the director, Herbert Wise, said, 'No, no, no!' He said, 'I will tell you how it has to work.' He said, 'Listen to me whilst I talk. It has to be big. It is very definite. It is very bold and it is up there and that is it, and I do not want any discussion.' As actors, we found that very difficult because it worked against the 'cool' way of generally working on television that I explained earlier, in bringing it down from theatre. In the end they had to put Episode 1 and 2 together because Episode 1 was not strong enough to show by itself. So that was an example of not getting the style right for that particular drama. I could not work out what I was doing wrong but I knew it was not working. I talked to Herbert about it. Once I realised that it was basically a family drama and the family was squabbling, I understood what he was after. Essentially it was soap opera. From then on I did not have a problem.

Acting in Period Drama

Period research

The value of period information and understanding for television actors portraying historical characters is clear across this chapter's interviews. However, the ways in which such period research is facilitated, under-taken and subsequently incorporated into contexts of performance are varied and complex. Acknowledged by all interviewees are the efforts made within the formal mechanics of period television production to empower actors with historical information. Phillips confirms that useful historical information has been made readily available to actors working on BBC period productions for many decades, commenting of *Shoulder to Shoulder* in 1974:

> The BBC at that time committed a lot of time to development and research. You went into the rehearsal room and there was a long trestle table with a host of books, swatches of fabric and so on. It was a big rehearsal room and the trestle table ran the whole length of it … We were offered so much information – details about eating and drinking, political pamphlets, and all the reference books you might need there on the table … The script was excellent but we did so much research that we all became experts on our characters and we all wanted additional stories from their lives included in the script as a result.

In this instance, it is clear that extensive production provisions of historical information for actors emboldened the cast in terms of their creative interest and investment in their work, to the extent that they wanted to make 'authorial' contributions in narrative terms, putting their research to good use by suggesting story elements that would further enrich the lives of their characters. Indeed, this example stresses the ways in which providing production-appropriate knowledge to actors can enhance their sense of 'authorial' legitimacy and therefore desire for valuable creative collaboration. Equally, however, Phillips recognises instances in which actors may find it more beneficial not to 'delve too much' into period research, suggesting the ways in which excessive information may result adversely in inhibiting intuitive responses in the moment of the scene. Echoing the beliefs of actor interviewees working in police and medical dramas, ultimately the emotional journey of the story must supersede other factors of 'authenticity' for the television actor. Supporting this, Farthing asserts: 'Whilst I would say that, if your priority is historical accuracy, you should go to a museum rather than watch a drama, it is still very important,' but clarifying: '[T]he most important thing has to be the story … you have to be in the scene and play the moment and be present.' Thus, as within other forms of television drama production, 'authenticity' in period formats is important in so far as it provides a plausible narrative environment within which writers can create engaging human stories and actors can generate moments of emotional sincerity.

Such importance of historical information in embodying period characters is articulated by both Wilton and Nicol when they discuss the usefulness of historical advisor Alastair Bruce in informing their work on *Downton Abbey*. Discussing an initial 'tour' of the sets and locations during which Bruce offered the cast historical details, Nicol stresses: 'That was far more valuable than reading a book because it personalised it and brought the history alive in that environment in which we would be working.' For Nicol, the true value of historical detail for the actor is activated in the performative environment in which action and emotion will take place. For example, Nicol discusses the ways in which historical advice regarding servant hierarchy on set enabled further depth of characterisation and interaction amongst the ensemble: 'The advisor lined us all up, as the downstairs staff, in order or importance … Once you had a clear sense of that hierarchy, the relationships on the pages of the script started to become even richer.' Moreover, Nicol highlights how her intuitive emotional responses to scripted material were inflected by historical advice, in ways which informed the emotional nuances of character relationships over prolonged periods:

> One thing that was a challenge, and the historical advisor helped here too, was that, as Mrs Patmore and Daisy became closer, you had to be increasingly aware of physical and emotional contact that was appropriate for the period … you had to fight against those modern expressions of intimacy and affection in front of the cameras, because that was not how it was in that period.

Nicol's insights reveal a further layer of complexity to the dynamic between 'authenticity' and the work of the actor within a period production context. Whilst Nicol does not contradict the assertions of other actors that story and emotional embodiment of story must always take priority, she points towards the ways in which historical awareness can help to shape an actor's emotional responses to scripted material, in ways which they feel increases the sincerity of emotional expression for their character. Wilton compounds this in stating: '[T]he style of the era and the etiquette was central to the way that we spoke to each other and the sorts of relationships that you would have with people.' It is clear Wilton felt her understanding of the internal and external emotional life of her character, along with her character's relationships, was illuminated and enhanced substantially by an awareness of historical context, particularly given the long-form historical span of *Downton Abbey* and the resultant opportunities for character development as social and cultural values surrounding her character changed:

> Isobel Crawley is a moderniser. However, even then, there are emotions that she feels which she can't express. To modern sensibilities, there is a reserved-ness to her manner, which is shared by other members of society at that time ... Each historical period allowed her views to be developed. It made her a very interesting and rewarding character to play.

In addition to historical research components that constitute part of the formal production process for actors, personal actor research is indicated within the interview material. Farthing's discussion of his personal research in advance of filming Series 1 of *Poldark* is most revealing in this regard. Farthing indicates the ways that, in dealing with a literary adaptation, his preliminary reading of the source texts for *Poldark* both inhibited and benefited his work on characterisation. Initially considering the appropriateness of his casting for the character of George, Farthing states: '[T]he description of George in the source novels ... isn't at all like me, whereas I thought I could fit more with the description of Francis in the books.' Hence, Farthing's opening research impeded his access to character as opposed to assisting it, but in ways which he rapidly overcame: '[Y]ou have to rely upon the perspective and the judgement of those people making these shows to see something in you ... it was a real gift for Mammoth to say "try this" and for me to have realised that it worked for me.' Alongside such suggestions of initial creative obstruction or misapprehension of character suitability through personal research of the source texts, Farthing also expresses the ways in which such research offered substantial reward. Referring to Graham's novels as 'an absolute treasure trove of detail', Farthing acknowledges how such details in terms of period and location offered him elements to 'hang on to' in embodying the thoughts, emotions and actions of his character. Farthing offers a particularly enlightening example when referring to his character's deceased father, who is a voice of reason and morality for his son in Graham's novels but does not appear in the television adaptation: 'In the absence of his father in our version, the way I've played it is that George's father's voice is still very much in his head, even though we never see his father on screen.' By stressing that he has not discussed this with other members of the cast, crew or creative team, Farthing further signals the importance of personal actor research in generating complexity of characterisation, in ways which may never achieve explicit expression on screen, but which nevertheless contribute substantially to the psychological and emotional richness of the final performative text. Indeed, reinforcing the opinions of numerous other interviewees across the soap opera and police and medical drama case studies, Farthing isolates personal research as the key distinguishing factor of television work for an actor: 'The main difference for me ... is that you have to do most of the work yourself, independently, in advance of the performance itself.'

The nature of Farthing's independent research in the historical context of his work on *Poldark* is elaborate. Farthing shares the ways in which his extended consumption of books and paintings of the time, along with films depicting the period, furnished his supportive framework of understanding and command in portraying his character:

> I just like to immerse myself in the world of the character and learn as much as I can. I like to feel as though I have a broad grasp on the context and the look of the time ... That's why it's nice to have research time in advance so you can do all that stuff before and then have it all in there, not necessarily consciously, and not that you always refer to it, but it's there.

In a similar manner to Niamh Walsh's understanding of the 'totemic' value of the annotated shooting script in the context of medical drama production (Chapter 3), Farthing discusses his use of a research notebook: 'That way, I have all these little details to refer to without trawling back through all that preliminary research. Often I won't even look at it but I always take it with me!' As Farthing implies, the notebook is a tangible manifestation of his preliminary period research efforts and is therefore not only a useful point of reference in a pragmatic sense but also a valuable symbolic reminder to carry during production, representing his awareness of the historical contexts required for effective character work. Interestingly, although Farthing found it natural to refer to Graham's source novels as part of the research process for *Poldark*, he saw no value in watching any of the BBC's earlier iconic adaptation: 'I think most of us actors actively avoided thinking about that too much because, of course, you want to offer your own take on the characters and the story.' Here, Farthing stresses the ways in which related 'artefacts' can be consciously omitted from the actor's research process as well as actively selected. Forms of personal research deemed of particular use to Farthing for *Poldark* were those connected to 'poise and pose' – with period portraits proving helpful in this regard – along with period writing offering advice on etiquette and the 'performance of gentility'. The value of these research components related to the specific nature of Farthing's character, as a man not born to nobility but desperate to escape his humble heritage and to convince others he should be accepted as a gentleman. Here, Farthing's comments suggest that, whilst shared forms of historical research offered to actors by the formalised mechanisms of production are of value, it is not a 'one-size-fits-all' process. Instead, historical research can be of enhanced value when tailored to the peculiar demands of individual characterisation. These modes of more bespoke historical research, it seems, remain subject largely to the personal choice, incentive and labour of the individual period television actor: some may choose to actively seek out such details to inform their work (from a historical advisor or alternative source) whilst others may not.

Period costumes and sets

Closely connected to the utility of period research for the television actor is the significance of period costumes and sets as part of a historical performative environment established for their work. Indeed, as this chapter's interviews attest, not only do such production components contribute to the final *mise en scène* in terms of aesthetic appeal or historical plausibility, they are also powerful conditioning factors influencing an actor's embodiment of character and sense of place within a story. From the vantage point of textual reading, Cardwell argues: 'The audience is aware of the fact that the props are rarely "real", and that the costumes are modified to fit the body shapes of [today's] actors, not 1800s' people.' (2002, 88) In a similar vein, Nelson observes of the BBC's 1995 adaptation of *Pride and Prejudice* that '[t]he décolletage revealing Jennifer Ehle's ample bosom as Elizabeth Bennett ... has more perhaps to do with the anticipated viewing pleasures of a heterosexual male segment of the contemporary audience than Regency English manners' (2008, 51). Despite the ways in which certain production decisions regarding period costume can be interpreted as anachronistic concessions to present-day viewing pleasures in the analysis of end texts, this chapter's interviewees nevertheless stress the ways in which costumes can add to the work of the television actor within the period production process. For instance, both Wilton and Nicol identify costume as an important means through which they accessed a physical sense of character on *Downton Abbey*, with Wilton recognising:

> You had to have very good deportment – which was something that was dictated by the corsets that we wore in the early series. This was also true of the men. The starched front panel of their dinner shirts was a nod towards armoured breastplates and again meant that they sat up with a very straight back. You can imagine that this becomes quite a challenge when you are filming all day. But it also allows you to really embody the period.

This sense of embodiment of period through costume is compounded by Phillips's reflections on her characterisation of Livia in *I, Claudius*:

> [V]ery little is known about Livia. I did no research. I let the costume department do their job – their own research, I let the make-up people do their research, and the wig department do theirs ... the costume department had been working on it for about a year. Everything had been researched endlessly and was ready to go ... That is a great help, and it gives one a lot of confidence.

Here, Phillips acknowledges how thoroughly researched costume and make-up can act in a similar fashion to (or, in some cases, replace) personal period research in empowering actors to physically realise their characters in the moment of performance. In the absence of biographical details regarding her character, Phillips looked instead to the meticulous work of the wardrobe and make-up departments to provide a structure of support in giving credible physical form to Livia. Moreover, unlike the characterisation processes of soap operas and police and medical dramas considered previously, in which actor–character correspondence and continuity are most often of benefit, effective period work can necessitate a sense of disconnect from the actor's contemporary identity and sensibilities, internally and externally, which can be assisted through the use of costume. Supporting this, Wilton comments of period costumes: 'From an acting point of view, these help you to see the character as being distinct from you. It makes you stand in a different way, behave in a different way.'

For Farthing's work on *Poldark*, costume took on a heightened significance due to the nature of his character. As Farthing explains: 'The meticulousness of George's clothes and his hair are an expression of who he wants to be rather than who he is ... He's desperate to sound right and appear right to his audience.' In this instance, the external components of costume act as important 'markers of what drives [George] internally', offering Farthing a route for physicalising the psychological and emotional landscape that he had already mapped out for his character. Resultantly, Farthing takes particular interest in discussions with the production's design team:

> I love talking to them about the details as part of the process. For example, the props team whilst filming recently said that they had this Malacca cane and so we talked about when might be appropriate to use it, in terms of the social contexts of certain scenes. I feel that those sorts of details are so defining for a character like George because everything about his appearance is so carefully selected.

Therefore, as with period research, an actor's engagement with the design process for costume can enhance their sense of creative investment in a role, particularly when costume decisions can be logically linked to the complex internal life and motivations of a character. In Farthing's case, his character's social performance through exterior presentation offered a further dimension of understanding: 'So much of being an actor is about pretending or about look or presentation, and so it's interesting when the character also chimes with those things ... George also goes through those things in his world. His life is a gruelling performance of sorts.'

Image 8   Jack Farthing as George Warleggan in *Poldark*

Alongside the usefulness of costume in embodying period characters, this chapter's interviewees recognise the significance of elaborate period sets in affording them a valuable performative environment in which to operate. Both Nicol and Farthing emphasise the immersive qualities of the constructed period locations in which they worked, with Farthing stating:

> As an actor, nothing beats walking onto a period set and feeling that it's real and that you've been transported somewhere. Nothing else can give you that same sense of context for your performance, so I think it's a huge advantage for an actor.

Moreover, both Nicol and Farthing recognise that much of the intricate period detail incorporated into these constructed environments is never seen in the finished texts, but nevertheless serves effectively to furnish a rich narrative world in which they can most plausibly and sincerely bring their characters to life in the moment of performance. However, Farthing also highlights the inhibiting potential of such performative contexts in relation to an actor's freedom and confidence in exploring different options:

> [C]reating these detailed, multifaceted environments takes longer to film than a contemporary piece. That can be a challenge because you're tied to a world for long periods that isn't entirely familiar. It can change how spontaneous and open you feel you can be because, to an extent, you have to remain within the parameters of historical accuracy.

Hence, in a similar manner to the creation of medical environments discussed in Chapter 3, period sets provide actors with plausible conditions which facilitate a sincerity of emotion, action and response. Furthermore, as with long-running medical productions, the cumulative experience of inhabiting such environments over prolonged periods increases this sincerity, with Nicol noting: '[A]s you live it and get immersed in it, it becomes easier.' Yet, because of the extent of the production efforts which go into generating and maintaining these period environments (not only for reasons of historical 'authenticity' but also to uphold the pre-established aesthetic standards and expectations of these dramas as 'high-end' heritage products), actors can also feel consequent challenges in terms of creative freedom and spontaneity, as Farthing suggests. Moreover, whilst the set is frequently deemed as supportive to the actor's work, Wilton's observation that sets can be modified at any time to meet filming needs, with chairs being replaced by stools to achieve appropriate eye-lines for example, stresses that the primary support mechanism for the television actor within the moment of performance is always his or her fellow actors. Other performative components serve first and foremost the image eventually realised on screen, not necessarily the work of the actor, and are thus not 'set' (as in permanent) but rather can prove changeable depending upon the shifting technical demands of production. Associated challenges present themselves also at the more practical levels of production intensity and time investment, and the resultant physical and mental labour related to period work for the television actor:

> [O]n a TV period drama, there's probably less time for everyone to do what they need to do, actors included, because the art department needs longer, wardrobe needs longer, hair and make-up need longer between takes and so on, because of the need to maintain that sense of period. So it's more work for everyone involved. (Farthing)

Period technical skills

The aforementioned commodity status of British period television dramas as highly polished, stylised heritage packages with an international appeal is reflected in the level of technical proficiency required of actors working within the form. For both Wilton and Nicol, in addition to the more generic challenges associated with filming out of continuity for television, at the centre of their professional experiences on *Downton Abbey* were the particular and sophisticated technical skills demanded by the production sensibilities of the drama. Wilton notes, for instance, that *Downton Abbey*'s prevailing 'focus on the ensemble', often employing wide shots that capture multiple characters simultaneously, along with the visual spectacle of their surroundings, as opposed to closer shooting techniques such as those which dominate scenes in soap opera, entailed an intensified focus and an increased awareness of the work of others around her during shooting – not only other actors but also camera crew and sound operators. Referring to the complex choreography of the dining room and party scenes, Wilton identifies the need to be attuned both to intricate technical issues – such as not placing cutlery down on the table so that the noise would disrupt dialogue – to the broader flow of action between cast and crew: 'The actors playing the waiting staff, those eating, and the sound and camera crew all had to be tightly choreographed ... It is a complex dance involving many people and the rhythms have to be just right.' The importance of achieving such rhythms in filming is recognised equally by Nicol in her descriptions of shooting the kitchen sequences. Not only does Nicol stress the need to be able to map out and undertake, in limited time, 'credible kitchen activity, and then knowing how to replicate that activity multiple times', but also the requirement to be aware of narrative time of day and its impact upon the intensity of action, communication and jeopardy within the kitchen scenes for the actors involved:

> If it was just before an important dinner upstairs, things would be more intense and tempers would be heightened. If a scene was after an important dinner, the pace would change completely. So timing and the rhythms of the house governed, and that was about authenticity but it also affected characters and their relationships at particular moments.

Image 9 Lesley Nicol as Mrs Patmore in *Downton Abbey*

Within such complex and often fast-paced rhythms of filming, the need for an actor's strong command of character is paramount. For example, Wilton highlights that the short length of many of the scenes within *Downton Abbey* meant that 'you had to get straight to the heart of the scene. There was no time for warming into it. You had to know exactly what you wanted to do with it'. Similarly, referring to his work on *Poldark*, Farthing identifies the ways in which 'constant revisions to the scripts during filming' demand a high level of adaptability from actors, which comes from both personal command of their character and a trust in other cast and crew members that they have an equal command of their responsibilities within these shifting rhythms of production.

Indeed, this chapter's interviewees recognise the ways in which the heightened technical demands of period production often necessitate a marked reliance upon the abilities of other cast and crew members, in ways which further underscore the collaborative nature of television 'authorship'. Articulating this, Wilton states:

> [Y]ou need to rely on the other actor. You feel the intensity of this reliance and it is one of the most satisfying things about television work … It becomes like a dance, and when it works well, you can feel it … One of the huge benefits of working on *Downton Abbey* was that the camera and sound operators worked on the show for many years and so they were skilled at working quickly and precisely with the actors. We were all very used to working together on this dance and when it all comes together it is a very satisfying feeling.

Moreover, as with other modes of drama discussed in previous chapters, if long-form, the command of the actor within these collaborative relationships can supersede that of other technical and creative agents within the process – even the director – due to the actor's often greater level of attunement to the particular rhythms of the production. As Nicol observes: '[O]n a long-running show, directors come and go but you are there all the time. So, in that sense, sometimes it is your job to make them feel comfortable.'

Conclusion

This chapter has considered some of the key processes behind actors' contributions to the 'history effects' (Higson 2011, 231) of period television drama, along with their involvement in fulfilling the demands of such productions as heritage commodities for international consumption. In so doing, the chapter has added further depth of insight to Cardwell's valuable discussion of the 'past/present dichotomy' (2002, 92) of the period drama as performative text, by sharing and analysing the perspectives of period television actors concerning their work.

Historical research is revealed to be of value across this chapter's actor interviews as a means of informing characterisation and increasing creative investment in production. However, the methods employed by actors to access such historical insights, along with the forms of information found to be of use, are varied and complex. Significantly, the interview data indicates that the primary utility of historical research for the actor lies in its ability to further furnish the internalised and externalised emotional lives and relationships of characters, with Nicol stressing that the true value of historical information is triggered when it can be connected directly to the performative environment in which the actor works or to specific moments of action and exchange within a script. Moreover, Farthing's comments regarding his personal historical research for *Poldark* suggest that the production-wide mechanisms for providing historical information to period actors, whilst undoubtedly of great use, sometimes require more tailored additions to better suit the more particular needs of individual characters, and that such additional research is left largely to the discretion of the actor. Equally, the interview insights of this chapter imply that there are limits to the efficacy of historical information in performance contexts, and that research saturation can threaten to impede rather than enhance an actor's ability to respond intuitively and sincerely to the material in the moment of the scene. As with other forms of television drama considered in previous chapters, the psychological and emotional dimensions of character, relationships and story must ultimately take precedence in period production.

Period costume is indicated to be of significance in enabling actors to access an embodiment of character which feels sufficiently distinct from their contemporary experiences and therefore adds to their sense of authenticity in a role. Indeed, period costume literally changes the physical conditions of the actor's work, often inflecting the ways in which they stand and move, and tying the actor more closely to the presentational codes and conventions of the historical period being depicted. As Phillips indicates, in the absence of readily available historical information regarding a character, the extended research efforts of wardrobe and make-up can offer a worthy substitute because of their ability to establish a supportive framework of credible physical conditions for the actor through which to realise their work. Additionally, as Farthing's reflections attest, in the case of particular period roles, costume can assume an enhanced level of importance in characterisation, because of the ways in which appearance can function as an external signifier of internal character complexity. Revealed to be of equal significance for the period actor are the elaborately constructed sets and locations of production, allowing actors to immerse themselves in the environments of their characters. However, the intensive and extensive production schedules often demanded by such period performative contexts are shown to pose clear challenges as well as advantages for the work of the television actor.

Alongside such emphases upon historical understanding and authentic embodiment of period character is the interviewees' acute awareness of the 'high-end' technical demands of period production. These demands foreground the complex, skilled rhythms of cast and crew in the moment of filming, underlining the importance of mutual trust and reliance in the collaborative creative processes of television drama production. It is clear from the insights of this chapter's interviews that actors have considerable parts to play in such processes, in ways which add further nuance to Cardwell's considerations of those 'whose job it is to "act" as if they were other people' (2002, 91) in period television drama.

References

BBC Media Centre, 2015, 8 April. 'BBC One Scores Record-breaking Q1 Performance in 2015 and Announces Recommission of Poldark'. Accessed at: www.bbc.co.uk/mediacentre/latestnews/2015/bbc-one-q1 (last viewed: 24 July 2016).

————2016, 6 July. 'Poldark Will Return to BBC One for a Third Series'. Accessed at: www.bbc.co.uk/mediacentre/latestnews/2016/poldark-series-three (last viewed: 24 July 2016).

BBC News, 2012, 18 January. 'Simon Schama Brands Downton "Cultural Necrophilia"'. Accessed at: www.bbc.co.uk/news/entertainment-arts-16609589 (last viewed: 24 July 2016).

Byrne, K., 2015. *Edwardians on Screen: from Downton Abbey to Parade's End*. London: Palgrave Macmillan.

Cardwell, S., 2002. *Adaptation Revisited: Television and the Classic Novel.* Manchester: Manchester University Press.

Caughie, J., 2000. *Television Drama: Realism, Modernism and British Culture.* Oxford: Oxford University Press.

Chapman, J., 2005. *Past and Present: National Identity and the British Historical Film.* London: I.B. Tauris.

Egner, J., 2013, 3 January. 'A Bit of Britain Where the Sun Still Never Sets: "Downton Abbey" Reaches Around the World'. *New York Times.* Accessed at: www.nytimes.com/2013/01/06/arts/television/downton-abbey-reaches-around-the-world.html?_r=1 (last viewed: 23 July 2016).

Frost, V., 2013, 19 January. 'Less Grit Please: The Rise of "Warm Bath" Television: Feelgood Dramas Are Spreading beyond Their Sunday Night Slots'. *The Guardian*, 17.

Geraghty, C., 2012. *Bleak House (BFI TV Classics).* London: BFI.

de Groot, J., 2008. *Consuming History: Historians and Heritage in Contemporary Popular Culture.* London: Routledge.

———2015. *Remaking History: The Past in Contemporary Historical Fictions.* London: Routledge.

Harper, S., 1994. *Picturing the Past: The Rise and Fall of the British Costume Film.* London: BFI.

Higson, A., 2001. 'Heritage Cinema and Television', in K. Robins and D. Morley (eds), *British Cultural Studies.* Oxford: Oxford University Press, 249–260.

———2003. *English Heritage, English Cinema: Costume Drama since 1980.* Oxford: Oxford University Press.

———2011. *Film England: Culturally English Filmmaking since the 1990s.* London: I.B. Tauris.

Hill, J., 1999. *British Cinema in the 1980s: Issues and Themes.* Oxford: Oxford University Press.

Hogg, C., 2013. 'The Punk-Rock King: Musical Anachronism in Period Film', *Media International Australia*, 148: 84–93.

ITV Press Centre, 2013, 10 November. 'ITV Commissions a Fifth Series of *Downton Abbey*'. Accessed at: www.itv.com/presscentre/press-releases/itv-commissions-fifth-series-downton-abbey#.Uu5drD1_uSp (last viewed: 23 July 2016).

Kamp, D., 2012, 8 November. 'The Most Happy Fellowes'. *Vanity Fair.* Accessed at: www.vanityfair.com/culture/2012/12/julian-fellowes-downton-abbey (last viewed: 24 July 2016).

Leggott, J. and J.A. Taddeo (eds), 2015. *Upstairs and Downstairs: British Costume Drama Television from The Forsyte Saga to Downton Abbey*. London: Rowman and Littlefield.

Monk, C., 2002. 'The British Heritage-Film Debate Revisited', in C. Monk and A. Sargeant (eds), *British Historical Cinema*. London: Routledge, 176–198.

Nelson, R., 2008. 'Costume Drama', in G. Creeber (ed.), *The Television Genre Book* (2nd Edition). London: BFI, 49–52.

Parker, J., 2013, 2 January. 'Brideshead Regurgitated: The Ludicrous Charms of *Downton Abbey*, TV's Reigning Aristo-Soap'. *The Atlantic*. Accessed at: www.theatlantic.com/magazine/archive/2013/01/brideshead-regurgitated/309194/ (last viewed: 24 July 2016).

Pearson, A., 2015, 26 April. 'Poldark, Series 1, Finale, Review: "Devastatingly Good"'. *The Telegraph*. Accessed at: www.telegraph.co.uk/culture/tvandradio/tv-and-radio-reviews/11564209/Poldark-series-1-finale-review-devastatingly-good.html (last viewed 24 July 2016).

Vidal, B., 2012. *Figuring the Past: Period Film and the Mannerist Aesthetic*. Amsterdam: Amsterdam University Press.

Notes

1   For more detailed consideration of these different descriptors, see, for example: Higson (2003), Monk (2002) and Vidal (2012).

6

Acting in British Television: A General Conclusion

This book proposes a new methodology for research into television, in which acting is positioned not as an aspect of textual analysis, readily discernible in the finished product, but rather as a process which is closely associated with, but – crucially – distinct from, the other areas of production. This acting work is largely hidden from view (not only from the public but also, often, from the writer, director and fellow actors). The only way to bring these processes into view is via detailed interviews with the actors themselves. By placing actor testimony at the heart of the analysis, this book locates the actor as a key creative agent in the success of these televisual forms. The 16 actor interviews in this work should not be taken as definitive, nor should they be regarded as typical, but they should be seen as indicative of the rich breadth of acting processes currently at work within British television.

The 16 interviews offered here are mainly with actors who have had significant success in their television work. Our choice of actors was based on two fundamental principles: firstly, that we wanted to highlight and examine the skill and innovation of actors, and the most likely people to exemplify this are those who are highly respected for what they do; secondly, we wanted to interview actors who represent the diversity of contemporary British television and who thus bring a variety of perspectives to their work. This means, however, that these actors often have more agency than might be experienced by an actor playing a visiting role on such programmes. John Hannah's discussions with Ian Rankin about *Rebus* and Rebecca Front's ideas about character that she shared with Armando Iannucci, for example, would have been an unrealistic component of the creative process for most television actors. However, across all of these interviews it was evident that the actors identified themselves as the custodians of their characters, and the experts on them. This is true of experienced actors as well as those at the start of their careers. Several elements of the industrial process of making these programmes (such as hot-seating sessions, improvisation, and actor–writer relationships) reinforced this belief. This gave the actors a clear stake in the storytelling and focused their energies on the specifics of their character's journey. Where this custodianship was compromised, such as through 'retcons' or due to storylines that they objected to but which were outside their control, they found that their work was undermined and often became deeply problematic.

Chapters 2 to 5 have demonstrated the unique demands of acting within prominent contemporary televisual genres, and the actors were clear that the opportunities and challenges they experienced were distinct from their work in theatre and film. Whilst each chapter includes a conclusion which draws together genre-specific findings, there are also wider connections, across all the interviews, which demand consideration.

Rehearsal/Preparation Distinction

We can clearly identify that rehearsal and preparation are very different things for these actors. Though some of the case-study productions (such as *Downton Abbey*, *W1A* and *Poldark*) included short rehearsal periods, much of the actors' preparation took place outside formalised spaces and was, rather, based on solo study by the actor, often immediately before filming commenced and in the evenings between shooting days. We had anticipated that actors would have longed for more time for rehearsal on these projects, and though some actors mentioned that this would have been advantageous, more common was their desire for more recording time through which to experiment with performative options. This emphasis tends to suggest that these actors located their craft in the act of filming, and that experimentation would ideally be caught by the camera rather than explored in rehearsal. This might be a reflection of the current industrial processes of television-making in which the notion of rehearsal is so far from an industry reality that the actors did not even consider it to be possible. The value that Siân Phillips retrospectively places on the extensive rehearsal in her work in the 1960s and 1970s suggests that this may be the case.

The actors' private work took a number of forms, including historical and cultural research into particular periods and contexts, the use of films and earlier television performances for inspiration, drawing on experiences from improvisation and experimentation earlier in the process, and the use of written sources to provide details about the world they were inhabiting. However, for many of the actors, this work was focused on a variety of approaches to script analysis. These approaches range from gaining an absolute linguistic precision, not only acknowledging punctuation and precise syntax, but also rhythms and structures in the dialogue between many characters (such as the precise verbal jousting experienced by Nina Sosanya and Jason Watkins in *W1A*), and a much freer approach to the text in which the actors could shape the lines according to their individual understanding of how their character would coin a phrase (such as in John Hannah's experience of *Rebus*, and Niamh Walsh's work on *Holby City*). At the heart of this breadth of approach are the different levels of reverence the actors afforded to the script. For some, this was like a piece of music in its complexity and their need to follow its detail; for others the script was 'totemic' and, whilst the sense was key, the minutia of the phrasing was the actor's province.

The range of approaches to script analysis also confronts one of the defining demands of acting on television: the lack of discrete narrative structures and resultant 'narrative flux' that was, in a variety of forms, present for almost all actors here. This was not, as we had expected, deemed to be a significant challenge across these interviews, and several actors aligned the lack of knowledge about the character's future with real life. Rather, the actors' preparation often focused on emotional and narrative structures within episodes, such as via improvisation for Rebecca

Front on *The Thick of It*, and via the identification and analysis of the two or three key scenes per episode for John Hannah when working on *McCallum* and *Rebus*. Indeed, in the experience of Hannah and many other actors here, the process of script development was focused on countering the challenge of character repetition and stasis, and finding elements in the narrative which emphasised change and development rather than repetition.

An unexpected feature of the actor's preparation was the experience of a close bond with the writer. Although this was not evident in all interviews, a recurring motif in their reflections was the way in which the script had been crafted for them. This is rare in an actor's career, and though actors might have experienced it in devising processes for theatre and via the presence of the writer in the rehearsal room, the complex nature of this relationship went a stage further to become exclusive to television. Not only did the actors in several of these programmes (*EastEnders*, *Holby City* and *The Thick of It*, for example) find that their ideas about the character had been incorporated, the long-running nature of the programmes analysed here meant that the writers could respond to the actor's performative contributions, and tailor future storylines according to their inclinations as the character. This uniquely televisual phenomenon flies in the face of the received wisdom about television acting, in which the formidable speed and complexity of the industrial process have been used to suggest how the actor's work is deprivileged.

The Act of Filming

The actors' experiences of filming were characterised by the close relationship between their work and the director's choice of shooting style. This comes as no surprise, but whilst analysis of shooting style (including analysis of shot choice and length, multi/single camera, location/studio shooting) is a well-trodden path for television researchers, this is the first time that shooting styles on television have been considered specifically in relation to acting. In these interviews, we can contrast the precision needed for continuity on single camera filming and the ways in which the actors negotiated this by attempting to psychologically justify all their moves so as to make repeating them a motivated and considered physical action, with the ways in which actors exploited the freedom of the docucom aesthetic in which continuity was not an issue, and physical and verbal inventiveness replaced precision and control as the dominant preoccupations when recording.

It was not just the shooting style which affected the actors' work, however. Costume and set can be identified as powerful conditioning factors here. Whether this was a particular historical context, such as in *Downton Abbey* and *Poldark*, the run-down offices of a junior minister in *The Thick of It*, or the particularly familiar and homely surroundings of a kitchen in *Coronation Street*, these actors' work was influenced and moulded by the material conditions that they acted in. This 'moulding' takes on a more literal meaning when the actors discussed costume and the ways in which tailoring and particular fashions altered their gait and gestural range. Though external, these factors had a significant effect on their approach to the role.

Importantly, we can identify that an actor's experience of a role on television is the experience of recording, not of rehearsal. In some theatre roles, the journey in rehearsals is as complex and imaginatively involving as the end product, and in theatre that end product will be repeated across the run of the show. On television, acting is, in large part, a matter of execution within the performative context of filming. It is therefore of little surprise that the actors here paid a great deal of attention to the act of filming. The actors debunked myths around television acting, particularly shorthand notions of scale. Acting on television is not a question of being smaller, but rather one of intensity and clarity of thought process, the physical precision of gesture and movement, and of being closely attuned to shifts in rhythm and pace. In addition, the actors here often noted the value of the first take, and the freshness of working within a scene for the first time. Again undermining the common belief that more rehearsals would support the actor, in fact they found repetition difficult, and valued the instinctive response they experienced when running the scene in front of the cameras in the first take. Where repeat takes were deemed useful, these tended to be opportunities to try something new and to take the scene in another direction (however subtle and nuanced that might be). This was heralded as being a much more creatively engaging process than correcting a mistake in an earlier take or capturing a scene from an additional angle.

Ways Forward

This work has placed actors at the heart of the analysis and has thus attempted to right the imbalance which has seen others (often academics, show-runners and writers) ventriloquising for actors and hypothesising about acting. We have probed existing terminology and the ways in which acting on television has been described in the past. In particular, we have attempted to avoid moulding the actors' testimony to fit existing theories of acting, such as those developed for the stage. In our interviews and subsequent analysis, we have responded to the interests and experiences of the actors as expressed to us, and have tried to analyse them on their own terms rather than making them conform to a pre-existing critical or theoretical framework. It is clearly impossible to analyse all the areas that the actors raise, and no doubt our own priorities in the analysis will not be universally shared. By including the full interview data alongside our analysis, we hope that others will use this data to explore their own interests and reach their own conclusions.

There is much in these interviews which will prove useful for actors approaching television work for the first time, and for those who are devising courses to train actors for the television industry. We hope that these experiences and our analysis will provide useful new information to actors in training as well as to their trainers. A noteworthy motif through the interviews was the actors' lack of training for the challenges they encountered. This is clearly changing, and this new material will contribute to the development of new pedagogies for television actor training.

We also hope that our investigative approach will be applied more widely, in order to further realise its benefits. We have demonstrated the reflective capacity of actors and the ways in which their individual experiences can be collated to provide a range of insights into hidden creative processes. If we were to interview another 16 actors, no doubt the picture would become even more complex and the range of approaches significantly extended. But the conversation has begun. We have provided not only new material across these 16 actor interviews but also, and more importantly, indicated a route and modus operandi for future fruitful analyses of television performance. This can now be applied to new areas such as new geographical contexts and television genres. Above all, this book set out to make the invisible components of television acting visible for the reader. In so doing, these 16 interviews demonstrate the skill, imagination and creative flair of actors working in British television today.

Index

A

Actor Training *see* Drama School
Addison, Chris   148, 172, 178,
    180, 195
Adler, Stella   135
Allam, Roger   148, 151, 153, 168,
    182–188, 192–194, 196, 198,
    200–202
Allen, Woody   219
Altman, Robert   183
Andrews, Carey   40, 69
Ansorge, Peter   79
Are You Being Served?   168
Armchair Theatre   248
Arts Educational Schools (ArtsEd)
    233
Asher, Jane   86
Ashes to Ashes   182
A Touch of Cloth   87
A Touch of Frost   225
Audience *see* Viewers
Auditions   20–21, 39–40, 50–51,
    58, 106–107, 114, 117–118,
    128, 155, 159, 162, 184, 235,
    239, 244
Austen, Jane   210
Ayckbourn, Alan   158

B

Babbington, Kylie   39, 45
BAFTA   164, 171, 216, 234, 246

Bailey, Nicholas   51
Basden, Tom   169
Bazalgette, Edward   216, 239
BBC   5, 18, 51, 55, 57–58, 79,
    85, 87, 90, 97, 106, 111, 114,
    147–150, 152, 154, 156, 160,
    164–165, 167, 170–171, 182,
    186–189, 194, 209, 216–217,
    225, 234, 237, 244, 246–249,
    251, 253, 258
BBC3   150
Beadle, Gary   18, 50–61, 70,
    72–74
Bellamy, Ralph   185
Benidorm   226
Best, Adam   107
Big Train   171
Birmingham School of Acting
    39, 50
Blackadder II   225
Black and Blue   95
Black, Bethany   22
Blandings   234–235
Bleak House   211
Bogart, Humphrey   185
Boleslavsky, Richard   191
Bonneville, Hugh   148, 155, 159,
    168–169, 192, 226
Brideshead Revisited   210
Bright, Rachel   18, 39–50, 61,
    64–66, 68–70, 193
Bristol Old Vic Theatre School   7

British Medical Association   82
Brooker, Charlie   87
Brooks, Charlie   52
Brookside   21, 58
Brown, June   42–43, 48
Bruce, Alastair   220, 254

C

Cable, Vince   150
Callow, Simon   88
Call the Midwife   210
Camera   5, 13n, 21, 26–27, 38–39,
    46, 69–70, 75, 92–93,
    103–104, 109–110, 120, 122,
    127, 151–153, 156–157, 160,
    163–164, 170–172, 174,
    176–179, 182–183, 185–186,
    198–199, 201–202, 218,
    222–224, 230–233, 243, 247,
    250, 254, 271–273
    Camera Crew   47, 77n, 152,
        219, 248, 262
    Camera Operator   121, 157,
        199, 223–224, 264
    Camera Work   6, 79, 157,
        198
    Portable Single Camera (PSC)
        28
Cameron, David   150
Cannon, John   114
Capaldi, Peter   148, 172–173, 177,
    181–182, 186, 202
Carnival Films   214
Carter, Jim   219
Casualty   85–86, 106, 113–115,
    225
CBS   80

Channel 4   22, 79, 87, 120, 149,
    153–154, 156
Character Stasis   130, 137, 141,
    272
Cilla   234
Cinema Vérité   151, 183, 186, 201,
    207n
Clerkenwell Films   85, 95
Cold Blood   87
Comedy   10, 40, 87, 106, 145–155,
    158–159, 164–165, 168,
    170–173, 177–178, 182,
    185–186, 189–192, 194,
    196–198, 203–204, 207n,
    234, 243, 252
    Restoration comedy   25
Comedy Vérité   151–153
Commissioners   16
Continuing drama   31, 37, 41, 44,
    62, 64, 66, 73–74, 89, 96,
    114, 117, 123, 126, 139, 210,
    272
Cookson, Catherine   20
Coronation Street   17–33, 35–39,
    58–60, 62–63, 66, 69–70, 74,
    112, 226, 273
Costume   2, 6, 44, 47, 67, 114,
    119, 139, 182, 209, 213, 215,
    229, 231, 233, 241, 247–248,
    251–252, 257–260, 265–266,
    273
Cucumber   22

D

Dallas   80
Dancing on the Edge   234
Dane, Clemence   247

Davies, Russell T 22
Davis, Phil 14n
Dennis, Les 62
Dexter, Colin 84
Dinnerladies 225
Director 2–3, 5, 20–21, 24, 26–30,
    34, 36–37, 40–41, 47, 55,
    67–68, 71, 75, 77n, 88, 94,
    96, 99, 103–104, 110, 112,
    114, 116, 119, 121, 126–127,
    140, 148, 153, 155–157,
    162–164, 183–184, 187, 189,
    191, 194–196, 199, 203, 216,
    226–227, 230, 234, 239–240,
    242–246, 249–252, 264,
    269, 272
Director of Photography 157
Doctors 225
Doctor Thorne 171
Doctor Who 161, 217, 224
Docucom 153, 198, 200,
    203–204, 273
Documentary-drama 82, 153
Docusoap 152–153
Dolan, Monica 168
Downton Abbey 210–211, 214–225,
    228, 230–233, 254–255, 258,
    262–264, 270, 273
Drama Centre London 217, 224
Drama School 38–39, 49, 54,
    97–98, 105–106, 113–114,
    119, 232–233, 244
    Actor training 3, 7–9, 14n, 20,
        38–39, 49–50, 68, 97, 106,
        113, 117–119, 135, 163–164,
        224, 232, 244, 249, 274
Dwelling Place, The 20
Dyer, Danny 62

E
Ealing Studios 223, 227
EastEnders 5, 17–18, 21, 39,
    42–43, 48–60, 62, 64–65,
    69–70, 73–74, 77n, 193, 272
Editing 2, 6, 162, 177, 183–184,
    194, 198–199, 228, 240
Editor 96, 119, 221
Educating Yorkshire 153, 156
Ehle, Jennifer 258
Emmerdale 31, 35–36, 39
Emotion 20, 24, 49, 63, 69, 77n,
    83, 93–94, 102, 105–106,
    111, 129, 131–132, 135–136,
    138–141, 143n, 185, 220,
    231, 238, 253–256, 259, 261,
    265, 271
Endeavour 182, 186–188
Ensemble 37, 44, 121, 123, 126,
    161, 190–191, 195, 198, 204,
    217–218, 254, 262
Equity 27
Evans, Shaun 187–188
Ever Decreasing Circles 217

F
Farthing, Jack 216, 234–246, 253,
    255–257, 259–263, 265
Fellowes, Julian 214, 217–218,
    222–223, 225–231
Ferguson, Murray 95
Finneran, Siobhan 226
Flanagan, Helen 31
Four Weddings and a Funeral 85,
    87–88, 95
Framing 2, 6
Frantic Assembly 250

Frontline Books   21
Front, Rebecca   148, 150,
    171–182, 188, 192–198,
    201–203, 270–272

G

Gébler, Ernest   248
Gielgud, John   186
Graham, Winston   216, 236–237,
    255–257
Granite   247
Grant, Cary   185
Graves, Robert   251
Guardian, The   150, 178, 221
Guildford School of Acting   7
Guildhall School of Music and Drama
    225, 232

H

Hagen, Uta   135
Halsall, Alan   27
Hannah, John   84–85, 87–96,
    125–134, 136, 139, 141,
    270–272
Harrison, Rex   249
Hat Trick Productions   165
Hawks, Howard   185
Hawley, Graeme   18, 30–39, 60,
    63–64, 66–67, 70–72, 129
HBO   61
Heartbreak House   248
Henshall, Paul   87, 106–113, 125,
    128–129, 134–136, 138–139,
    141
Hercules and the Amazon Women
    164

Hesmondhalgh, Julie   17–18, 19–30,
    36, 58–59, 64, 66, 68, 73–74
His Girl Friday   185, 202
Historical Advisor   220, 226–227,
    231, 238, 254
Hoggart, Simon   23
Holby City   85–87, 106–110,
    113–119, 121–123, 126, 128,
    130, 134, 137–138, 141, 225,
    271–272
Hollyoaks   120
Horsfield, Debbie   216, 236–237,
    239, 244
House & Garden   158
Houston, Donald   248
Howitt, Peter   85
Hynes, Jessica   149, 159

I

Iannucci, Armando   148, 150,
    171–174, 176–178, 180–186,
    192, 194–195, 197, 201–202,
    270
I, Claudius   210, 216–217, 246,
    251–252, 258
Improvisation   65, 94, 106, 109,
    155, 157, 168, 172–173,
    175–176, 183–184, 189–190,
    192–195, 197–198, 200–201,
    204, 231, 238, 270–271
I'm with Stupid   106
Independent, The   86, 150
Inspector Morse   84–85, 182
ITV   17, 20, 31, 58, 83–85, 87,
    106, 112, 154, 171, 182, 185,
    187, 209, 214, 225–226, 234,
    248

J

James-Collier, Rob   226
Jones, Rufus   157, 200
Jones, Suranne   63

K

Kitchen Sink   82
Knowing Me, Knowing You   171

L

Lancashire, Sarah   6, 63
Langham, Chris   148, 156,
    171
La Plante, Lynda   83
Last Tango in Halifax   154
Lawson, Wilfrid   248
Lesser, Anton   188
Lewis   171, 176
Lewis, Russell   187
Lighting   2, 6, 26, 77n, 79, 162,
    170, 177, 179, 197, 201, 222,
    230, 249
Little Britain   146
Location   5, 13n, 28, 103, 151,
    199, 203, 223, 226, 237, 241,
    254–255, 260, 266, 272
Logan, Phyllis   229
London Academy of Music and
    Dramatic Art (LAMDA), the
    7, 19–20, 113–114, 118,
    234
Lord Chesterfield's Letters to His Son
    238
Love, Nina   164
Luther   57
Lynch, Bet   21

M

Make-up   44–45, 77n, 114,
    241–242, 251, 258–259,
    262, 265
Malik, Art   86, 112
Mamma Mia   233
Mammoth Screen   187, 235–236,
    255
Manchester Metropolitan
    University   30, 106, 113
Marcella   154
Marion and Geoff   152
Marsh, Kym   62
Masterpiece   214
Match Point   219
McAlpine, Jennie   30, 34–37, 67
McCallum   85, 87, 90–91, 94,
    132–133, 136, 272
McGregor, Will   216
McShera, Sophie   227–228
Medical Advisors   82, 86, 107, 118,
    138
Medical Drama   10, 79–83, 85–86,
    89–90, 113, 123–124, 126,
    130, 134–141, 145, 210, 215,
    225, 253, 256, 259, 261
Meisner, Sanford   135
Messiah   85, 97, 99–101
Method Acting   17, 53, 135,
    180
Milliband, Ed   150
Mirren, Helen   83
Mockumentary   151–152, 158,
    177–178
Morton, John   148, 152, 154–161,
    165–169, 189–190, 197, 199,
    204
Moscow Art Theatre   191

Mountview Academy of Theatre
Arts   97
Mr Selfridge   210
Mullan, Peter   95

N

National Theatre, The   83
Naturalism   26, 62–63, 116,
122–123, 128, 140, 145,
154, 155–156
Neilson, David   19, 24, 29, 36
Newell, Mike   85, 88
New Street Law   87, 92
Nicholson, Jack   88
Nicol, Lesley   215, 225–234, 254,
258, 260–265
Nighty Night   171
Norwood, Ricky   42, 69

O

Off Their Rockers   106

P

Pack, Roger Lloyd   23
Parades End   182
Parish, Sarah   149
Pasco, Richard   248
PBS   214
People Like Us   152–156, 159
Period Drama   10, 209–217,
219–220, 226–227, 231, 235,
238, 241–242, 246, 251–254,
256–261, 263, 265–266
Phillips, Siân   210, 216–217,
246–252, 253, 258–259,
262, 265, 271

Platonov   249
Playing the Field   106, 113
Pleasence, Donald   247
Poldark   209, 216, 234–235,
238–244, 255–257, 259–260,
263, 265, 270, 273
Police Drama   10, 13n, 79–85,
89–90, 93, 96–97, 99–100,
102, 123–124, 126, 130–141,
145, 210, 215, 225, 253, 256,
259
Powell, Robert   86, 109, 112
Pramface   234
Pride and Prejudice   210, 258
Prime Suspect   83
Producer   2, 16, 21, 31–33, 40–41,
43–44, 51–52, 55, 65, 69–70,
73, 90, 94, 100, 104, 110,
114–116, 126–129, 132, 140,
155–156, 163, 165, 187–188,
193, 215, 217, 225, 235, 239
Pulman, Jack   251–252

R

Rankin, Ian   84–85, 87, 94–95,
102, 127, 130, 270
Rebus   84–85, 89, 97, 99–101,
124, 127–128, 131–132,
270–272
Reed, Heida   235
Rehearsal   5, 26, 29, 33, 48, 51,
53–54, 70–71, 74–75, 87–88,
99, 102–104, 109–110, 112,
119, 126, 130, 147, 159–160,
169, 174–176, 180–181, 185,
188, 193–194, 204, 223, 228,
230–231, 242–243, 248–249,
270–273

Camera Rehearsal   26, 45–46, 70, 103, 223, 248
Rehearsal room   35, 227, 244, 251, 253
Reid, Anne   229
Renaissance Pictures   164
Research   8, 10–11, 14n, 22, 65, 75, 86, 91, 102, 108, 119, 139, 141, 147, 173, 191, 213, 226, 238–239, 251–253, 255–256, 258–259, 265, 269, 271
Richard, Wendy   43
Ripper Street   210
Rising Damp   185, 202
Roache, William   18
Romeo and Juliet   234
Rossiter, Leonard   185
Royal Academy of Dramatic Art (RADA)   7–8, 14n, 164, 246, 249
Royal Central School of Speech and Drama   7
Royal Scottish Academy of Music and Drama   87
Royal Shakespeare Company   83
Russell, Rosalind   185

S

Satire   148–149, 153, 165, 169
Scale   122, 140, 273
Scanlan, Joanna   148, 172, 178, 180–181, 195
Scherfig, Lone   234
Schlesinger, Paul   155, 157, 165
Scottish Television (STV)   84–85, 90, 95–96, 132

Script Analysis   50, 54, 141, 175, 191, 194, 204, 271
Script Changes   43, 52–53, 65, 74–75, 115, 121, 123, 188
Script Editor   24, 44, 47, 65, 94, 167
Script Supervisor   46, 105
Scriptwriter *see* Writer
Secret Army   97
Series   16, 67, 80, 82, 85, 92, 141, 148–150, 154, 156, 158–162, 168–169, 171–172, 179, 181–182, 190, 198, 200, 209, 214, 216–217, 219, 221–224, 228, 237, 242–243, 252, 255, 258
Set   5, 25, 27–28, 30, 34, 46–47, 67, 70, 107–108, 114, 118, 122, 170, 209, 213, 218, 222–224, 229–231, 236, 241–243, 247–248, 254, 257, 260–261, 266, 273
Set Design   2
Shakespeare's Globe   234
Shoulder to Shoulder   217, 246, 251–253
Show-runner   2, 274
Silent Witness   90
Silk   154, 234
Sitcom   16, 145–147, 151, 153–154, 158–159, 171, 178, 189–190, 204, 217, 225
Skinner, Hugh   161
Sky   87, 164
Sliding Doors   85, 95
Smith, James   148, 177, 180, 195, 203
Smith, Maggie   226

Soap Opera   5, 10, 15–19, 21,
        23–27, 31, 34–37, 39, 49–51,
        53–54, 56, 58–63, 67–68,
        70–71, 73–76, 80, 82, 86, 88,
        125–126, 135, 145, 193,
        210–211, 215, 252, 256,
        259, 262
    Soap Actor   17, 25, 61, 127, 129
    'Soapification'   4
    'Soapisation'   4, 16, 80
Soller, Kyle   235
Sorapure, John   157
Sosanya, Nina   149, 152–153,
        154–164, 169, 189–192,
        198–200, 202, 204, 271
Stanislavski   97, 135, 139, 143n,
        191
    Actioning   191
    Objectives   191
Star/Celebrity   3, 13n, 62, 84, 95,
        127, 209, 211, 214, 226
    Fame   25
Stevens, Dan   221
Stoll, Liz   114
Stoppard, Tom   182
Storylines   20–24, 30–32, 35–36,
        39–42, 44, 46–47, 50–52, 56,
        58, 60, 63–66, 69, 73, 80–81,
        83, 86, 101, 108, 116–117,
        128, 130, 133, 135, 137, 179,
        198, 218, 221, 243, 270, 272
    Story Arc   31–32, 38, 66, 68,
        71–72, 89, 91, 95, 102, 130,
        137, 233
    Backstory   31, 33, 51, 70–71,
        74, 95, 130
    Narrative Flux   63, 66, 74, 271
    Narrative Repetition   80, 130,
        136–137, 141

Narrative Structures   16–17, 19,
        81, 130–131, 271
Stott, Ken   84–85, 97–106,
        124–125, 127, 132–133,
        136–137, 139, 141
Strangers in the Room   248
Strasberg, Lee   135, 139, 143n
Studio   8, 13n, 24, 28, 43, 46–47,
        53, 62, 77n, 96, 120, 122,
        151, 210, 224, 247, 250, 272

T

Taggart   85, 90
Tarmey, Bill   27
Teachers   154
Tennant, David   149, 151
Thaw, John   84
The Bill   20, 225
The Creatives   182
The Day Today   171
The Flintstones   176
The Jewel in the Crown   210
The Jury   182
The Last Detective   225
*The Lost Honour of Christopher
        Jefferies*   164–165, 170
The Missing   182, 187
The Office   146, 149, 151–152, 178
The Paradise   210
The Riot Club   234
The Singing Detective   97
The Sopranos   61
The Thick of It   147–153, 168,
        171–172, 175–177, 179,
        182–189, 192–194, 196–204,
        207n, 272–273
The Vice   85, 97, 99–100, 133
The Windsors   149

Timmer, Damien   235
Torrens, Pip   237
Tour, Frances de la   185
Trollied   164
Trubridge, Liz   225–226
Turner, Aidan   216, 235
Twenty Twelve   148, 152–156, 159, 165, 170, 189

U

Upstairs, Downstairs   209
Up The Women   171

V

Viewers   17, 34, 43, 51, 56, 60–63, 73, 81, 86, 90, 93, 132, 137, 153, 158, 161, 209, 212, 245
   Audience   16–17, 21, 34, 38, 42, 59–62, 72, 75, 80–81, 83–84, 86, 90, 98, 101, 130, 132, 137, 145, 151, 156–157, 161, 169, 171, 211–212, 215–216, 229, 240, 258–259

W

W1A   147–161, 163–165, 167–171, 188–190, 192, 197–200, 202, 204, 270–271
Wade, Laura   234
Wainwright, Sally   6
Walsh, Niamh   87, 113–122, 123–127, 130, 137–140, 256, 271

War and Peace   171
Watkins, Jason   149, 164–171, 188–192, 197–198, 200–201, 204, 271
West, Timothy   62
Wilton, Penelope   215, 217–225, 254–255, 258–259, 261–264
Wise, Herbert   252
Women Can Be Monsters   248
Wood, Jake   47
Writer   2, 21, 23–24, 27, 29, 33–34, 40–43, 52–53, 55, 65, 67–69, 71–75, 91–92, 94, 96, 99, 108, 110–111, 115–117, 124, 126–129, 140, 148, 158, 163, 169, 171–176, 183–184, 186–187, 189, 193, 228, 239, 246, 254, 269, 272, 274
   Author   84, 194
   Authorial Agency   2, 126–129, 253, 270
   Authorship   123, 126, 140, 143n, 264
   Screenwriter   214, 216
   Scriptwriter   65, 67–68
   Writer-Director   149, 158, 188–189, 203

Y

Yes, Minister   207n
Yes, Prime Minister   207n
Yorke, John   55
YouTube   58, 73

Printed by Printforce, the Netherlands